Making
Sense of
GOD

REDEEMER

Making Sense of GOD

An Invitation to the Skeptical

Timothy Keller

VIKING

VIKING

An imprint of Penguin Random House LLC
375 Hudson Street
New York, New York 10014
penguin.com

ISBN 9780525954156 (hardcover)
ISBN 9780698194366 (e-book)

Printed in the United States of America
1   3   5   7   9   10   8   6   4   2

Set in ITC Galliard Std
Designed by Alissa Rose Theodor

To all my colleagues who have worked to communicate faith in a skeptical age

*Especially
Craig Ellis, Mai Hariu-Powell
and my son, Michael Keller*

CONTENTS

Preface

⸻◇◇◇⸻

The Faith of the Secular

I have been a Christian minister in Manhattan for nearly thirty years. Most people in the city that is my home are not religious believers. Nor are they what used to be called "C and E" (Christmas and Easter only) Christians. Rather, most would identify as "no religious affiliation" or as "secular."

Recently the *New York Times* ran a story about a weekly discussion venue our church holds for people who are skeptical that there is a God or any supernatural reality. The ground rules of the group assume neither that any religion nor that secularism is true. Instead, multiple sources are consulted—personal experience, philosophy, history, sociology, as well as religious texts—in order to compare systems of belief and to weigh how much sense they make in comparison with one another. Most participants certainly come to the discussion with a point of view and have some hope of seeing their own worldview look stronger by way of this process of appraisal. But each person is also urged to be open to critique and willing to admit flaws and problems in their way of looking at things.[1]

After the article ran, several Internet message boards and forums discussed it. Many heaped derision on the effort. One commenter said that Christianity "makes *no* sense in the real, natural world we live in" and so has "no [rational] merit" at all. Many objected to the view that secularism was a set of beliefs that could be compared with other systems. On the contrary, they said, it was merely a sensible assessment of the nature of things based on a purely rational evaluation of the world. Religious people try to impose their beliefs on others, but, it was said, when secular people make their case, they just have facts, and people who disagree are closing their eyes to those facts. The only way to be a Christian, another said, is to assume the fairy tales of the Bible are true and to close your eyes to all reason and evidence.

In another forum the participants couldn't understand why any secular skeptics would ever come to such a group. "Do they think 'nones' [those without religious affiliation] in America have never heard the 'good news'?" one man asked incredulously. "Do they think that secular people will come to such a place and listen and say, 'why has no one told me of this?'" Another wrote, "People aren't 'nones' because they aren't familiar with religion—they're nones because they *are*."[2]

However, over the years I have been in too many of these kinds of discussion groups to count, and the guesses of these critics about them are largely wrong. Believers *and* nonbelievers in God alike arrive at their positions through a combination of experience, faith, reasoning, and intuition. And in these forums I routinely hear skeptics say to me, "I wish I'd known before that this kind of religious belief and this way of thinking about faith existed. This doesn't necessarily mean I'm going to believe now, but I've never had this much food for thought around these issues offered before."

The material in this book is a way of offering to readers—especially the most skeptical who may think the "good news" lacks cultural relevance—the same food for thought. We will compare the beliefs and claims of Christianity with the beliefs and claims of the secular view, asking which one makes more sense of a complex world and human experience.

Before we proceed, however, we should take a moment to explore how we will be using the word "secular." There are at least three ways the word is used today.

One applies the term to the social and political structure. A *secular society* is one in which there is a separation of religion and the state. No religious faith is privileged by the government and the most powerful cultural institutions. "Secular" may also be used to describe individuals. A *secular person* is one who does not know if there is a God or any supernatural realm beyond the natural world. Everything, in this view, has a scientific explanation. Finally, the term may describe a particular kind of culture with its themes and narratives. A *"secular age"* is one in which all the emphasis is on the *saeculum*, on the here-and-now, without any concept of the eternal. Meaning in life, guidance, and happiness are understood and sought in present-time economic prosperity, material comfort, and emotional fulfillment.

It is helpful to distinguish each of these aspects of secularity, because they are not identical. A society could have a secular state even if there were very few secular people in the country. Another distinction is very common. Individuals could profess to not be secular people, to have religious faith. Yet, at the practical level, the existence of God may have no noticeable impact on their life decisions and conduct. This is because in a secular age even religious people tend to choose lovers and spouses, careers and friendships, and financial options with no higher goal than their own present-time personal happiness. Sacrificing personal peace and affluence for transcendent causes becomes rare, even for people who say they believe in absolute values and eternity. Even if you are not a secular person, the secular age can "thin out" (secularize) faith until it is seen as simply one more choice in life—along with job, recreation, hobbies, politics—rather than as the comprehensive framework that determines all life choices.[3]

In this book I will be using the word "secular" in the second and third ways and will be offering often sharp critiques of these positions. I am, however, a great supporter of the first kind of secularism. I do not want the church or any religious institution to control the state nor for the state to control the church. Societies in which the state has adopted and promoted one true faith have often been oppressive. Governments have used the authority of the "one true religion" as a warrant for violence and imperialism. Yet ironically the wedding of church and state ends up weakening the privileged religion rather than strengthening it. When people have religion imposed on them through social pressure instead of choosing it freely, they often embrace it in a halfhearted or even hypocritical way. The best option is a government that promotes neither a single faith nor a doctrinaire form of secularist belief that denigrates and marginalizes religion.

A truly secular state would create a genuinely pluralistic society and a "marketplace of ideas" in which people of all kinds of faith, including those with secular beliefs, could freely contribute, communicate, coexist, and cooperate in mutual respect and peace. Does such a place exist? No, not yet. It would be a place where people who deeply differ nonetheless listen long and carefully before speaking. There people would avoid all strawmen and treat each other's objections and doubts with respect and seriousness. They would stretch to understand the other side so well that their opponents could say, "You represent my position in a better and more compelling way than I can myself." I admit that such space does not exist, but I hope this book is a small, imperfect contribution toward its creation.

Some years ago I wrote a book called *The Reason for God*, which, as the title suggests, provides a case, a set of reasons, for belief in God and Christianity. While that book has been helpful to many, it does not begin far back enough for many people. Some will not even begin the journey of exploration, because, frankly, Christianity does not seem relevant enough to be worth their while. "Doesn't religion call for leaps of blind faith in an age of science, reason, and technology?" they ask. "Surely fewer and fewer people will feel the need for religion and it will die out."

This volume begins by addressing those objections. In the first two chapters I will strongly challenge both the assumption that the world is getting more secular and the belief that secular, nonreligious people are basing their view of life mainly on reason. The reality is that every person embraces his or her worldview for a variety of rational, emotional, cultural, and social factors.

After that first section of the book, in the next chapters I will compare and contrast how Christianity and secularism (with occasional reference to other religions) seek to provide meaning, satisfaction, freedom, identity, a moral compass, and hope—all things so crucial that we cannot live life without them. I will be arguing that Christianity makes the most emotional and cultural sense, that it explains these life issues in the most trenchant ways, and that it gives us unsurpassed resources for meeting these inescapable human needs.

The Reason for God also does not address many of the background beliefs that our culture presses on us about Christianity, which make it seem so implausible. These assumptions are not presented to us explicitly by argument. Rather, they are absorbed through the stories and themes of entertainment and social media. They are assumed to be simply "the way things are."[4] They are so strong that even many Christian believers, perhaps secretly at first, find their faith becoming less and less real in their minds and hearts. Much or most of what we believe at this level is, therefore, invisible to us *as* belief. Some of the beliefs that I will address are:

- "You don't need to believe in God to have a full life of meaning, hope, and satisfaction" (chapters 3, 4, and 8).

- "You should be free to live as you see fit, as long as you don't harm others" (chapter 5).

- "You become yourself when you are true to your deepest desires and dreams" (chapters 6 and 7).

- "You don't need to believe in God to have a basis for moral values and human rights" (chapters 9 and 10).

- "There's little or no evidence for the existence of God or the truth of Christianity" (chapters 11 and 12).

If you think Christianity doesn't hold much promise of making sense to a thinking person, then this book is written for you. If you have any friends or family who feel this way (and who in our society doesn't?) this book should be full of interest for you and them as well.

After one of the "skeptics welcome" discussions at our church, an older man approached me. He had come to many of our sessions. "I realize now," he said, "that both in my younger years when I was going to church *and* in the years in which I have lived as an atheist, I never really looked this carefully at my foundations. I've been too influenced by my surroundings. I haven't thought things out for myself. Thanks for this opportunity."

My hope is that this book will allow readers both inside and outside of religious belief to do the same.

PART ONE

Why Does Anyone Need Religion?

One

———

Isn't Religion Going Away?

Y ou have picked up this book, which shows you have some interest in the question of whether religious belief is possible in our time. But really, should you keep reading? Isn't a book about the relevance of religion nothing but a desperate, rear-guard action? Isn't the greater reality that "nonbelief is on the march"? That religion in general and Christianity in particular are spent forces, inevitably declining? Aren't increasing percentages of the population, especially millennials, finding that they have less need for God and faith in their lives?

A woman in my church brought a colleague from the business world to visit a Sunday worship service. The man, in his late fifties, was stunned to see several thousand professionals present, mostly young and living in Manhattan. He found the service helpful, thought provoking, and even moving. Afterward he admitted to her that the experience was unnerving. Why, she asked? He answered: "It has always been a settled belief of mine that religion is dying out, at least among educated people and certainly among the young. Oh, I can understand young adults being attracted to the Christian rock-concert-type things. But my experience here puts something of a hole in that assumption."

After a major new study by the Pew Research Center, the *Washington Post* ran an article titled "The World Is Expected to Become More Religious—Not Less." While acknowledging that in the United States and Europe the percentage of people without religious affiliation will be rising for the time being, the article distilled the research findings, namely, that in the world overall religion is growing steadily and strongly.

Christians and Muslims will make up an increasing percentage of the world's population, while the proportion that is secular will shrink. Jack Goldstone, a professor of public policy at George Mason University, is quoted: "'Sociologists jumped the gun when they said the growth of modernization would bring a growth of secularization and unbelief. . . . That is not what we're seeing,' he said. 'People . . . need religion.'"[1]

Many readers of the *Washington Post* article had the same reaction as the man who had visited our church. They found the study's findings unbelievable. One opined, "It's easy to get rid of religion just by educating people about other religions, or even giving them a secular, non-biased look at the history of the religion that any given kid has been raised in."[2] In other words, as long as education levels rise and modernization advances religion *has* to die out. In this view, people feel they need religion only if they are untutored in science, history, and logical thinking.

The Pew study, however, threatened all these deeply held beliefs about why people are religious. Not long ago, leading scholars in Western society were also nearly unanimous in thinking that religion was inevitably declining. They thought the need for religion would go away as science provided explanations and aid against the natural elements better than God ever did. In 1966 John Lennon represented this consensus when he said, "Christianity will go. It will vanish and shrink. I needn't argue about that; I'm right and will be proved right."[3]

However, this hasn't happened as advertised. As the Pew study proves, religion is on the rise, and the emergence of the more strident and outspoken "new atheists" may be in fact a reaction to the persistence and even resurgence of vibrant religion.[4] Nor is the flourishing of faith happening only among less educated people. Over the last generation philosophers such as Alasdair MacIntyre, Charles Taylor, and Alvin Plantinga have produced a major body of scholarly work supporting belief in God and critiquing modern secularism in ways that are not easy to answer.[5]

Demographers tell us the twenty-first century will be less secular than the twentieth. There have been seismic religious shifts toward

Christianity in sub-Saharan Africa and China while evangelicalism and Pentecostalism have grown exponentially in Latin America. Even in the United States the growth of the "nones" has been mainly among those who had been more nominal in their relationship to faith while the devoutly religious in the United States and Europe are growing.[6]

Belief in God makes sense to four out of five people in the world and will continue to do so in the foreseeable future.[7] The immediate question is, then, why? Why does religion still grow amid so much secular opposition? Some might answer that most people in the world are simply undereducated, while others might be a bit more blunt and respond, "Because most people are idiots." But a more thoughtful, less misanthropic answer is in order. There are two good answers to the question of why religion continues to persist and grow. One explanation is that many people find secular reason to have "things missing" from it that are necessary to live life well. Another explanation is that great numbers of people intuitively sense a transcendent realm beyond this natural world. We will look at both of these ideas in turn.

An Awareness of Something Missing

Some years ago a woman from China was doing graduate work at Columbia University in political theory, and she began attending our church. She had come to the United States to study partially because there was a growing opinion among Chinese social scientists that the Christian idea of transcendence was the historic basis for the concepts of human rights and equality.[8] After all, she said, science alone could not prove human equality. I expressed surprise at this, but she said this was not only something that some Chinese academics were arguing, but that some of the most respected secular thinkers in the West were saying it too. Through her help, I came to see that faith was making something of a comeback in rarefied philosophical circles where secular reason—rationality and science without any belief in a transcendent, supernatural reality—has increasingly been seen as missing things that society needs.

One of the world's most prominent philosophers, Jürgen Habermas, was for decades a defender of the Enlightenment view that only secular reason should be used in the public square.[9] Habermas has recently startled the philosophical establishment, however, with a changed and more positive attitude toward religious faith. He now believes that secular reason alone cannot account for what he calls "the substance of the human." He argues that science cannot provide the means by which to judge whether its technological inventions are good or bad for human beings. To do that, we must know what a good human person is, and science cannot adjudicate morality or define such a thing.[10] Social sciences may be able to tell us what human life *is* but not what it ought to be.[11] The dream of nineteenth-century humanists had been that the decline of religion would lead to less warfare and conflict. Instead the twentieth century has been marked by even greater violence, performed by states that were ostensibly nonreligious and operating on the basis of scientific rationality. Habermas tells those who are still confident that "philosophical reason . . . is capable of determining what is true and false" to simply look at the "catastrophes of the twentieth century— religious fascist and communist states, operating on the basis of practical reason—to see that this confidence is misplaced."[12] Terrible deeds have been done in the name of religion, but secularism has not proven to be an improvement.

Evidence for Habermas's thesis comes from recent research on the history of the eugenics movement in the early twentieth century. Thomas C. Leonard of Princeton University shows that a century ago progressive, science-based social policies were broadly understood to entail the sterilization or internment of those persons deemed to have defective genes.[13] In 1926 John T. Scopes was famously tried under Tennessee law for teaching evolution. Few people remember, however, that the textbook Scopes used, *Civic Biology* by George Hunter, taught not only evolution but also argued that science dictated we should sterilize or even kill those classes of people who weakened the human gene pool by spreading "disease, immorality, and crime to all parts of this country."[14] This was typical of scientific textbooks of the time.

It was the horrors of World War II, not science, that discredited eugenics. The link between genetic makeup and various forms of antisocial behavior has never been disproved; indeed, the opposite is true. Recent studies, for example, show that a particular receptor gene decreased boys' likelihood to stay in school, even with compensatory support and help from teachers and parents.[15] There are many links of heredity to disease, addictions, and other problematic behavior. Thomas Leonard argues that "eugenics and race science were not pseudosciences in the . . . Progressive Era. They were sciences."[16] It was perfectly logical to conclude that it would be more socially and economically cost effective if those genetically prone to nonproductive lives did not pass on their genetic code. However, the death camps aroused the moral intuition that eugenics, while perhaps scientifically efficient, is *evil.* Yet if you believe that it is, you must find support for your conviction in some source beyond science and the strictly rational cost-benefit analysis of practical reason. Where can you look for this support? Habermas writes: "The ideals of freedom . . . of conscience, human rights and democracy [are] the direct legacy of the Judaic ethic of justice and the Christian ethic of love. . . . To this day there is no alternative to it."[17]

None of this denies that science and reason are sources of enormous and irreplaceable good for human society. The point is rather that science *alone* cannot serve as a guide for human society.[18] This was well summarized in a speech that was written for but never delivered at the Scopes "monkey trial": "Science is a magnificent material force, but it is not a teacher of morals. It can perfect machinery, but it adds no moral restraints to protect society from the misuse of the machine. . . . Science does not [and cannot] teach brotherly love."[19] Secular, scientific reason is a great good, but if taken as the sole basis for human life, it will be discovered that there are too many things we need that it is missing.

Facing Death and Finding Forgiveness

A popular book that makes similar points is the best-selling *When Breath Becomes Air*, the reflections of a young neurosurgeon, now deceased, who wrote about a journey back toward faith when he was dying of cancer.[20] Paul Kalanithi had been an "ironclad atheist." His primary charge against Christianity was "its failure on empirical grounds. Surely enlightened reason offered a more coherent cosmos . . . a material conception of reality, an ultimately scientific worldview."[21] But the problem with this whole conception became evident to him. If everything has to have a scientific explanation and proof, then this "is to banish not only God from the world but also love, hate, meaning— . . . world that is self-evidently *not* the world we live in."[22]

All science can do, Kalanithi argues, is "reduce phenomena into manageable units." It can make "claims about matter and energy" but about nothing else. For example, science can explain love and meaning as chemical responses in your brain that helped your ancestors survive. But if we assert, which virtually everyone does, that love, meaning, and morals do not merely *feel* real but actually are so—science cannot support that. So, he concluded, "scientific knowledge [is] inapplicable" to the "central aspects of human life" including hope, love, beauty, honor, suffering, and virtue.[23]

When Kalanithi realized that there was no scientific proof for the reality of meaning and virtue, things he was sure existed, it made him rethink his whole view of life. If the premise of secularism led to conclusions he knew were not true—namely that love, meaning, and morals are illusions—then it was time to change his premise. He found it no longer unreasonable to believe in God. He came to a belief not only in God but also in "the central values of Christianity—sacrifice, redemption, forgiveness—because I found them so compelling."[24] Paul Kalanithi had also found that, in Habermas's phrase, the completely secular point of view had too many things "missing" that he knew were both necessary and real.

Kalanithi refers in passing to forgiveness as one reason he left secularism behind. He does not elaborate, but another account may shed light on this. Author and teacher Rebecca Pippert had the opportunity to audit some graduate-level courses at Harvard University, one of which was "Systems of Counseling." At one point the professor presented a case study in which therapeutic methods were used to help a man uncover a deep hostility and anger toward his mother. This helped the client understand himself in new ways. Pippert then asked the professor how he would have responded if the man had asked for help to forgive her.[25] The professor responded that forgiveness was a concept that assumed moral responsibility and many other things that scientific psychology could not speak to. "Don't force your values . . . about forgiveness onto the patient," he argued. When some of the students responded with dismay, the professor tried to relieve the tension with some humor. "If you guys are looking for a changed heart, I think you are looking in the wrong department." However, as Pippert observes, "the truth is, we *are* looking for a changed heart."[26] Secular reason, all by itself, cannot give us a basis for "sacrifice, redemption, and forgiveness," as Paul Kalanithi concluded in his final months.

A Sense of the Transcendent

A second reason why, even in our secular age, religion continues to make sense to people is more existential than intellectual. Harvard professor James Wood, in a *New Yorker* article "Is That All There Is?" tells of a friend, an analytic philosopher and a convinced atheist, who sometimes wakes in the middle of the night haunted by a visceral angst:

> *How can it be that this world is the result of an accidental big bang? How could there be no design, no metaphysical purpose? Can it be that every life—beginning with my own, my husband's, my child's, and spreading outward—is cosmically irrelevant?*[27]

Wood, who is a secular man himself, admits that "as one gets older, and parents and peers begin to die, and the obituaries in the newspaper are no longer missives from a faraway place but local letters, and one's own projects seem ever more pointless and ephemeral, such moments of terror and incomprehension seem more frequent and more piercing, and, I find, as likely to arise in the middle of the day as the night."[28]

What is this "incomprehension" that can suddenly grip even secular persons? Wood's friend's questions reveal more an intuition than a line of reasoning. It is the sense that we are more and life is more than what we can see in the material world. Steve Jobs, when contemplating his own death, confessed that he felt that "it's strange to think that you accumulate all this experience . . . and it just goes away. So I really want to believe that something survives, that maybe your consciousness endures." It seemed to Jobs untrue to reality that, for something as significant as the human self, death would be just an "off switch," so it is merely "*Click!* And you're gone."[29]

Lisa Chase, the widow of the prominent journalist Peter Kaplan, also rejects the closed, totally secular view of the world. She believes her departed husband is still alive in spirit. At the end of her essay in *Elle* she quotes her grieving son, who says, "I wish we lived in a magic world [rather than one] where science wasn't the answer to everything." Chase, though living in the heart of sophisticated, progressive Manhattan, concludes that her son's description of a "magic world" *is* closer to the truth than the secular one.[30] Her intuitions about the reality of the transcendent beyond the natural became too strong.

Sometimes this intuition triggers a protest against the way secularism seems to flatten and reduce life so that "all our getting and spending amounts to nothing more than fidgeting while we wait for death."[31] Other times it is a more positive apprehension of realities that our objective reason tells us can't really be there. Julian Barnes, for example, finds himself moved deeply by certain works of art that he realizes should not really do so. Mozart's *Requiem* relies on the Christian understanding of death, judgment, and afterlife for its stunning grandeur. With his objective reason Barnes rejects these ideas. He believes there is nothing after death but extinction. Nevertheless, the *Requiem* moves him—and not merely the sounds but the words. "It is one of the haunting hypotheticals for the nonbeliever," he writes. "What would it be like 'if [the *Requiem*] were true'[?]"[32]

Philosopher Charles Taylor asks if people like Barnes can explain *why* such art affects them so deeply. There are times when we are "hit" with such experiences of overwhelming beauty that we feel forced to use the term "spiritual" to explain our reaction. Consistently secular thinkers such as Harvard scientist Steven Pinker teach that the origin of our aesthetic sense must be, like everything else about us, something that helped our forebears stay alive and then came down to us through our genes.[33]

Reductive explanations such as Pinker's, however, actually make Taylor's case. Most people, and not just nonreligious ones, will protest "No!"—that beauty cannot be only that. "Here the challenge is to the unbeliever," Taylor writes, "to find a non-theistic register in which to respond to [great works of art] without impoverishment."[34] I believe Taylor means something like this. If you are being swept up in joy and wonder by a work of art, it will impoverish you to remind yourself that this feeling is simply a chemical reaction that helped your ancestors find food and escape predators, and nothing more. You will need to shield yourself, then, from your own secular view of things in order to get the most out of the experience. It is difficult to get "very serious pleasure from music if you know and remember that its air of significance is a pure illusion."[35] Leonard Bernstein famously admitted that when he heard great music and great beauty he sensed "Heaven," some order behind things. "[Beethoven] has the real goods, the stuff from Heaven, the power to make you feel at the finish: something is right in the world. There is something that checks throughout, that follows its own law consistently: something we can trust, that will never let us down."[36]

Is it possible, then, that art will continue to provoke in people the inescapable intuition that there is more to life than scientific secularism can account for?

The Experience of Fullness

Religion also makes sense to many people because of a direct experience of the transcendent that goes beyond the fainter intuitions of the aesthetic experience.

In his essay "Is That All There Is?" Wood discusses Charles Taylor's description of "fullness."[37] Sometimes one experiences a fullness in which the world suddenly seems charged with meaning, coherence, and beauty that break in through our ordinary sense of being in the world.[38] Some who experience this know unavoidably that there is infinitely more to life than just physical health, wealth, and freedom. There is a depth and wonder and some kind of Presence above and beyond ordinary life. It may make us feel quite small and even unimportant before it, and yet also hope filled and unworried about the things that usually make us anxious.

These experiences are probably more frequent than is thought, because most people who tell of them do so very reluctantly, knowing that their friends and family will think they have gone off the rails. Frank Bruni wrote in the *New York Times* about experiences like this that leave people feeling in the middle "between godliness and godlessness" because they seem to lead to the conclusion that there is something beyond the material, seen world.[39] Philosophers Hubert Dreyfus and Sean Kelly call the experience "The Whoosh."[40] English philosopher Roger Scruton speaks of the sense of a "sacred order" that keeps erupting into our consciousness.[41]

A classic example of this is what happened to Lord Kenneth Clark, one of Great Britain's most prominent art historians and authors, and the producer of the BBC television series *Civilization*. In an autobiographical account, Clark writes that when he was living in a villa in France he had a curious episode.

> *I had a religious experience. It took place in the church of San Lorenzo, but did not seem to be connected with the harmonious beauty of the architecture. I can only say that for a few minutes, my whole being was radiated by a kind of heavenly joy,*

far more intense than anything I had ever experienced before. This state of mind lasted for several minutes . . . but wonderful as it was, [it] posed an awkward problem in terms of action. My life was far from blameless. I would have to reform. My family would think I was going mad, and perhaps after all, it was a delusion, for I was in every way unworthy of such a flood of grace. Gradually the effect wore off and I made no effort to retain it. I think I was right. I was too deeply embedded in the world to change course. But I had "felt the finger of God" I am quite sure and, although the memory of this experience has faded, it still helps me to understand the joys of the saints.[42]

A similar experience happened to Czech writer and revolutionary-turned-statesman Václav Havel. One day when he was in prison he looked out into the crown of a great tree and suddenly was "overcome by a sensation" that he had stepped "outside time in which all the beautiful things I have ever seen and experienced existed in a total 'co-present'"—what traditionally would have been called eternity. He was "flooded with a sense of ultimate happiness and harmony" and felt he was standing "at the very edge of the infinite."[43]

Atheism with a Wild God

While Clark and Havel gave religious interpretations to their encounters with fullness, there are others who maintain disbelief in God yet have no way to account for the experience rationally.[44] In the *Paris Review* Kristin Dombek writes, "I have been an atheist now for more than fifteen years, and I have been able to explain to myself almost everything about the faith I grew up in, but I have not been able to explain those experiences of God so real he entered the bedrooms of his own accord, lit them up with joy, and made people generous. . . . It [was] like you've glimpsed the world's best secret: that love need not be scarce."[45]

Atheist Barbara Ehrenreich, best known for her seminal work *Nickel and Dimed*, wrote a memoir titled *Living with a Wild God*, which centers on a life-changing mystical experience she had in May 1959 as a seventeen-year-old. She had begun a "quest" at the age of thirteen to find answers to the questions What is the point of our brief existence? and What are we doing here and to what end?[46] Ehrenreich was raised by atheist parents, and her efforts to answer these questions were carried out on a strictly rationalistic basis. This led her into what she calls the "morass" of solipsism. She felt there was no way to know right from wrong or true from false.[47] But then at age seventeen, on an empty street just before dawn, "I found whatever I had been looking for since the articulation of my quest." It was an experience that, as others have also said, could not be described. "Here we leave the jurisdiction of language, where nothing is left but the vague gurgles of surrender expressed in words like 'ineffable' and 'transcendent.'"[48]

> *There were no visions, no prophetic voices or visits by totemic animals, just this blazing everywhere. Something poured into me and I poured out into it. This was not the passive beatific merger with "the All," as promised by the Eastern mystics. It was a furious encounter with a living substance. . . . "Ecstasy" would be the word for this, but only if you acknowledge [that it] does not occupy the same spectrum as happiness or euphoria, that it . . . can resemble an outbreak of violence.*[49]

Now that she had every evidence that there was at least the "possibility of a nonhuman agent . . . some mysterious Other . . . could I still call myself an atheist?"[50] She decided she could. Why? She says that her experience bore no resemblance to the "religious iconography" she had grown up with.[51] First, this Presence did not seem to be solicitous toward humans at all. "The most highly advertised property of the Christian . . . God [is] that he is 'good.'" But her experience had connected her with something "wild," unconditioned, even dangerous and violent, not anything she could consider nice or good. Second, her experience did not come "with ethical instructions." She heard no voices. "Whatever I had seen *was what it was,* with no . . . reference to human concerns." And yet, she says, the immediate result was that she was shaken out of her claustrophobic philosophical conundrums and swept out into "the great plain of history—the downtrodden against those who do the down-treading, the invaded against the invaders. I had been swept up in this struggle."[52] She became a social activist and has remained so for the rest of her life.

Contrary to her interpretation of her experience, however, it does indeed fit in with much of the Christian and biblical theology of God. She says that it was a "wild, amoral Other," not "the enforcer of ethics," but a reading of the book of Job that shows that human beings have encountered him as both.[53] In biblical accounts of encounters with the divine (see Exodus 3 and 33 and Isaiah 6) the human recipients feel utterly insignificant. These texts also reveal a God whose presence is violently traumatic and lethal yet compelling and attractive at the same time. Augustine, in his *Confessions,* describes a preconversion experience of God that he could describe only as "the flash of one tremulous glance" that gave him a dazzling but threatening glimpse at something wholly other.[54] Later, after he met God through Christ, Augustine's encounters with the divine were marked by "the union of love and dread" (*Confessions* XI, 11). Oxford historian Henry Chadwick, in his book on Augustine's theology, explains:

> *The dread [was] induced by the contemplation of the unapproachable Other so distant and 'unlike', the love by the awareness of the Other who is so similar and so near.*[55]

Even Ehrenreich's offhanded comment that *it was what it was* sounds like God's word to Moses "I am who I am" (Exodus 3:14). The "wildness" Ehrenreich describes fits in completely with many of the descriptions of God in the Bible.[56] God appears as a hurricane (Job 38:1); in other places he comes as a blazing fire (Exodus 3:2) or as a smoking furnace or searing lightning (Genesis 15:17).[57] Ehrenreich's experience sounds uncannily like Rudolf Otto's famous description of the "Holy."

She had come, as he writes, "upon something inherently 'wholly other,' whose kind and character are incommensurable with our own, and before which we therefore recoil in a wonder that strikes us chill and numb."[58]

Despite all this, she remains an atheist. Nevertheless, we might say that her strictly secular frame is no longer complete or closed. She says she is "no longer the kind of scornful, dogmatic atheist my parents had been." When asked on a TV show about her atheism,

> *I said only that I did not "believe in God," which was true as far as it went. Obviously I could not go on to say, "I don't have to 'believe' in God because I know God, or some sort of god anyway." I must have lacked conviction because I got a call from my smart, heroically atheist Aunt Marcia saying she's watched the show and detected the tiniest quaver of evasion in my answer.*[59]

Charles Taylor argues that "fullness" is neither strictly a belief nor a mere experience. It is the perception that life is greater than can be accounted for by naturalistic explanations and, as we have seen, it is the widespread, actual lived condition of most human beings regardless of worldview.[60] The challenge for both believers and nonbelievers is how to make sense of this lived condition of fullness within their belief structures. If this life is all there is, why do we long so deeply for something that doesn't exist and never did? Why are there so many experiences that point beyond the world picture of secularism, even by those who do not welcome such perceptions? And if this life is all there is, what will you do with these desires that have no fulfillment within the closed secular frame?

Why It Is So Natural to Wonder

The limits of secular reason, the ordinary experience of transcendence in the arts, and the extraordinary experiences that rend the secular frames even of hardened atheists—all of these explain why religious belief keeps reasserting itself even in the heart of the secular West.

Actually, it is quite natural to human beings to move toward belief in God. As humanities scholar Mark Lilla has written: "To most humans, curiosity about higher things comes naturally, it's indifference to them that must be learned."[61] Strict secularism holds that people are only physical entities without souls, that when loved ones die they simply cease to exist, that sensations of love and beauty are just neurological-chemical events, that there is no right or wrong outside of what we in our minds determine and choose. Those positions are at the very least deeply counterintuitive for nearly all people, and large swaths of humanity will continue to simply reject them as impossible to believe.

Many ask: Why do people feel they need religion? Perhaps now we see that the way this question is phrased doesn't explain the persistence of faith. People believe in God not merely because they feel some emotional need, but because it makes sense of what they see and experience. Indeed, we have seen that many thoughtful people are drawn toward belief somewhat unwillingly. They embrace religion because they think it is more fully true to the facts of human existence than secularism is.

But Still—Isn't Religion in Decline?

I can certainly imagine a reader at this point conceding much of what I have been saying, that secularism cannot account for many aspects of human experience, and that a great number of people have a strong sense of a transcendent reality. But, you may counter, nevertheless, are not far more people losing their faith than are gaining one? One writer in the *Times* of London assured readers that religion is inevitably waning among the people of the world, "as the unfairness of divine justice, the irrationality of the teaching, or the prejudice . . . begin to bother them." He concluded that "secularism and milder forms of religion will win in the long run."[62]

Many people have a great investment in this account of things. Nevertheless, the evidence is strongly against it. Sociologists Peter Berger and Grace Davie report that "most sociologists of religion now agree" that the secularization thesis—that religion declines as a society becomes more modern—"has been empirically shown to be false."[63] Countries such as China are becoming more religious (and Christian) even as they modernize.[64] Other sociological studies, such as the pathbreaking work by Georgetown professor José Casanova, have found no simple downward trend for religion as societies become modern.[65]

Most striking of all are the demographic studies that predict that it is not religious populations but secular ones that are in long-term decline. The April 2015 Pew study projects that the percentage of atheists, agnostics, and the religiously unaffiliated will slowly but steadily decline, from 16.4 percent of the world's population today to 13.2 percent forty years from now. University of London professor Eric Kaufmann, in his book *Shall the Religious Inherit the Earth?*, speaks of "the crisis of secularism" and argues that the shrinkage of secularism and liberal religion is inevitable.[66]

Why? There are two basic reasons. One has to do with the trends of retention and conversion. Many point to the rising percentage of younger adult "nones" in the United States as evidence for the inevitable shrinkage of religion. However, Kaufmann shows that almost all of the new religiously unaffiliated come not from conservative religious groups but from more liberal ones. Secularization, he writes, "mainly erodes . . . the taken-for-granted, moderate faiths that trade on being mainstream and established."[67] Therefore, the very "liberal, moderate" forms of religion that most secular people think are the most likely to survive will not. Conservative religious bodies, by contrast, have a very high retention rate of their children, and they convert more than they lose.[68]

The second main reason that the world will become more religious is that religious people have significantly more children, whereas the more irreligious and secular a population, the less often marriage happens and the smaller the families.[69] This is true across the world and holds within every national group, within every educational level, and within every economic class. So, for example, it is not the case that religious people have more children because they are less educated. Religious people, when they become more educated and urban, continue to out produce their less religious counterparts "by a landslide."[70]

It should be clear that no one is making the case that always "the more children, the better." Columbia economist Jeffrey Sachs has argued well that overpopulation and exorbitant birthrates are major contributing factors to world poverty.[71] Nevertheless, it would be a mistake to think there is no opposite problem. Cultures that do not have a replacement-level birthrate die out as they are displaced by other populations and cultures. As Kaufmann and others show, the most secular societies are maintained through the immigration of more religious peoples.[72]

In the United States and Europe, liberal religious bodies will continue to lose members, who are swelling the numbers of the secular and unaffiliated, while traditional, orthodox religions will grow.[73] This is hard for cultural elites to grasp, since liberal religions are the only ones that secular thinkers believe are viable. In the Broadway hit *The Book of Mormon* the main characters are missionaries with traditional views, but in the end they come to regard the stories of their scripture as only metaphors which lead us to love and make the world a better place. Certainties about the afterlife and even God are unnecessary. This "all horizontal and no vertical" liberal religion plays well to secular American audiences, but as the sociologists have shown, it is the kind of faith that is dying out most quickly in the world.[74] Meanwhile, the faiths that rely on conversion are growing exponentially.

Some years ago I spoke to a man who had been a minister in a liberal, mainline denomination in Manhattan for four decades. He told me that when he had been trained for ministry in the early 1960s, he was confidently told by his teachers that the only religion that would survive in the future was the most mild, modern kind that did not believe in miracles or the deity of Christ or a literal, bodily resurrection. But when

I spoke to him he was nearing retirement, and he observed that most of his generation of ministers presided over empty church sanctuaries and dwindling, aging congregations. "Ironically," he observed, "they can only keep the doors open by renting them out to growing, vibrant churches that believe all the doctrines we were told would soon be obsolete."

It turns out, then, that the individualism of modern culture does not necessarily lead to a decline in religion. Rather, it leads to a decline of *inherited* religion, the sort one is born into.[75] Religion that wanes comes with one's assigned national or ethnic identity, as in "You are Indian, so you are Hindu; you are Norwegian, so you're Lutheran; you are Polish, so you're Catholic; you are American, so you should be a good member of a Christian denomination." What is not declining in modern societies is *chosen* religion, religion based not on ethnicity or solely on upbringing but on personal decision.[76] For example, only evangelical Protestants, among all religious bodies in the United States, are converting more people than they are losing—which is exactly what Berger, Casanova, Davie, and other sociologists would lead us to expect.[77]

In the non-Western world the growth of Christianity is stunning. Last Sunday there were more Christians attending church in China than there were in all of "Christian Europe."[78] By 2020 Christianity will have grown from 11.4 million Christians in East Asia (China, Korea, Japan) in 1970 and 1.2 percent of the population, to 171.1 million and 10.5 percent of the population.[79] In 1910 only 12 million people, or 9 percent of Africa's population, were Christians, but they will number 630 million, or 49.3 percent of the populace, by 2020.[80] Last Sunday in *each* of the nations of Nigeria, Kenya, Uganda, Tanzania, and South Africa there were more Anglicans in church than there were Anglicans and Episcopalians in all of Britain and the United States combined.[81]

Kaufmann, a Canadian academic and a secularist, answers the question of his book's title—*Shall the Religious Inherit the Earth?*—on the last page of his book with an unequivocal *yes.*[82] In an interview with *New Humanist*, Kaufmann was asked whether secularism might turn the tide and "do a better job of winning over [people]." He answered: "Religion does provide that enchantment, that meaning and emotion, and in our current moment we [secularists] lack that."[83]

Why to Keep Reading

So why read this book? One reason is practical. In this chapter I have not addressed whether religion is true. I have only sought to make the case that it is by no means a dying force. Rabbi Jonathan Sacks, in his book *Not in God's Name*, concludes that "the twenty-first century will be more religious than the twentieth.[84] He touches on many of the realities we have observed in this chapter. Secularism in the twentieth century has not proven it can give moral guidance to technology or the state. Many intuit faintly or strongly that we human beings and our loves and aspirations cannot be reduced to matter, chemistry, and genes. Finally, citing the low birthrates of secular countries, he argues that religion provides a basis for the growth rather than the decline of human communities. We need, then, to jettison the view that religious belief is not worthy of our attention because it is becoming irrelevant. I invite you to keep reading even if you're not interested in Christianity, at least for the sake of understanding the faith of growing millions of people who are finding faith appealing.

The other reason to keep reading is a personal one. You may find that the descriptions of "fullness" and other such intuitions resonate with your own experience. But what if they don't? You may say, "I feel no need for God in my life." Faith, however, is not produced strictly by emotional need, nor should it be. Many of the secular thinkers we have cited have rather reluctantly moved toward religion not out of emotional need but because faith in God makes more sense of life than nonbelief. As we have noted, people come to faith in God through a mix of rational, personal, and relational reasons. We will be exploring all of these categories in this book.

Consider too what Saint Augustine says to God in his *Confessions,* that "our heart is unquiet until it rests in you."[85] In other words, if you are experiencing unquiet and dissatisfaction in your life, they may be signs of a need for God that is there but which is not recognized as such. That is Augustine's theory. It would be worth your time to explore whether or not he is right.

Two

Isn't Religion Based on Faith and Secularism on Evidence?

Today's media and literature are full of what could be called "deconversion" stories. S. A. Joyce gives us his.

> *In the years after leaving the military I went back to college—not as a serious attempt to earn a degree, but just to improve myself. . . . I came across and pieced together, bit by bit, a humanistic set of values which turned out to be far more self-consistent and pertinent to the modern world than a petrified Decalogue of biblical taboo. It was becoming clear to me that the universe behaved pretty much as might be expected if God didn't exist, or at least didn't care. It gradually dawned upon me that in the grand scheme of things there was in fact no grand scheme. . . . God performed no observable function and had no valid purpose. The question entered my mind, "What is a God without purpose and for which there is no evidence?" "Nonexistent," came the obvious answer. The blinders of dogma and the yoke of dread were finally off. For me the universe now shone in a wholesome new light, the comforting glow of reality no longer distorted, either by the almost cartoonish artificial "glory" of myth and miracle or by the dreadful glare of hellfire. I was free!*

He titles his deconversion testimony "One night I prayed to know the truth. The next morning I discovered I was an atheist."[1]

If we read or hear scores of these loss-of-faith accounts, as I have, some patterns can be discerned. I have quoted S. A. Joyce because his story is almost prototypical. The narrators recount that they were confronted by the lack of empirical evidence for the claims of religion, and had to come to grips with the problem of evil in a world supposedly overseen by a good, all-powerful God. They decided that the universe shows no trace of the traditional God. If for a moment they worried that life without God would be purposeless, they soon discovered thoughtful nonbelievers who were much more passionately committed to justice and equality than most religious people they knew. They concluded that human beings don't need God to lead a good life and build a good world for all to live in. In fact, we can better carry out these tasks without any religion at all. After struggling with the implications of all these discoveries, and counting the cost of "coming out" as skeptics, they finally decided to face reality and tell the truth.[2]

This is a powerful story line. It depicts nonbelief as the result of a quest for truth and the courage to face life as it is. It implies that the nonbeliever is ready to engage any believer who can rise to the same level of objectivity and truthfulness. One secular commenter wrote: "I find it ludicrous that any thinking adult can believe in God given there has NEVER been even one tiny bit of PROOF for His existence. I'm open to anyone who thinks they have such proof trying to prove their belief to me."[3]

Deconversion accounts often testify to a desire for a world no longer divided endlessly between true believers and infidels. Newly secular persons feel they are now more accepting of all people. A Web site titled "A Good Life Without God" argues that without the influence of religion we will finally be able to achieve "a tolerant, open society where [there is] mutual respect and equality for all people, no one view of the universe but lots of views, and all people will be able to realize their potential."[4]

Behind these stories, however, lies a deeper narrative, namely, that religious persons are living by blind faith, while secular and nonbelievers in God are grounding their position in evidence and reason. Most who have lost their faith say that they are simply following the dictates of rationality. But anthropologists such as Talal Asad counter that they are actually shedding one set of moral narratives—with its insiders and outsiders, heroes and heretics, and unprovable assumptions about reality— for another. Assad calls the typical deconversion story one of going "from a jungle of darkness into the light."[5] The plotline is one in which the hero has the courage to think for him- or herself.

Charles Taylor calls this narrative the "subtraction story."[6] People claim that their secular outlook is simply what was left after science and reason subtracted their former belief in the supernatural. Once that superstition was gone, they were able to see things that had been there all along—that reason alone can establish truth, and the "humanistic values" of equality and freedom. However, each of these ideas is a new belief, a value-laden commitment that can't be empirically proven. To move from religion to secularism is not so much a loss of faith as a shift into a new set of beliefs and into a new community of faith, one that draws the lines between orthodoxy and heresy in different places.

This is one of the main reasons many secular people do not think it worth their while to explore and weigh the claims for believers in God and Christianity. They assume that belief is mainly a matter of faith while nonbelief is mainly based on reason. In this chapter I want to strongly challenge this view. I know that for most readers this idea—that secularity is a set of faith beliefs—is a new one. So I will begin by making those secular beliefs more visible.

Exclusive Rationality

The first set of beliefs that many secular people adopt is what I will call "exclusive rationality." Exclusive rationality is the belief that science is the only arbiter of what is real and factual and that we should not believe anything unless we can prove it decisively using empirical observation. The things that we can prove are the only things worthy of being called "truth." Everything else one might say or think lies in the realm of unreliable human feeling and opinion. This view of reason is fundamental to the secular claim that religion simply cannot prove its claims that there is a God and a supernatural realm.

In our society today this might seem like a perfectly levelheaded position. However, many who have thought this view out to its logical conclusion have seen it to be deeply problematic. I once knew a young man who was a devoted philosophy student. Like his hero, the French philosopher René Descartes, he started with the only certainty, namely, that he existed and could think. From there he tried to proceed by piecing together a view of life that was in every part absolutely rational and proven. To his dismay, he discovered that he could get almost nowhere. He couldn't prove that the universe wasn't an optical illusion, a trick played on him by some demon. He also couldn't prove by what standard something was "proven." He fell into a kind of intense, radical agnosticism, unable to know that anything existed outside of his own self and mind.

In her spiritual biography, Barbara Ehrenreich testifies that she arrived at the same place as a teenager. "The whole logical enterprise began to come apart, as I suppose it's bound to when you confront the world with only 'I' as a given," she wrote. When a Christian friend chastised her for not believing in God, she responded that it was hard enough to believe in *her*. "Believing in her, or even my family members for that matter, as independent minds, took all the effort I could muster."[7] Both Ehrenreich and the young man used exclusive rationality—the belief that you cannot know anything unless you can prove it empirically—and came to the conclusion that, therefore, they could hardly know anything at all. We should not see these cases as eccentric outliers. In many ways they foreshadowed the path of philosophical thinking over the last century.

William Kingdon Clifford, the British mathematician and philosopher, crystallized exclusive rationality in his famous essay "The Ethics of Belief" (1877). He wrote, "It is wrong always, everywhere, and for anyone to believe anything on insufficient evidence," and by "sufficient evidence" he meant empirical verification that would convince any reasonable person who is capable of assessing it.[8] Even though most secular people today have never heard of Clifford, this is the operating principle most of them use for rejecting religious belief.[9] There are innumerable challenges by atheists on the Internet who say to religious people, "If you want me to believe in God, you must prove his existence."

However, this view of reason is now seen to have insurmountable problems. For one thing, it cannot meet its own standard. According to Clifford's thesis, we should not believe something unless we can prove it empirically. But what is the empirical proof for *that* proposition?

Another problem is that few of our convictions about truth can be proven scientifically. While we may be able to demonstrably prove to any rational person that substance X will boil at temperature Y at elevation Z, we cannot so prove what we believe about justice and human rights, or that people are all equal in dignity and worth, or what we think is good and evil human behavior. If we used the same standard of evidence on our other beliefs that many secular people use to reject belief in God, no one would be able to justify much of anything. The only things that would be "ethical" to believe in would be things that could be proven in a laboratory.[10] Philosopher Peter van Inwagen points out that the Clifford essay is often assigned in religion classes today but never in classes on epistemology (which addresses how we know what we know). That is because, Van Inwagen says, there are almost no teachers of philosophy in the West who believe in Clifford's view of reason anymore.[11]

An additional problem is that even the criteria for proof are widely contested. That means that even statements of agnosticism can contain declarations of belief about rationality. To say, for example, that you don't believe that P is proven accepts by faith some standard of "proof" that not everyone accepts.[12] Obviously, you cannot prove a norm of rational proof without using it. So reason can make a case that it is the way to truth only by appealing to itself. One philosopher writes, "That seems to some like defending the trustworthiness of a car salesman by having him swear that he always tells the truth."[13]

That statement is unfair. Reason is a crucial and irreplaceable way to help us weigh competing beliefs. But it is impossible to claim that we should believe only what is proven and that therefore, since religion can't be proven, we shouldn't embrace it. All of us have things we believe— including things we would sacrifice and even die for—that cannot be proven. We believe them on a combination of rational, experiential, and social grounds. But since these beliefs cannot be proved, does this mean we ought not to hold them, or that we can't know them to be true? We should, therefore, stop demanding that belief in God meet a standard of universally acknowledged proof when we don't apply that to the other commitments on which we base our lives.

"The View from Nowhere"

So reason and proof must start with faith in reason and belief in some particular concept of proof. However, there is even more faith involved in ordinary rationality that that. Twentieth-century thinkers such as Martin Heidegger, Maurice Merleau-Ponty, Ludwig Wittgenstein have argued that all reasoning is based on prior faith commitments to which one did not reason.[14]

For example, reason depends on the faith that our cognitive senses— our eyes and ears, our minds and memories—are not tricking us. Yet there is no noncircular way to establish that. We cannot test their reliability without using and therefore assuming their reliability. Ludwig Wittgenstein showed that it is impossible to disprove the claim that the earth is only one hundred years old and that it came into existence with all the marks of being old.[15] To explain what Wittgenstein means, consider the movie *The Matrix*. Can you prove that you aren't actually in a vat somewhere with plugs coming out of the back of your head feeding you an alternate reality? We cannot, then, prove these fundamental premises for the operation of reasoning. We take them on faith and are defensively dismissive of those who question those beliefs, because we know we can't "get behind" them in order prove them.

Also, even the assertion that science and empirical evidence are the only sure ways to understand reality assumes a view of the universe that can be known only by faith. For example, American philosopher C. Stephen Evans writes, "Science by its very nature is not fit to investigate whether there is more to reality than the natural world."[16] Because science's baseline methodology is to always assume a natural cause for every phenomenon, there is no experiment that could prove *or* disprove that there is something beyond this material world. For example, there would be no way to empirically prove that a miracle has occurred since a scientist would have to assume, no matter what, that no natural cause had been discovered *yet*. If there actually had truly been a supernatural miracle, modern science could not possibly discern it.

Evans argues, then, that both the statement "there is no supernatural reality beyond this world" and the statement "there is a transcendent reality beyond this world" are philosophical, not scientific, propositions. Neither can be empirically proven in such a way that no rational person can doubt.[17] To state that there is no God *or* that there is a God, then, necessarily entails faith. And so the declaration that science is the only arbiter of truth is not itself a scientific finding. It is a belief.

All this is because deeper beliefs about the nature of being, traditionally called "ontology," are unavoidable and yet empirically unprovable. Indian Hindu philosophy holds that the world is the emanation of an absolute spirit and therefore much of reality can be truly discerned only through contemplation. Western science assumes instead that things exist on their own—and therefore that all material effects are contingent on previous material causes.[18] If the Indian view is right, reality is not ultimately predictable. Western science, however, assumes a closed system of natural causes and that, therefore, given enough empirical knowledge, all things could be predicted. There can be no experiment that can test out whether the Indian or the Western view is right, and that's the point. As eighteenth-century philosopher David Hume has extensively argued, our science is based on beliefs about the universe that can't be proven or disproven.[19]

In short, no one can purge him- or herself of all faith assumptions and assume an objective, belief-free, pure openness to objective evidence. There is no "view from nowhere."

Background Beliefs

Scientist and philosopher Michael Polanyi has argued that every individual act of human knowing works on two levels—"focal awareness," in which the knower gives direct attention to an observed object, and "subsidiary awareness," in which the knower employs a host of assumptions that are tacit and not recognized as we use them.[20] Polanyi shows that all people have innumerable beliefs about reality and relevance that come to us through bodily experience, authorities we trust, and communities we are part of. These beliefs pass into us and we hold them as tacit knowledge, barely conscious beliefs, and "paradigms" of reality.[21] So we always come to observe anything with a "preunderstanding" of existing beliefs, expectations, and values that controls what we see, what seems plausible, and what does not.[22]

This tacit knowledge, of which we are barely aware, shapes our conscious reasoning more than we know. Often we find certain arguments compelling mainly because of our background beliefs, and when these beliefs shift, usually not through argument but through experience and intuition, it makes arguments that formerly felt strong begin to feel weak.

The problem of evil is a good case study of how background beliefs control our supposedly strictly rational thought. James Wood and Barbara Ehrenreich explain how the problem of evil and suffering in the world was decisive in preventing them from believing in God as young adults. Wood, who was raised in an evangelical Christian home, says that the cruelty and evil of actual human life would make life pointless even if God exists.[23] Wood calls this objection to the existence of God "so obvious and so old," but that isn't really the case. The book of Job, for example, presents the outrageousness of undeserved suffering as well as any ancient text, yet in no way does it present it as an objection to the existence of God. Ancient people were arguably much more acquainted with brutality, loss, and evil than we are. Their literature—and the book of Job is only one example—is filled with laments about inexplicable suffering. Yet there is virtually no ancient thinker who reasoned from such evil that, therefore, there couldn't be a God. Why does this argument against God's existence seem so rational and convincing today?

Charles Taylor explains why modern people are far more likely to lose their faith over suffering than those in times past. He says it is because, culturally, our belief and confidence in the powers of our own intellect have changed. Ancient people did not assume that the human mind had enough wisdom to sit in judgment on how an infinite God was disposing of things. It is only in modern times that we get "the certainty that we have all the elements we need to carry out a trial of God."[24] Only when this background belief in the sufficiency of our own reason shifted did the presence of evil in the world seem to be an argument against the existence of God.

There is, then, a significant backdrop of faith behind modern arguments against God on the basis of evil. It is assumed, not proven, that a God beyond our reason could not exist—and therefore we conclude that he doesn't exist. This is, of course, a form of begging the question. Our background beliefs set up our conscious reasoning to fail to find sufficient evidence for God. So the young James Wood and Barbara Ehrenreich, brilliant young thinkers that they were, found the thesis of the "monotheistic God" wanting. But it wasn't true that their reasoning had undermined their faith. Instead it was that a new kind of faith, one in the power of human reason and ability to comprehend the depths of things, had displaced an older, more self-effacing kind of faith.

The Critique of Doubt

So even our most rigorous rational thinking is shot through with various forms of faith. Michael Polanyi goes a step further, however, and shows that even skeptical doubt always contains an element of belief. In his essay "The Critique of Doubt" Polanyi argues that doubt and belief are ultimately "equivalent." Why? "The doubting of any explicit statement," he writes, "denies [one] belief . . . in favor of other beliefs which are not doubted for the time being."[25] You can't doubt belief A except on the basis of some belief B you are believing instead at the moment. So, for example, you cannot say, "No one can know enough to be certain about God and religion," without assuming at that moment that you know enough about the nature of religious knowledge to be certain about *that*.

Some years ago a man began attending our church. He had begun life with a general belief in God, but he had been assailed with doubts during his college years and had lived for decades without any religious faith. After a number of months of attending our congregation he told me that faith in God was looking much more plausible to him. When I asked how that was happening, he said that a turning point had been a talk he heard me give on "doubting your doubts." He said, "I had never realized that there had to be some faith under my doubts. And when I looked at the things I did believe, I discovered that I didn't have good reasons for *them*. When I started to examine some of the bases for my doubts, faith in God didn't seem so hard."

What does it mean to do that? As I got to know this man and he became a friend and eventually a member of my church, I went through the series of the things that had triggered his first doubts. Later I discovered an atheist blogger who made an almost identical list:

> *The first cause that plants the initial seed of doubt varies from person to person. However, some of the common reasons include: meeting a real atheist and finding that they are not the immoral, unhappy misanthropes the believer has been led to*

expect; witnessing a good and faithful fellow believer suffer hor-
ribly seemingly for no reason; witnessing institutionalized
corruption or hypocrisy in the believer's religious hierarchy; real-
izing the basic unfairness of the doctrines of Hell and salvation;
or finding an unanswerable contradiction or error in the
believer's scriptures of choice.[26]

Here's how my friend doubted his doubts.

**Meeting a real atheist who was not an immoral, unhappy mis-
anthrope.** This doubt is based on the implicit belief that religious people are saved by God because of their goodness and morality. If that is
the case, then atheists by definition ought to be bad and immoral. When
he learned the biblical teaching that we are saved only by undeserved
grace, not by our moral character, he realized that there was no reason
why an atheist might not be a far better person than a Christian. The
belief under his doubt crumbled, and so his doubt went away.

**Witnessing a good and faithful believer suffer horribly for no
good reason.** This doubt stems from a belief that if we human beings
can't discern a sufficient reason for an act of God, then there can't be any.
My friend came to realize this assumed that, if there was an infinite God,
a finite mind should be able to evaluate his motives and plans. He asked
himself how reasonable it was to believe that, to have such confidence in
his own insight, and the doubt began to erode.

Witnessing corruption or hypocrisy in a religious institution.
This might be the most warranted basis for doubting the truth of a particular faith. But my friend realized that the moral standards he was
using to judge hypocritical believers came mainly from Christianity itself.
"The worst thing I could say about Christians was that they weren't being Christian enough, but why should they be, if Christianity wasn't true
at all?"

**Realizing the basic unfairness of the doctrines of hell and salva-
tion.** This doubt, my friend said, largely came from the underlying beliefs of his culture. He had a Chinese friend who did not believe in God,
but who said that, if he existed, God certainly would have a right to

judge people as he saw fit. He then realized that his doubt about hell was based on a very white, Western, democratic, individualistic mind-set that most other people in the world did not share. "To insist that the universe be run like a Western democracy was actually a very ethnocentric point of view," he told me.

An unanswerable contradiction or error in the Scripture. This doubt, my friend said, was based on a belief that all religious believers had a naive, uncritical trust in the Bible. "Since coming to your church I realize that there have been a thousand PhD dissertations written on every single verse, and that for every contention that one verse contradicts another or is an error, there are ten cogent counterpoints." He rightly lost his faith that he could ever find a difficulty in the Bible that was "unanswerable."

A Balance of Reason and Faith

Nothing I have said should be read as an argument for irrationality or belief based on emotion and impulse alone. Nonrational leaps of faith, prejudice, and unquestioning traditionalism are wrong. Theses and propositions should be rationally tested for both inner consistency and alignment with what we know about reality. We should have as many good reasons for what we believe as possible. However, there is both an objective pole and a subjective pole to knowledge. The Enlightenment, following René Descartes and John Locke, refused to see the subjective as true knowledge at all. On the other hand, twentieth-century thinkers such as Jacques Derrida and Michel Foucault, being sensitive to how power shapes public perceptions of truth, attacked the idea that there was any objective pole at all. No one, they thought, should be certain of anything.

But Michael Polanyi is convincing that both these positions—of pure objectivism or subjectivism—are self-defeating and ultimately impossible to hold. The objectivists can't account for the host of values they unavoidably *know* though they can't be proven. And the subjectivists make their own assertions meaningless and contradictory. Where do they get the certainty of knowledge necessary to say that no one has the right to be certain? Polanyi's goal was "to restore the *balance* of our cognitive powers."[27] Social scientists have argued that we arrive at what we consider to be "truth" through a range of methods including analytic thinking, experience, empathy or "mentalizing," and intuition.[28] Augustine understood that reason and faith work always together and that reason always operates "under the guidance of antecedent belief."[29]

The Christian believer is using reason and faith to get to her beliefs just as her secular neighbor is using reason and faith to get to hers. They are both looking at the same realities in nature and human life, and both are seeking a way to make the best sense of them through a process that is rational, personal, intuitive, and social. Reason does not and cannot operate alone.

Contemporary secularity, then, is not the absence of faith, but is instead based on a whole set of beliefs, including a number of highly contestable assumptions about the nature of proof and rationality itself.[30]

Humanistic Morality

Besides a set of beliefs about rationality, most secular people today also hold a set of ethical beliefs about the nature of human life. Many would describe themselves as "liberal humanists" who are committed to science and reason, to progress and the good of humanity, and to the rights, equality, and freedom of every individual human being.[31] Secularity is marked by a call "to take active responsibility for the progressive improvement of the world . . . [to] work for the betterment of other humans, even strangers beyond our shores."[32] And, it is argued, removing the influence of religion in the world will help us realize these values.

However, where did these values come from? Not only can none of these humanistic moral standards be proven empirically, but they don't follow logically from a materialistic view of the world. This problem seems invisible to many. For example, a commenter on a *New York Times* article about the meaning of life writes:

> *When the Hubble space telescoped [sic] pointed to a black spot in the sky about the size of an eraser head for a week it found 30,000 galaxy [sic] over 13 billion years old with many trillions of stars and many many more trillions of inferred planets. [So] how significant are you? . . . You are not a unique snowflake, you are not specials [sic], you are just another piece of decaying matters [sic] on the compost pile of this world. Nothing of who you are and what you will do in the short time you are here will matter. Everything short of that realization is vanity. So celebrate life in every moment, admire its wonders, [and] love without reservation.*[33]

The first part of this statement provides a bracing, no-holds-barred materialistic view of the world. You are made strictly of matter without any soul. You were not created for any special purpose. There is no afterlife. The world will eventually burn up in the death of the sun. Nothing you do here, be it kind or cruel, will make any difference in the end. But then, with the word "so" indicating a logical sequence, we are told that we should therefore live a life of celebration and love.

However, if we are just a decaying piece of matter in a decaying universe and nothing more significant than that, how does it follow that we should live a life of love toward others? It doesn't. Why shouldn't we live as selfishly as we can get away with? How do beliefs in individual freedom, human rights, and equality arise from or align with the idea that human beings came to be what they are through the survival of the fittest? They don't, really. Russian philosopher Vladimir Solovyov sarcastically summarized the ethical reasoning of secular humanism like this: "Man descended from apes, therefore we must love one another."[34] The second clause does not follow from the first. If it was natural for the strong to eat the weak in the past, why aren't people allowed to do it now? I am not, of course, arguing that we should not love one another. Rather, I'm saying that, given the secular view of the universe, the conclusion of love or social justice is no more logical than the conclusion to hate or destroy. These two sets of beliefs—in a thorough-going scientific materialism and in a liberal humanism—simply do not fit with one another. Each set of beliefs is evidence against the other. Many would call this a deeply incoherent view of the world.

If the values of secular humanism cannot be inferred or deduced from a materialistic universe, then where did they come from?

The answer is that they have a "genealogy," a history. French philosopher Jacques Derrida has said: "Today the cornerstone of international law is the sacred . . . the sacredness of man as your neighbor . . . made by God or by God-made man. . . . In that sense, the concept of crime against humanity is a Christian concept and I think there would be no such thing in the law today without the Christian heritage, the Abrahamic heritage, the biblical heritage."[35] We have already heard Jürgen Habermas express the growing consensus of many scholars,[36] namely that the modern "ideals of freedom . . . of conscience, human rights and democracy" come from the Bible's teaching on justice and love, and that secular society has found no good alternative way to ground these ideals.[37] Derrida and Habermas are acknowledging that the humanistic moral values of secularism are not the deliverances of scientific reasoning but have come down to us from older times, that they have a theological history. And modern people hold them by faith alone.

The Legacy of Christianity

In *A Brief History of Thought* Luc Ferry tells the story of how the Christian faith grew and supplanted classical Greco-Roman culture and pagan thought in the West.[38] One reason it did so was because "Christianity gave to the world . . . [ideas that] . . . many modern ethical systems would adopt for their own purposes."[39] One was that of human equality.

The Greek worldview rested "entirely on the conviction that there exists a natural hierarchy. . . . Some men are born to command, others to obey." But "in direct contradiction, Christianity was to introduce the notion that humanity was fundamentally identical, that men were equal in dignity—an unprecedented idea at the time, and one to which our world owes its entire democratic inheritance."[40] Max Horkheimer writes that, while Greek thought gave us a partial idea of a limited democracy only for the highborn and educated, the biblical idea of "God's creation of man in his own image and Christ's atonement for all mankind" strengthened the Western idea of the value of the individual "immeasurably."[41]

Christianity provided not merely a general idea of equality but also the resources for an understanding of "natural" human rights. Who ever came up with the idea that a human being had "rights" not granted by the state and that could be appealed to against the state? Where did the thought come from that some things are owed to *all* persons, regardless of their social status, gifts, or abilities, just by virtue of their being human? While it is popularly thought that human rights were the creation of modern secularism over and against the oppressiveness of religion, the reality is that this concept arose not in the East but in the West, and not after the Enlightenment but within medieval Christendom. As Horkheimer in the 1940s and Martin Luther King Jr. in the 1960s recognized, the idea of human rights was based on the biblical idea of all people being created in God's image.[42]

Another thing that Christianity gave us, in contrast to the views of the Greeks and other ancients, was a positive view of the body and of emotions. Peter Brown, in his landmark work *The Body and Society*, explains that for the governing classes in the Greco-Roman world, "the soul had been thought of as ruling the body with the same . . . authority as the well-born male ruled those inferior and alien to himself."[43] Ancient pagan culture believed the mind and reason (resident in the soul) needed to subordinate the "alien" body and the emotions resident within the body. But the Bible has a different understanding. It sees both body and soul as equally good and equally affected by sin.[44] It teaches that the great human struggle is not between mind and body but takes place within our hearts, "the hidden core of self that could respond to or reject the will . . . [and God's] fatherly love" or not.[45]

Christianity, then, saw the battle for human virtue as no longer one of head versus heart (becoming more rational), nor mind over matter (getting more technical mastery over the world). The battle was over where to direct the supreme love of your heart. Will it be toward God and your neighbor, no matter who that neighbor is? Or will it be toward power and wealth for yourself and your tribe?[46] Augustine was the first to formulate this, drawing on biblical teaching. Cambridge historian Henry Chadwick argued that Augustine "marks an epoch in the history of human moral consciousness."[47] For the first time the supreme goal of life was not self-control and rationality but love. Love was required to redirect the human person away from self-centeredness toward serving God and others. Augustine's *Confessions* laid the groundwork for what we would call psychology in a way that non-Christian classical thought could not have done.[48] The older idea of the body being bad and the soul good—of the emotions (resident in the body) as bad and reason as good—changed under Christianity.

And these new views of the importance of the body and the material world laid the foundation for the rise of modern science. The material world was no longer understood as an illusion or simply something to be spiritually transcended. Nor was it just an incomprehensible mystery but, according to the Bible, it was the creation of a personal, rational being. Therefore it could be studied and understood by other personal, rational beings.[49]

In general, Christianity brought an unprecedented idea of the importance of the individual. "For the Buddhist, the individual is but an illusion, something destined for dissolution and impermanence; for the [Greek] Stoic the individual self is destined to merge into the totality of the *cosmos*; Christianity on the contrary promises immortality of the individual person: his soul, his body, his face, his beloved voice—as long as he is saved by the grace of God."[50] It also undermined the elitism of antiquity. "Salvation" for the Greeks had to do with philosophical contemplation, something only people with training and leisure could do. For Christians, however, salvation came through dependent, trusting faith that Jesus had saved them, doing what they could not do. That was something anyone could do. In this sense it was much more egalitarian than other kinds of ancient and classical thought.

The "Ghost at the Atheist Feast"

Where, then, did the moral values of Western, liberal, secular culture come from, including the importance of the individual, equality, rights, love, and concern for the poor, and the necessity of improving material conditions for everyone? Many scholars have made a strong historical case that they came down to us from Jewish and Christian thought.

In response, someone might say, so what? Even if we no longer believe in God or the Bible, is there any problem with just keeping the moral values if we like them? In many ways, there is.

This "package" of Christian moral beliefs made great sense in an intensely personal universe. When the Gospel of John called Jesus Christ the *Logos*—a word that meant to the Greek philosophers the supernatural order behind the cosmos—it was revolutionary. For the Greeks, the claim that the "universal cosmic order" could be identified with an individual human being was "insanity."[51] For Christians, however, it meant a radical "personalizing" of the universe. It was the unprecedented idea that the power behind the world was love, a personal God.[52] The doctrine of the Incarnation, that God had become human, had "an incalculable effect on the history of ideas," lifting the human person to the highest possible status, and without it "the philosophy of human rights to which we subscribe today would never have established itself."[53]

In ancient thought the highest power had been either the impersonal Platonic "Idea of the Good" or a divine God whose "defining characteristic was *apatheia*" ("without passions"). In that kind of universe a society made sense that was built on the warrior ethic, on stoicism, on respect for strength, hierarchy, and power.[54] Convictions about the value and equality of every person and the importance of loving the weak arose only in a society that believed in a universe with a personal God who made all to have loving communion with him. Modern secularism has largely kept these moral ideals of biblical faith while rejecting the view of the personal universe in which those ideals made sense and from which they flowed as natural implications.[55]

No one has made this point more forcefully than Friedrich Nietzsche. Nietzsche's great insight was simple. If there is no God and supernatural realm, and this material world and life are all there is, then "there does not exist any perspective higher than life itself." There is no transcendent reality beyond or outside of this life that can serve as a standard by which to determine what parts of the world are right or wrong. There is no point of view privileged enough to escape being part of the same "tissue of forces" in which everything else exists. For example, your moral evaluation comes from a human brain operating in a human culture, processing necessarily limited human experience. Why should your brain stand in judgment on other brains, cultures, and experiences? To simply choose and elevate one part of real life and call it "good" over another that we call "bad" is an arbitrary act.[56] So, Nietzsche wrote: "Judgments, value judgments concerning life, for or against, can in the last resort never be true."[57] Literary critic Terry Eagleton writes:

> *Nietzsche sees that [Western] civilization is in the process of ditching divinity while still clinging to religious values, and that this egregious act of bad faith must not go uncontested. . . . Our conceptions of truth, virtue, identity, and autonomy, our sense of history as shapely and coherent, all have deep-seated theological roots. . . .*[58]

Nietzsche's point is this. If you say you don't believe in God but you do believe in the rights of every person and the requirement to care for all the weak and the poor, then you are still holding on to Christian beliefs, whether you will admit it or not.[59] Why, for example, should you look at love *and* aggression—both parts of life, both rooted in our human nature—and choose one as good and reject one as bad? They are both part of life. Where do you get a standard to do that? If there is no God or supernatural realm, it doesn't exist.

Nietzsche's critique of secular humanism has never really been answered. In a note on the writings of George Eliot, Nietzsche observes presciently that the English-speaking world would try to abandon belief in God yet maintain the values of compassion, universal benevolence, and conscience. But he predicts that in societies that reject God, morality itself will eventually become "a problem."[60] It will be harder and harder to justify or motivate morality, people will become more selfish, and there will be no way but coercion to control them. In his book *Beyond Good and Evil* he mocks the philosophy of the utilitarians—those who promote human rights and compassion as simply practical wisdom, the best way to pursue "the greatest good for the greatest number." How, he asks, can you promote unselfish behavior using selfishness as the motivation?[61] It won't work, and "rights talk" will simply be the way whatever party is in power keeps itself there.

I do not want to give the impression that no one has ever tried to respond to Nietzsche's critique. Law professor Ronald Dworkin has perhaps been the most insistent that those who do not believe in God can nonetheless believe in "the independent reality of . . . value and purpose"[62] Dworkin startled many people, however, by saying that belief in humanistic values was an act of religious faith. Indeed, though not believing in a personal God (and therefore maintaining his identification as an atheist), he professed faith in "something beyond nature" that is the source of beauty and morality which "cannot be grasped even by finally understanding the most fundamental of physical laws."[63] This is not, then, really a refutation of Nietzsche's challenge. It is a confirmation that the German philosopher was right. When secularists endorse human dignity, rights, and the responsibility in order to eliminate human suffering, they are indeed exercising religious faith in some kind of supranatural, transcendent reality.

The humanistic beliefs, then, of most secular people should be recognized as exactly that—beliefs. They cannot be deduced logically

or empirically from the natural, material world alone. If there is no transcendent reality beyond this life, then there is no value or meaning for
anything.[64] To hold that human beings are the product of nothing but
the evolutionary process of the strong eating the weak, but then to insist
that nonetheless every person has a human dignity to be honored—is an
enormous leap of faith against *all* evidence to the contrary.

Even Nietzsche, however, cannot escape his own scalpel. He blasted
secular liberals for being inconsistent and cowardly. He believed that
calls for social bonding and benevolence for the poor and weak meant
"herd-like uniformity, the ruin of the noble spirit, and the ascendency of
the masses."[65] He wanted to turn from the "banal creed" of modern liberalism to the tragic, warrior culture (the "Ubermensch" or "Superman") of ancient times. He believed the new "Man of the Future" would
have the courage to look into the bleakness of a universe without God
and take no religious consolation. He would have the "noble spirit" to be
"superbly self-fashioning" and not beholden to anyone else's imposed
moral standards.[66]

All of these declarations by Nietzsche compose, of course, a profoundly moral narrative. Why is the "noble spirit" noble? Why is it good
to be courageous, and who says so? Why is it bad to be inconsistent?
Where did such moral values come from, and what right does Nietzsche
have, by his own philosophy, to label one way of living noble or good and
other ways bad?[67] In short, he can't stop doing what he tells everyone else
to stop doing.

Thus, Eagleton observes, Nietzsche's "Man of the Future" has not
abolished God at all. "Like the Almighty, he rests upon nothing but
himself." We see that there is no truly irreligious human being. Nietzsche
is calling people to worship themselves, to grant the same faith and authority to themselves that they once put in God. Even Nietzsche believes.
"The autonomous, self-determining Superman is yet another piece of
counterfeit theology."[68] We have seen that the secular humanism Nietzsche despised lacks a good grounding for its moral values.[69] However,
the even greater dangers of Nietzsche's antihumanism are a matter of
historical record. Peter Watson details how Nietzsche's views were

important inspirations in the twentieth century to totalitarian figures of both the Left and Right, of both Nazism and Stalinism.[70]

Revisiting the Deconversion Story

We have seen, then, that people neither adopt nor discard faith in God through pure, objective reasoning, because no such thing is possible. We also have seen that moral values are always grounded in faith assumptions with a cultural history. In light of this, can we get a better understanding of what happens in deconversion experiences we cited earlier in this chapter?

A young academic, David Sessions, is a former evangelical Christian who "deconverted" from the faith. In a blog post he relates how he read Charles Taylor's *A Secular Age* with great interest. He summarizes Taylor's contention that "countless loss-of-faith stories follow the familiar path of an earnest believer agonizing with the realities of science and concluding he must grow up and give up his childish religious illusions." He adds, "This is the story I would have told about myself at a certain point."

He had what he calls a fundamentalist education that taught him that "Darwinism was a hoax, Columbus was a God-ordained missionary to the savages, the American founders were Biblical literalists, liberal elites were trying to set up a 'one-world government,' etc." When he was exposed to "the power of alternative answers to the deepest questions in films and novels; books on history, anthropology and natural science," it turned him into a "materialist, a believer overwhelmed by the facts." That is how he would have described his journey at one time.

He now concedes, however, that while "rational arguments played a significant role in undermining" his faith, that was not all there was to it. Sessions sides with Polanyi and others against the naive view of reason so many secular people adopt to justify their deconversion. "The background world of what makes sense to us shifts ahead of us having theoretical reasons for why we changed our mind," he writes. His move from a small, conservative town to living in New York City "shattered many of the stereotypes, prejudices, and preconceived notions that made up the environment where my faith had once made sense."

As we have seen, much of what makes a way of thinking credible is not simply the logical cogency of its explicit tenets. Also involved are one's "tacit," barely perceived supportive beliefs. When people are presented with the Christian faith, the actual doctrines are often given against a backdrop of other implicit beliefs, attitudes, and expectations. That often includes ideas about what nonbelievers must be like, how life ought to go for a true believer in God, and what sinning and violations of the rules should feel like. All of these background beliefs are instilled in a variety of implicit ways, and they become an important part of the supportive tissue that helps Christianity make sense. If they give way, so may faith in the explicit doctrines.

For example, a person might have a tacit belief that "if I'm a Christian, and God loves me, there's a limit to how badly life can go for me." Such an idea is not part of formal Christian doctrine. Indeed, the life of Jesus, the suffering servant, contradicts it. Yet it can seem to be a necessary inference from some Christian texts and teachings and it can be absorbed from the attitudes of others in a community. Then, if the believer's life begins to go terribly wrong and this tacit belief begins to crumble, all the other teachings of the faith can seem unconvincing as well.

Also, many Christians are led to believe that all nonbelievers will be more selfish, unscrupulous, and unhappy than believers. But what if the believer falls in with a band of well-adjusted, altruistic, honest and committed secular people? When the background belief is disproven, the foreground beliefs all seem less compelling. Or what if a young person raised to believe sex outside of marriage is a sin also picks up the thought that therefore any experience of premarital sex would make him feel empty and unfulfilled? What if, instead, the experience makes him feel wonderful and alive? When the tacit belief is found to be wrong through new lived experience, it undermines the plausibility of the whole Christian sex ethic. Are any of these "preunderstanding" background beliefs actually part of the historical Christian faith? No, they aren't, yet they are part of Polanyi's "subsidiary awareness," the loss of which, if it is unexamined, can lead to the loss of the whole faith.

As Sessions began to slide away from his former beliefs, some of his Christian friends charged that he was being affected by his secular environment, that he wanted to be "cool." In response, he countered that his loss of faith was strictly "the product of Serious Reading and Good, Solid Intellectual Arguments." But he now recognizes that something more than arguments was driving the change. There was also "the changing sense of what kind of person I wanted to become." His experience was shifting, and so did many background intuitions and beliefs, and this made him open to new kinds of intellectual arguments.

Today he is willing to say that coming to a secular, materialist viewpoint is "a matter of a new, more or less equally faith-based story eclipsing the old one's explanatory power. . . . What happened here was not that a moral outlook bowed to brute facts. Rather we might say that one moral outlook gave way to another." He agrees with Nietzsche that his humanistic moral values don't really follow from his view of the universe. "There are as many value judgments in liberal humanism as there are in its parent religion, and many people who come to the point of unbelief are happy to accept them despite objecting to [what they consider] the similar ungroundedness of Christianity. . . . It's amusing now how little [my values] intrinsically had to do with the materialism I'd become convinced of. Nothing about individual liberty, human rights, or civilizational progress follow automatically from the fact that God is dead."

Sessions concludes by calling for secular people to be more cognizant of the fact that their viewpoint is a "construal," a way of interpreting reality, and not simply the only objective, factual account of reality. He writes: "One needn't remain religious to admit potential harm in the lack of self-awareness in certain secular construals of the world, and to be able to see religious belief, with a kind humility and respect, as a construal that can be equally as plausible as our own. And one that is to be studied carefully . . . for its crucial insights about human be-ing." Sessions goes on to urge Christians to show greater humility too, to forgo their triumphalism, and to stop thinking they can win the field strictly through rational proofs and arguments. "If you can begin to pull your religion out of that abyss, there's no telling what a powerful countercurrent it might become."[71]

What This Means

I hope by now my more skeptical readers will see that neither secularism nor Christianity has the main "burden of proof." Western secularity is not the absence of faith but a new set of beliefs about the universe.[72] These beliefs cannot be proven, are not self-evident to most people, and have, as we shall continue to see, their own contradictions and problems just as other religious faiths do.[73] One significant problem is that modern secularism's humanistic values are inconsistent with—even undermined by—its belief in a material-only universe. The other problem we have addressed is that many secular people base their nonbelief on a rigid and simplistic view of reason. They will not acknowledge that there are different, contested approaches to rationality and that all of them include the exercise of faith.

Empirical reason can prove neither the claim that there is a supernatural, transcendent reality nor the claim that there is none. That does not mean there is no way to weigh and evaluate such philosophical or religious statements. It means only that using demanding, demonstrable, unquestionable proof for them is inappropriate. Blaise Pascal sums this all up well in *Pensée* 406. "We have an incapacity for proving anything which no amount of dogmatism can overcome. We [also] have an idea of truth which no amount of skepticism can overcome."[74]

Rather than unfairly asking only religious people to prove their views, we need to compare and contrast religious beliefs and their evidences with secular beliefs and theirs. We can and should argue about which beliefs account for what we see and experience in the world. We can and should debate the inner logical consistency of belief systems, asking whether they support or contradict one another. We can and should consult our deepest intuitions.

My aim from here on through the book is to do just that, and, I hope, to show that Christianity makes the greatest sense in every way—emotionally, culturally, and rationally.[75] In the process, I hope to show readers that Christianity offers far greater and richer goods for understanding, facing, enjoying, and living life than they had previously imagined.

PART TWO

Religion Is More Than You Think It Is

Three

A Meaning That Suffering
Can't Take from You

There may be no more fundamental question than What is the meaning of life? Many thinkers, however, regard this as a bogus query. After all, they say, we don't talk about whether a cave is meaningful or meaningless, or whether a snowstorm is true or false. We may love a breathtaking seascape, but we don't expect the sea to love us back. "Meaning," it is said, is not a property of anything in the world—it's just how we humans happen to feel about it at the moment. In this view, each of us can decide if a particular object is meaningful to us, but to ask what is the meaning of life itself is nonsensical. Life can't have a meaning of its own.

At the end of his book *What Does It All Mean?* philosopher Thomas Nagel wonders if the "Meaning-capital-M" question comes from too great a sense of our own importance.[1] He proposes that since "the grave is [life's only] goal, perhaps it's ridiculous to take ourselves so seriously." It should be enough to simply take life as it comes and enjoy it as much as we can. Many want more than that. They want a reason to believe that our lives "matter from the outside."[2] That is, they want their lives to be connected to something beyond their mere pleasures and comforts, to be significant of something higher. That, Nagel says, is asking too much. Why torture ourselves?

Nevertheless, we do. When asked whether they think about the meaning and purpose of life, nearly three fourths of people across the globe say that they do often or sometimes. Regional variations are small, ranging from 89 percent in sub-Saharan Africa to 76 percent in Asia.[3] And the meaning question is not likely to decline in its influence. Martin

Heidegger argues convincingly in *Being and Time* that human beings are distinguished from other living things "by their capacity to put their own existence into question. They are creatures for whom existence as such, not just particular features of it, is problematic."[4]

But what are we actually asking when inquiring about the meaning of life? In common usage the term "to mean" has two overlapping senses. The first sense has to do with *purpose*. Something has meaning if there is intention behind it, as in "did you mean to hurt her like that?" The second sense has to do with *significance*. Something has meaning if it signifies, if it acts as a sign pointing to something beyond itself, as in "this medal means bravery above and beyond the call of duty." Of course, the two senses can come together. We might ask "do these rocks on the ground mean anything?" If they were put there on purpose to point the way to the next town, we answer that they do. If the rocks simply fell off the hill after a rainstorm, we answer that they do not.

In the same way, if people say that their lives feel meaningless, it doesn't necessarily mean that they don't have good jobs, family and friends, and the means to live in a materially comfortable way. It means that they are not sure what all the activity is being done *for*. Put another way, they are not sure that all their making and getting actually matters, makes a difference, or accomplishes anything beyond itself.

So to have meaning in life is to have both an overall purpose for living and the assurance that you are making a difference by serving some good beyond yourself.

The psychological need for this is inarguable. Physician, professor, and author Atul Gawande tells of a doctor working at a nursing home who persuaded its administrator to bring in dogs, cats, parakeets, a colony of rabbits, and even a group of laying hens to be cared for by the residents. The results were significant. "The residents began to wake up and come to life. People who we had believed weren't able to speak started speaking. . . . People who had been completely withdrawn and nonambulatory started coming to nurses' station and saying, 'I'll take the dog for a walk.' All the parakeets were adopted and named by the residents."[5]

The use and need for psychotropic drugs for agitation dropped significantly, to 38 percent of the previous level. And "deaths fell 15 percent."

Why? The architect of these changes concluded, "I believe that the difference in death rates can be traced to the fundamental human need for a reason to live."[6] Gawande goes on to ask "why simply existing—why being merely housed and fed and safe and alive—seems empty and meaningless to us. What more is it that we need in order to feel that life is worthwhile? The answer . . . is that we all seek a cause beyond ourselves."[7]

The Crisis of Meaning

Heidegger says that humans are the only living beings who wonder about the meaning of life. And yet the question was not something that bothered people in ancient times the way it has bothered us today. The twentieth century's writers and thinkers acknowledged a new meaning-shaped hole in the center of the culture. They spoke of existential dread, angst, and despair, of absurdity and nausea.

In Chekhov's play *The Three Sisters*, the character Masha says that life must have "meaning" and adds, "I think man ought to have faith or ought to seek a faith, or else his life is empty, empty. . . . You've got to know what you're living for or else it's all nonsense and waste."[8] In Franz Kafka's book *The Trial*, a man is arrested by a faceless bureaucracy for a crime that is never named. The main character, Joseph K., asks: "What . . . is the purpose of this enormous organization? . . . How are we to avoid those in office becoming deeply corrupt when everything is devoid of meaning?"[9] Jean-Paul Sartre, in *Being and Nothingness*, wrote, "Man is a useless passion."[10]

Albert Camus famously argues in *The Myth of Sisyphus* that human life is absurd. "The absurd is born of this confrontation between the human need and the unreasonable silence of the world."[11] We want to find meaning in things but the universe does not cooperate. We are all like Sisyphus in the Greek myth, rolling the rock up the hill only to see it inevitably roll back. We try to do good for the people we love, but what we do never lasts, nor do they. To Camus, death is not a gateway into another life but a "closed door." All our greatest hopes are frustrated by it.[12] Inevitable death, then, makes life absurd. He writes: "We want love to last and we know that it does not last; even if, by some miracle, it were to last a whole lifetime, it would still be incomplete. . . . In the final analysis, every man [is] devoured by the overpowering desire to endure and possess . . . those whom he has loved."[13] Even the steely philosopher Bertrand Russell argued that the secular view—that all human labor, love, and genius are "destined to extinction in the vast death of the solar system"—results "henceforth" in the "unyielding despair" of the soul.[14]

But this crisis of meaning that was felt by artists and philosophers of the late nineteenth and twentieth centuries is resisted by many in the twenty-first. Cosmopolitan secular people today tend to cringe at the phrase "the meaning of life" as they would at "God, country, Mom, and apple pie." Literary critic Terry Eagleton observes: "In the pragmatist, streetwise climate of advanced postmodern capitalism, with its skepticism of big pictures and grand narratives . . . 'life' is one among a whole series of discredited totalities. . . . Even 'meaning' becomes a suspect term for postmodern thinkers. . . . It assumes that one thing can represent or stand in for another, an assumption which is felt by some to be *passé*."[15] If the universe is truly indifferent and meaningless, why think it *ought not* to be that way?

Nagel agrees that if you have this expectation that there ought to be meaning, then you might experience life as absurdity. But if you stopped railing at the world for simply being what it is, the sense of angst and absurdity would go away. Life is meaningless only if you insist it be meaningful, he concludes.[16] In fact, say some, "only by breaking with the whole notion of 'deep' meaning, which will always tempt us to chase the chimera of the Meaning of meanings, can we be free."[17] Why might the relinquishment of meaning be liberating? To say life itself has meaning would assume that there is some moral standard of "right living and being" to which we all must conform. That would mean there is a single right way to live and be, and that would mean the loss of our freedom to determine for ourselves how to live. If *the* Meaning of life exists, then we are not free to create that meaning for ourselves. So Harvard scientist Stephen Jay Gould wrote that there simply is no meaning to life but that this fact "though superficially troubling, if not terrifying, is ultimately liberating. . . . We must construct those answers for ourselves."[18] It is, in this view, liberating to believe there is no Meaning to life.

In the modern era we mourned the loss of the Meaning of life, but in the postmodern era, an age of freedom, we say good riddance to the very idea.[19]

God and Modern Meaninglessness

Or do we? And who is "we"?

The second season of the television series *Fargo*, with one of its episodes titled "The Myth of Sisyphus," made Camus' modern pessimism about meaning one of its themes. In an early episode a teenage girl, Noreen, intones, "Camus says knowin' we are all gonna die makes life a joke."[20] The story line does indeed seem to fit Camus' absurdist philosophy, with the people who are trying to do the right thing being threatened or frustrated at every turn. But another character in the series, Peggy, falls under the influence of a thinker more postmodern than the gloomy Frenchman. She discovers John Hanley Sr., the founder of Lifespring, a company dedicated to helping you find your "best you." "He who seeks meaning finds nothing but contradiction and nonsense," Hanley writes. "Don't think about the person [you] want to be, just be that person."[21] Don't try to find the meaning of life—just create your own meaning.

Peggy's quest for an actualized self, however, leads to disaster, and her husband, Ed, dies trying to save both her and his dream of having a family. A good cop, Lou Solverson, explains the tragedy to Peggy with an unwitting Camus reference. "Your husband said he was going to protect his family, no matter what, and I acted like I didn't understand, but I do. It's the rock we all push. Men. We call it our burden, but it's really our privilege." For Lou Solverson, loving your family even to your own hurt and death is not absurd at all. It is what gives life meaning.

To get at the roots of the Solversons' ability to find life nasty, brutish, and short but nevertheless meaningful, we get a word from Lou's wife, Betsy, a young mother dying of cancer. The sullen Noreen looks at her and says, "Camus says knowin' we're gonna die makes life absurd." Betsy responds, "Nobody with any sense would say something that foolish. We're put on this earth to do a job, and each of us gets the time we get to do it." She looks at her young daughter Molly and continues. "And when this life is over, and you stand in front of the Lord, well, you try telling him it was all some Frenchman's joke."[22]

The Solversons are looking at life through lenses without the slightest bit of rose-colored tint. They see the darkness of the world. Yet they are neither modern people struggling with a lack of purpose nor postmodern people who feel they are free to forge the meanings that they prefer. What makes the difference is their belief that their life tasks have been given to them by "the Lord" and a final approval exists for those who have not sought their own path but been faithful to the call.

The works of modern authors Chekhov, Kafka, Sartre, and Camus (not to mention Joseph Conrad, Virginia Woolf, E. M. Forster, and Samuel Beckett) reveal "the persistent need for meaning and the gnawing sense of its elusiveness."[23] All of them have said, in one way or another, that today we can no longer look to God and religion to infuse our lives with meaning. But in these kinds of statements, what does the term "we" mean? Does it mean "we, most human beings"? As we saw in chapter 1, that is untrue and it is unlikely to ever be true. The Solversons are an example of how a family can look unflinchingly into the abyss of the evil and suffering of this life, without sentimentality or naïveté, and experience great tragedy—and yet live a life infused with meaning because of their belief in a divine calling and purpose in life.

God and Postmodern Meaning

Despite *Fargo*'s warnings, many secular thinkers and writers sound a lot like John Hanley Sr. of Lifespring. As we saw, Stephen Jay Gould says that a purposeless cosmos means we are liberated to construct our own individual meanings for our lives. University of Chicago professor Jerry Coyne says the same:

> *Cosmology doesn't give one iota of evidence for a purpose . . . or for God. . . . Secularists see a universe without apparent purpose and realize that we must forge our own purposes and ethics. . . . But although the universe is purposeless, our lives aren't. . . . We make our own purposes, and they're real.*[24]

Postmodern culture understands any claim that there is *a* Meaning to *all* life to be a form of bondage. In its view, no one (and certainly no religious institution) has the right to tell us how we should be living. As Coyne says, we get to forge and make our own meanings. The world and the human race have no purpose, but that liberates us to create our own. In a typical blog post, "Does Atheism Make Life Meaningless?" a secular writer explains that he used to be a Christian but he is no longer. "It is true I do not have an absolute purpose in life—I am not dedicated to 'glorifying God' anymore. But I find creating my own purpose thrilling. I am the author of a novel, and the book is my life. The freedom is exhilarating. . . . Life is as happy and meaningful as you make it."[25]

Is it? There are two questions to ask those who take this remarkably sunny approach to a meaningless universe. Is this a cogent, consistent position? And does it work, practically, for living your life?

Let's look first at the issue of consistency. Terry Eagleton points out that when postmodernism denounces all absolute values and inherent meanings in the name of freedom, it "secretly smuggles . . . an absolute into the argument."[26] Why, for example, is freedom so important? Why is *that* the absolute, unquestioned "good"—and who gets to define it as such? Are you not assuming a value-laden standard that you are using to critique all other approaches to life? And are you not, then, actually giving a universal answer to the Meaning question, namely, that the meaning of life is to have the freedom to determine your own meaning? Are you not, then, doing the very thing you say should not be done?

So the postmodern approach to meaning is not very consistent. However, is it workable at a practical level? Eagleton finds it wanting at this level as well. He finds the "life is what you make it" view "seems troublingly narcissistic. Do we ever get outside of our own heads? Isn't a genuine meaning one which we feel ourselves running up against, one which can resist or rebuff us? . . . Surely life itself must have a say in the matter?"[27] He questions whether we can really take anything in life and "construct" a meaning around it of our own. "Nobody actually believes this," he answers, and gives an example. You could try with all your might to "read" tigers as animals that are coy and cuddly, but if you try to do that, you would "no longer be around to tell the tale," because to some degree the world is "independent of our interpretations of it."[28]

I once knew a young man who had grown up to be far below average in height, size, and weight. Yet he wanted to play football. He was continually injured as he competed with players who were far bigger than average. His parents tried to dissuade him from football, but he reminded them that all his life he had always been told by his teachers that he could be absolutely anything he chose to be and that life was what he made of it. "And didn't you see the movie *Rudy*?" he asked them. Someone should have gently but firmly given him Eagleton's illustration and conclusion. Life isn't simply what you make it. Often it is what it is. We are not fully free to impose our meanings on life. Rather we must honor life by discovering a meaning that fits in with the world as it is.

So is meaning in life without God practically possible? Public discourse is filled with loud religious voices insisting that life without God is inevitably pointless, bleak, and unworkable. On the other side there are plenty of secular people who insist that they not only have satisfying meaning in life but also have a kind of freedom that religious people do not.

Who is right? Can we have meaning in life without any belief in God at all? To be fair to all, I would argue that the answer is both yes and no.

I say yes because both by our definition and by lived experience secular people can certainly know meaning in life. We defined "meaning" as having both a purpose and the assurance that you are serving some good beyond yourself. If you decide that the meaning of your life is to be a good parent, or to serve a crucial political cause, or to tutor underprivileged youth, or to enjoy and promote great literature—then you have, by definition, a meaning in life. Plenty of secular people live like this without being tortured and gloomy in the manner of a Camus. It is quite possible to find great purpose in the ordinary tasks of life, apart from knowing answers to the Big Questions About Existence.

But I also say no. Secular people are often unwilling to recognize the significant difference between what have been called "inherent" and "assigned" meanings. Traditional belief in God was the basis for *discovered*, objective meaning—meaning that is there, apart from your inner feelings or interpretations. If we were made by God for certain purposes, then there are inherent meanings that we must accept.

The meanings that secular people have are not discovered but rather *created*. They are not objectively "there." They are subjective and wholly dependent on our feelings. You may determine to live for political change or the establishment of a happy family, and these can definitely serve as energizing goals. However, I want to argue that such created meanings are much more fragile and thin than discovered meanings. Specifically, discovered meaning is more rational, communal, and durable than created meaning.

Discovered Meaning Is More Rational Than Created Meanings

It sounds strange to say that I think Christianity is more *rational* when it comes to meaning in life. But I am talking of how meaning in life is sustained at a practical level.

Thomas Nagel, in his essay "The Absurd," agrees that in order to find some activity meaningful, like work and making money, we must answer the question What is it all *for*? What is the point of it? He agrees that we feel we must attach things we do to "something larger than ourselves." So what is the point of caring for our health? We answer—so we can work. But what then is the point of working? We may answer—so we can make money and care for our family, or so we can create jobs and give to charity in order to alleviate poverty.[29] But the problem is that there is always the same question coming again. We can always ask, What, then, is the point of *that*? What difference does *it* make? And as we move up this chain we find the answers get more and more difficult to find. For example, if your meaning is attached to personal relationships, well, people die.[30] If you say you are thinking of future generations or how to help the planet, all those things will pass away too. We have defined meaning in life as "making a difference," but for the secular point of view, in the end, the universe gives you a final answer: Nothing makes a difference. Nagel writes:

> *Even if you produce a great work of literature which continues to be read thousands of years from now, eventually the solar system will cool or the universe will wind down and collapse and all trace of your effort will vanish. . . . The problem is that although there are justifications for most things big and small that we do within life, none of these explanations explain the point of your life as a whole. . . . It wouldn't matter if you had never existed. And after you have gone out of existence, it won't matter that you did exist.*[31]

If this life is all there is, and there is no God or life beyond this material world, then it will not ultimately matter whether you are a genocidal maniac or an altruist; it won't matter whether you fight hunger in Africa or are incredibly cruel and greedy and starving the poor. In the end what you do will make no difference whatsoever. It might make some people happier or sadder for a brief time while they are on the planet, but beyond that, your influence—good or bad—will likely be negligible when viewed on any grand scale. Everything you do, and everyone you have done things with and to, will be gone forever. Ultimately, everything we do is radically insignificant. Nothing counts forever.

Now, as we have said, many people in the postmodern culture believe we should train ourselves to *not* ask this "metaquestion" about the point of life. We should discipline ourselves not to think about the ultimate outcome of all we do, which in the secular view is sheer nothingness. We should put that out of mind and concentrate on today. But this establishes my first point. When secular people seek to lead a meaningful life, they must have discipline to *not think* so much about the big picture. They must disconnect what their reason tells them about the world from what they are experiencing emotionally. That is getting a feeling of meaningfulness through a lack of rationality, by the suppression of thinking and reflection.

The great Supreme Court justice Oliver Wendell Holmes Jr. once wrote to a friend and said that if one "thinks coldly," a modern person has to admit that there is "no reason for attributing to man a significance different in kind from that which belongs to a baboon or a grain of sand." By this he meant that if the modern secularist thinks out the implications of his view of a strictly materialistic world in which all life evolved randomly and accidentally, human beings have no importance at all. But then he added that when he begins thinking like this it is time to "go down stairs and play solitaire." No one with this set of beliefs can get peace and meaning for daily life unless he stops thinking about the implications of his beliefs.[32]

The problem is that it is hard to stop thinking, and the big picture may keep breaking in on you.

In *A Confession* Leo Tolstoy tells how he was leading a very successful life until around the age of fifty he began to realize that every loved one would be taken away from him and all he had written would eventually be forgotten. In light of that, "the question was: 'Why should I live, why wish for anything, or do anything? . . . Is there any meaning in my life that the inevitable death awaiting me does not destroy?'" He also asked: "How can we fail to see this? . . . That is what is surprising! One can only live while one is intoxicated with life; as soon as one is sober it is impossible not to see that it is all a mere fraud and a stupid fraud!"[33] He had "sobered up" and was now thinking rationally (or "coldly" as Holmes named it). He could not now go back to writing his novels and loving his family, because the lack of any objective, lasting meaning had dawned on him. He could not go back to his prereflective state.

C. S. Lewis describes this same problem Tolstoy had with the added color of a modern belief in evolutionary biology. He writes:

> *You might decide to simply have as good a time as possible. The universe is a universe of nonsense, but since you are here, grab what you can. Unfortunately . . . [y]ou can't, except in the lowest animal sense, be in love with a girl if you know (and keep on remembering) that all the beauties both of her person and of her character are a momentary and accidental pattern produced by the collision of atoms, and that your own response to them is only a sort of psychic phosphorescence arising from the behavior of your genes. You can't go on getting very serious pleasure from music if you know and remember that its air of significance is a pure illusion, that you like it only because your nervous system is irrationally conditioned to like it. You may still, in the lowest sense, have a "good time"; but just in so far as it becomes very good, just in so far as it ever threatens to push you on from cold sensuality into real warmth and enthusiasm and joy, so far you will be forced to feel the hopeless disharmony between your own emotions and the universe in which you [think you] really live.*[34]

By contrast, life meaning and purpose play out for a Christian believer in the very opposite direction. Christians do not say to themselves: "Stop thinking out the implications of what you believe about the universe. Just try to enjoy the day." No, if a Christian is feeling downcast and meaningless, it is because, in a sense, she is not being rational enough.

She is not thinking enough about the implications of what she believes about the universe.

Christians believe that there is a God, who made us in love to know him, but that as a human race we turned away and were lost to him. However, he has promised to bring us back to himself. God sent his Son into the world to break the power of sin and death, at infinite cost to himself, by going to the cross. Christian teaching is that Jesus rose from the dead and passed through the heavens and now is ruling history and preparing a future new heaven and a new earth, without death and suffering, in which we will live with him forever. And then all the deepest longings of our hearts will find their fulfillment.

It is fair to say that if you are a Christian with those beliefs—about who you are to God and what is in store for you—but you are not experiencing peace and meaning, then it is because you are not thinking enough. There is a kind of shallow, temporary peace that modern people can get from not thinking too much about their situation, but Christianity can give a deep peace and meaning that come from making yourself as aware and as mindful of your beliefs as possible.

If you believe there is no discovered meaning in life, only created meaning, then if you really start to think globally—about the fact that nothing you do is going to make any difference in the end—you are going to begin to experience the dread or nausea of the modernists. And, of course, you don't have to think like this—you can put it out of mind—and that is certainly how most people in a secular culture live today. But that is my first point. This is not a very rational way to have meaning in life. Created meaning is a less rational way to live life than doing so with discovered meaning.

Discovered Meaning Is More Communal Than Created Meanings

Until the modern age our main sources of meaning in life—religion, family, and art—were tightly interrelated and public matters. In fact, it was not thought good or possible for individuals to find a meaning in life of or on their own.[35] Harvard philosopher Josiah Royce in 1908 wrote *The Philosophy of Loyalty*, in which he sought to answer the question of why human beings needed meaning. Why wasn't it enough to simply work, eat, sleep, and do the normal activities of daily life? His answer was that human beings could not live without dedication to a cause more important than their individual interests. They needed a cause for which we were willing to sacrifice greatly. He believed that we are happy only if we make our meaning in life something greater than our happiness.[36]

Royce therefore believed that finding meaning in life could be done only if we rejected individualism. "The individualist puts self-interest first, seeing his own pain, pleasure, and existence as his greatest concern." Modern individualists see loyalty and self-sacrifice as an alarming mistake, leaving oneself open to exploitation and tyranny. To them "nothing could matter more than self-interest, and because when you die you are gone, self-sacrifice makes no sense."[37] Now, tyranny is certainly a great evil but individualism, according to Royce, was the wrong way to overcome it. If every individual seeks his or her own meaning, we will have fewer shared values and meanings, which will erode social solidarity and public institutions. All this will lead to intractable polarization and fragmentation. And ironically, Royce argued, individualism undermines individual happiness. We need "devotion to something more than ourselves for our lives to be endurable. Without it, we have only our desires to guide us, and they are fleeting, capricious, and insatiable."[38]

In the first decade of the twentieth century Royce saw the beginning of the erosion of communally held, discovered meanings in favor of individually created meanings. Charles Taylor, lecturing in the last decade of the century, could see that modern individualism had triumphed. He defined our cultural consensus this way: "Everyone has the right to develop their own form of life, grounded in their own sense of what is really important or of value. . . . No one else can or should try to dictate its content."[39] Taylor argues that individualistic created meaning leads inevitably to a "soft relativism," because, it is thought, no one should challenge the meanings or values of anyone else as being wrong. And this in turn leads to what he calls "extraordinary inarticulacy" about what our society's ideals should be.[40]

For example, we may believe that it is wrong to starve the poor, but in a culture of created meanings we are unable to say why it is so. Your meaning in life might be to help the needy, but my meaning in life might be to get rich by trampling on them. How, in the context of self-created meanings, can you explain why my chosen meaning in life is wrong? How can you do that without telling me that there is different meaning I *ought* to have? On what basis will you do that?

Taylor argues that today, unlike in the past, "moral positions are not in any way grounded in reason or in the nature of things but are ultimately just adopted by each of us because we find ourselves drawn to them."[41] This means there is no way to have a conversation with someone who has not got the same inner feelings that you do. There is no shared authority that can adjudicate moral disputes, because everyone is free to determine his or her own meanings. You may counter, "Yes, you are free, but not if you use your freedom to harm others." Yet we can't define what "harm" actually is unless we first define what a good human life looks like. There are many different views of that—whose definition is going to be imposed on the rest of us? And how can this be done consistently with the belief that we must all seek and create our own visions of the good life?

In the end, if anyone you are disagreeing with about the poor "still feels like holding on to his original position, nothing further can be said to gainsay him."[42] Without socially shared *discovered* meaning we have no basis for saying to somebody else: "You need to stop doing that!" Created meanings cannot be the basis for a program of social justice. Martin Luther King Jr., for example, did not tell white Christians in the South that they should support civil rights because everyone should be free to live as he or she sees fit. In his "I have a dream" speech he quoted Amos 5:24, calling for justice to roll down on the nation.[43]

Terry Eagleton notices that the common secularist proposal to create your own meaning sounds suspiciously like the consumerism of late-modern capitalism. "Capitalist modernity" he says, turns everything into a private commodity. Things that used to be communally held and accomplished achievements—from child rearing to listening to a concert to prayer and worship—are now seen as private choices that can be measured, priced, and consumed by you according to your tastes and convenience.[44] "The meaning-of-life question was now in the hands of . . . the technologists of piped contentment, and chiropractors of the psyche."[45]

Ironically, then, those who say that they are free to create their own meaning might be less liberated and more captive to consumerist, individualist culture than they think.

Discovered Meaning Is More Durable Than Created Meanings

So created meanings work less rationally and communally than discovered meanings. They are also less durable, less able to get you through adversity and suffering.

Secularism is the only worldview whose members must find their main meaning within this life. All other ways of understanding the world hold that "this life is not the whole story," but with secularism, it is. That is why all previous religions and cultures have been able to find in suffering and death a way to affirm something that matters beyond and more than just this life.[46] When secular people create their meanings, however, it must be around something located inside the material world. You might be living for your family or for a political cause or for career accomplishments. To have a meaningful life, therefore, life must go well. But when suffering disrupts this, it has the power to destroy your very meaning. The secular approach to meaning can leave you radically vulnerable to the realities of how life goes in this world.

Viktor Frankl was a Jewish doctor who survived the death camps during World War II. His famous book *Man's Search for Meaning* explored the reason why some people under those horrendous conditions seemed to stay strong and kind while others simply gave up or even became collaborators in order to survive.[47] His conclusion was that it had to do with a person's meaning in life. Many people had made career or social status or family their meaning. These meanings were based on things in this life that the death camp swept away from them completely. Some collapsed psychologically and spiritually and often died by simply "giving up."[48] Some collapsed morally; "they were prepared to use every means . . . even brutal force, theft, and the betrayal of their friends, in order to save themselves."[49] Those who did not crumble often had a different kind of reference point that transcended the circumstances of this life. Many prisoners turned back to a "depth and vigor of religious belief" that "surprised the new arrivals."[50] One woman in the camp said, "In my former life I was spoiled and did not take spiritual accomplishments seriously."[51] When Dr. Frankl spoke to prisoners, in order to infuse their suffering with "dignity and meaning" he would say that "someone looks down on each of us in difficult hours—a friend, a wife, somebody alive or dead, or a God—and he would not expect us to disappoint him."[52]

Frankl discovered that the only way for the prisoners' humanity to survive was to relocate the main meaning of their lives to some transcendent reference point, something beyond this life and even this world. All other religions and cultures outside of secular society do this. The Meaning of life may be escaping the cycle of reincarnation to go into eternal bliss, or escaping the illusion of the world to merge with the all-soul of the universe, or resting with your ancestors after living an honorable life in faithfulness to your family, or, as in the Christian faith, becoming like Christ and living with God and others in love and glory forever. In each case, the Meaning of life cannot be destroyed by adversity. If, for example, your Meaning in life is to know, please, emulate, and be with God, then suffering can actually *enhance* your Meaning in life, because it can get you closer to him. Anthropologists have observed that all nonsecular cultures give their members resources for actually being edified by suffering. Though not welcoming it, they see it as meaningful and help toward the ultimate goal. Only secular culture sees suffering as accidental and meaningless, just an interruption or destruction of what we are living for. And so our society makes it difficult to fully affirm the goodness of *all* life, even life in the midst of affliction.[53]

As we have seen, Camus argued that what we most want in life is to not lose our love relationships. The knowledge of our impending death, he concluded, takes love away and so makes life meaningless. Many people find Camus to be too gloomy, but the older one gets, the more one feels the force of his words. If you believe death really is the end of love, then you will not want to think about it too much as you get older. However, if you believe, as Christians do, that death is actually the entrance into greater and endless love relationships, then thoughtful reflection will only make it easier to face whatever is coming.

Western societies are perhaps the worst societies in the history of the world at preparing people for suffering and death, because created meaning is not only less rational and communal, but also less durable.[54]

The End of Meaninglessness

It is very important for believers and skeptics not to insult each other unnecessarily in these discussions, even where there are sharp disagreements. Subjective, created meanings do serve human life well, and believers must not say to secular friends, "Your life is meaningless." But I hope those without belief in God might now see why many who have found faith in Jesus Christ might feel that their pre-Christian lives were not infused with rich Meaning. Previously, their purpose in life was fragile, weakening quickly under too much thinking or adversity. Now, they find that sustained thought and even suffering only drive them deeper into it.

Part of the richness of the Christian life lies in the ways Christianity gives Meaning that are distinct from not only secularism but from other religions as well. Unlike the concept of karma, Christianity teaches that suffering is often unfair, not merited by actions from a former life. Unlike Buddhism, Christianity teaches that suffering is a terrible reality, not an illusion to be transcended with stoic detachment. Unlike ancient fatalism, such as the Greek Stoics, or other shame-and-honor cultures, Christianity finds nothing particularly noble about suffering—it should not be welcomed. Yet unlike secularism, Christianity teaches that suffering can be meaningful, that it can make you something great. The reason for all these differences is that the Christian view of the universe is so different. A secular anthropologist, Richard Shweder writes:

> For the man of antiquity . . . the external world was happy and joyous, but the world's core was deeply sad and dark. Behind the cheerful surface of the world of so-called merry antiquity there loomed "chance" and "fate." For the Christian, the external world is dark and full of suffering, but its core is nothing other than pure bliss and delight.[55]

How can Christians be sure this is in store for them? The book of Ecclesiastes in the Hebrew Old Testament famously explores the search for meaning. It opens with the cry "Meaningless! Meaningless! . . . Everything is meaningless." (Ecclesiastes 1:2) The author's thesis is that life is meaningless "under the sun" (Ecclesiastes 1:2–3; 2:11,17,20,22). He conducts an elaborate thought experiment—how shall we regard life on earth apart from the existence of the supernatural, God, or eternity? He tries to find a way to find all his comfort, happiness, and meaning within the confines of this material world. He then explores in turn sensual pleasure, philosophy and learning, and work and achievement. He finds that all of them fail to provide meaning in the face of life's realities and death.

The book of Ecclesiastes is enigmatic, difficult, fascinating, and feels extraordinarily up-to-date. Yet it fits well into the story line of the whole Bible. If life "under the sun" is thin on meaning, then we all experience something of its ennui and alienation, because we are all cut off from a direct relationship with the God for whose fellowship we were created. The Christian teaching is that the entire human race is removed from the presence and love of God through our self-centeredness and sin. Therefore all people wrestle at times with a sense of purposelessness.

But when Jesus Christ died on the cross, he cried out: "My God, my God, why have you forsaken me?" (Matthew 27:46) Christianity teaches that he died to take upon himself the penalty for our sin. He then was experiencing the darkness—the meaninglessness—of life without God. We deserve this eternal nausea, what Søren Kierkegaard called, in his 1849 book, the "sickness unto death."[56] The Christian teaching is that Jesus was cut off from God as we deserved, and paid the debt we owed, so that when we believe in him we can receive God's love and forgiveness. On the cross Jesus Christ got life without God so we could have life with God. He was putting himself into our lives—our misery, our mortality— so we could be brought into his life, his joy, and immortality.

As we saw in an earlier chapter, Christians believe that Jesus is the *Logos* that the Greeks intuited—the meaning behind the universe, the reason for life. But unlike the philosophers, Christians believe that the *Logos* is not a concept to be learned but a person to be known. And therefore we don't believe in a meaning we must go out and discover but in a Meaning that came into the world to find us. Embracing him by faith can give you a purposeful life that is death camp proof.

Four

A Satisfaction That Is Not Based on Circumstances

P sychologist Jonathan Haidt's book *The Happiness Hypothesis* provides a historical survey of thinking about happiness.[1] He begins his chapter with a book of the Bible we have just looked at, Ecclesiastes. The author writes: "A person can do nothing better than to . . . find satisfaction in their own toil" (Ecclesiastes 2:24), but that is exactly what eludes him. He describes a life of accomplishment that very few achieve.

> *I undertook great projects: I built houses for myself and planted vineyards. . . . I amassed silver and gold for myself, and the treasure of kings and provinces. I acquired male and female singers, and a harem as well—the delights of a man's heart. . . . I denied myself nothing my eyes desired; I refused my heart no pleasure." (Ecclesiastes 2:4,8,10)*

Nevertheless, he says, "I hated life. . . . My heart began to despair over all my toilsome labor under the sun." (Ecclesiastes 2:17,20) Haidt summarizes, "The author of Ecclesiastes wasn't just battling the fear of meaninglessness; he was battling the disappointment of success. . . . *Nothing brought satisfaction.*"[2] This is an abiding human problem, and there is plenty of modern empirical research that backs it up. Studies find a very weak correlation between wealth and contentment, and the more prosperous a society grows, the more common is depression.[3] The things that human beings think will bring fulfillment and contentment don't. What should we do, then, to be happy?

Haidt says that the answer—of the Buddha and Chinese sages like Lao Tzu in the East and the Greek Stoic philosophers in the West—constituted the "early happiness hypothesis" of ancient times. The principle was this: We are unhappy even in success because we seek happiness *from* success. Wealth, power, achievement, family, material comfort, and security—the external goods of the world—can lead only to a momentary satisfaction, which fades away, leaving you more empty than if you had never tasted the joy. To achieve satisfaction you should not seek to change the world but rather to change your attitude toward the world. Epictetus, a Stoic philosopher, wrote, "Do not seek to have events happen as you want them to, but instead want them to happen as they do happen, and your life will go well."[4] If we do that, the Buddha taught, "when pleasure or pain comes to them, the wise feel above pleasure and pain."[5] In short, don't try to fulfill your desires; rather, control and manage them. To avoid having our inner contentment overthrown by the inevitable loss of things, do not become too emotionally attached to anything.[6]

However, many people have found this approach to satisfaction not very satisfying. Haidt, for example, believes that Buddha and the Greeks "took things too far."[7] He argues that modern research shows *some* external circumstances *do* correlate with increased satisfaction. In particular, love relationships are important, and therefore the advice of emotional detachment may actually undermine happiness.[8] Philosopher Alain de Botton agrees that loving relationships are fundamental to happiness. Indeed, he thinks our quest for the external goods of status and money is really just another quest for love.[9] Another obvious problem with the ancient happiness hypothesis was that it undermined any motivation for seeking major social change. Rather than change the world as it is, we were to resign ourselves to it.

Haidt takes a very modern attitude toward our ancestors. He says we can agree with any wisdom from the past that is backed by empirical research. The ancients warn us about the disappointment of overacquisitiveness, and the social science confirms that, he says. But what Haidt describes as modern culture's operational "happiness hypothesis" is only a slightly chastened version of what the author of Ecclesiastes was trying to do. While warning against overdoing it, modern culture encourages its members to find satisfaction through active efforts to change our lives, not to just accept life as it is.[10]

Back Where We Started

If we stand back to ask what we have learned about happiness over the centuries, it is striking to see our lack of progress. Think of how we have surpassed our ancestors in our ability to travel and communicate, in our accomplishments in medicine and science. Think of how much less brutal and unjust to minorities many societies are today compared with even one hundred years ago. In so many ways human life has been transformed, and yet though we are unimaginably wealthier and more comfortable than our ancestors, no one is arguing that we are significantly happier than they were. We are struggling and seeking happiness in essentially the same ways our forebears did and doing a worse job of it, if we use the rise of depression and suicide as an indicator.

The author of Ecclesiastes deserves the final word here. "Whatever is has already been, and what will be has been before." (Ecclesiastes 3:15) Despite all our modern efforts, with regard to happiness we are essentially back where we started.

One response is to ask, "So what?" and insist that there is little real problem here. Julian Baggini thinks that there is no genuine problem, that no one is perfectly happy or needs to be. Most people get by fine without it, so we shouldn't worry about how happy we are but instead should simply do things that matter.[11] Thomas Nagel observes that, according to empirical studies, most people are pretty happy most of the time.[12]

Terry Eagleton, however, responds that the problem is masked rather than revealed by the term "happiness." The very word is a "feeble, holiday-camp sort of word, evocative of manic grins and cavorting about."[13] For most people—including those who answer researchers' survey questions—the term does not have much depth to it. It refers to a range of conditions from simply "being okay" to "having fun." To be okay is not too hard to achieve. When asked by either friends or social psychologists, "How are you today?" we instinctively say, "Fine, thanks." But conflicts and anger flare up so quickly, and the statistics on depression and suicide always startle, and all this indicates things are not as good as we say they are.

To get at our condition more accurately, we should ask about joy, fulfillment, and satisfaction in life. Are we achieving *those* things? The thesis of this chapter is that we have much thinner life satisfaction than we want to admit to researchers or even to ourselves. On the whole, we are in denial about the depth and magnitude of our discontent. The artists and thinkers who talk about it most poignantly are seen as morbid outliers, but actually they are prophetic voices. It usually takes years to break through and dispel the denial in order to see the magnitude and dimension of our dissatisfaction in life.

The Dimensions of Our Discontent

Roman poet Horace asked, "How comes it to pass . . . that no one lives content with his condition . . . ?" He concludes that "all . . . think their own condition the hardest."[14] Why is no one content with his or her life?

One reason can be seen in a line from the poem "Sunday Morning" by Wallace Stevens. "But in contentment I still feel the need for an imperishable bliss."[15] As we have seen, travel, material goods, sensual gratification, success, and status give quick spikes of pleasure and then fade. Stevens's line helps us understand why. Even as we taste a moment of contentment, we sense how fleeting it is, that it will soon be wrenched from our grasp. It begins to fade away even as we try to embrace it or even to savor it. The ephemeral nature of all satisfaction makes us long for something we can keep, but we look in vain. However, this is not the whole problem. We do not only want a satisfaction that lasts longer but also one that goes much deeper.

In 1969 the singer Peggy Lee recorded the song "Is That All There Is?" written by Jerry Leiber and Mike Stoller and based on an 1896 Thomas Mann novella called *Disillusionment*.[16] The woman speaking in the song tells about being taken as a twelve-year-old to the circus that was called "The Greatest Show on Earth," but as she watched she "had the feeling that something was missing. I don't know what, but when it was over I said to myself, 'Is that all there is to a circus?'" Later she says that she fell "so very much in love" with the "most wonderful boy in the world." And then one day he left her, and she thought she'd die. "But I didn't. And when I didn't, I said to myself, 'Is that all there is to love?'" At every turn everything that should have delighted and satisfied her did not—nothing was big enough to fill her expectations or desires. There was always something missing, though she never knew what it was. Everything left her asking, "Is that it?"

So every stanza of her life, like a song, went back to the same refrain:

Is that all there is?
Is that all there is?
If that's all there is my friends,
Then let's keep dancing.
Let's break out the booze and have a ball,
if that's all—
there is.

The lack of any deep or lasting satisfaction drives her to joyless partying. As we gradually discover that everything we thought would be fulfilling is not, we become less able to look forward to life, more numb, jaded, and cynical, or worse. The woman speaking in the song realizes that her listeners might wonder why she doesn't commit suicide. But she predicts that the experience of dying will be every bit as disappointing as life has been, so there is no reason to hurry it.

I know what you must be saying to yourselves.

"If that's the way she feels about it why doesn't she just end it all?"

Oh, no, not me.

I'm in no hurry for that final disappointment.

'Cause I know just as well as I'm standing here talking to you,

That when that final moment comes and I'm breathing my last breath

I'll be saying to myself—

Is that all there is?

The Leiber-Stoller song echoes the experience of *Village Voice* columnist Cynthia Heimel, who saw friends go from anonymity to Hollywood stardom only to find, to their horror, they were no more fulfilled and happy than before, and the experience actually deepened their emptiness, turning them "howling and insufferable." She surmises that "if God really wants to play a rotten practical joke on us, he grants our deepest wish and then giggles merrily as we begin to realize we want to kill ourselves."[17] Henrik Ibsen, the Norwegian playwright, helps us understand what happened to Heimel's friends. "If you take away the life-illusion from an average man, you take away his happiness as well."[18] Within Ibsen's play *The Wild Duck*, a life illusion is the belief that some object or condition will finally bring you the satisfaction for which you long. But this is an illusion. At some point reality will destroy it, and nothing destroys it like actually achieving your dreams.

If you are younger, it is natural to say to yourself, "I have heard about these disillusioned celebrities and wealthy people who say their life isn't happy. But if I get anything like what I'm hoping for, I'll be different." No you won't. Though there is a spectrum of experience, nobody in the end has ever been different. That's what the wisdom of the ancients and all the anecdotal evidence in the world will tell you. C. S. Lewis put it in perhaps the classic way in his wartime BBC radio talk on hope.

Most people, if they really learn how to look into their own hearts, would know that they do want, and want acutely, something that cannot be had in this world. There are all sorts of things in this world that offer to give it to you, but they never keep their promise. The longings which arise in us when we first fall in love, or first think of some foreign country, or first take up some subject that excites us, are longings which no marriage, no travel, no learning can really satisfy. I am not speaking of what would ordinarily be called unsuccessful marriages or trips and so on; I am speaking of the best possible ones. There is always something we grasped at, in that first moment of longing, that just fades away in the reality. The spouse may be a good spouse, the scenery has been excellent, it has turned out to be a good job, but "It" has evaded us.[19]

The Strategies of Our Discontent

So what do we do when we discover that we lack "it"—the "something missing but we don't know what"? There are at least seven strategies that people take toward their discontent. There are two broad approaches—you can either live life assuming that satisfaction in life is quite possible, that *"it" is still out there*, or you can live in the conviction that satisfaction is not possible, that *there is no "it."* But within these two categories we can discern four strategies in the first and three strategies in the second.

"IT" IS STILL OUT THERE

The young. The normal way people start adult life is to travel hopefully in anticipation of a joyful arrival. We think, "If I get the right love partner, if I get the right spouse, if I get the right career and make some money—then I will have life satisfaction." James Wood refers to the pursuit of "jobs, family, sex, and so on—the usual distractions" by which we hide from ourselves the emptiness of our lives.[20] Actually we may be quite discontent, but we don't recognize it because we are so busy in the process of getting ready to be happy. "Of course I am restless. I haven't gotten to do all the things I am going to do." We think we just have to get over this hill or get around that bend and then things will be great. This strategy, of course, is only effective temporarily.

The resentful. However, as time goes on, we begin to realize we are not getting "it." One of the main reactions is to blame the obstacles that have kept us from achieving the things we think will satisfy us. We may be the victim of prejudice or discrimination, or we may find ourselves in a community that is not open to many of the things we want to be and do. Rather than social structures, we may identify individuals who blocked our progress or who have wronged us. And so we blame them, saying "I would be quite happy if it wasn't for (fill in the blank)." Now, this might in the short run lead to some good—we might channel our anger constructively into becoming social activists. Even less constructive anger, such as complaining and venting, can in the short run be a kind of relief—but it is only in the short run. And if our efforts actually break the barriers and get us to the next level of accomplishment, we will find that "it" is still not there to be found. That means we will need the third strategy.

The driven. By definition, a secular culture puts the most emphasis on the here-and-now. We think that accruing possessions and accomplishments will bring satisfaction. What happens if, unlike the young and resentful, we find we actually reach many of our material goals? We will, as the ancients did, still find something significant missing. What do we do? Many people begin to blame the things we have. We assume that if we got a better spouse, a better job, a better income, or a better home, then we would feel much better too. If we take this path, we may become among society's most productive members—and also the most driven. We go through houses and spouses and jobs and the constant reinvention of our lives, assuring ourselves that at the next level "it" is going to finally be there. But psychologists call this merely speeding up the "hedonic treadmill."[21] On an exercise treadmill a change of speed does not translate into a change of location; we only work harder to maintain our position and eventually become too weary to keep on going. So too the enjoyment that attainment initially brings wears off, so that we need more and more of the same kinds of attainment just to maintain the same pleasure. Eventually, as on a physical treadmill, we will find ourselves too exhausted to continue.

The despairing. What if we don't find "it," even after removing obstacles and achieving more and more, but we nonetheless continue to assume it exists? In some cases, rather than blaming other things, we may blame ourselves. That means saying, "There is something wrong with *me*—I haven't done well enough. I haven't gone far enough up the career ladder. I haven't attracted the best romantic partners. I'm a failure." If we take an honest look at ourselves, it is never too hard to see some ways we have contributed to our own frustration. British author Francis Spufford writes that for a time we can live in denial of our active tendency to "break stuff—'stuff' here including promises, relationships we care about, our own well-being, and other people's." But the day comes when "you're lying in the bath and you notice you are thirty-nine and that the way you're living bears scarcely any resemblance to what you thought you always wanted, and yet, you realize you got there by a long series of choices."[22] So we hate ourselves.

"IT" DOESN'T EXIST

All of these strategies are based on the assumption that human beings can and ought to live a life of satisfaction and fulfillment. However, many people question that very premise. They conclude that it is our expectations of life that are out of line. We may start out life naively in pursuit of "it," but eventually we see that it does not exist, and we should get used to life as it is. This has affinities with the ancient "happiness hypothesis." There are at least three ways to live based on this outlook, and all three of them seem to be an improvement over the naïveté, resentment, anxiety, and despair we have been looking at. But on closer look, each one of these strategies is extremely problematic as well.

Altruism. Often people who have devoted the earlier part of their lives to personal advancement turn away from it toward social causes, philanthropy, and improving the lives of others. Sometimes their story goes like this. "I thought I would find satisfaction in acquisition, but now I realize that it is only through giving and serving that I can have a fulfilling life." Of course, this is to be fully encouraged. One writer in the *New York Times*, typical of this approach, relates how in earlier years he thought that satisfaction and self-esteem could be found. He sought to fill his "sense of deficit"—his inner emptiness and need for satisfaction—through success and wealth. But then he learned a better way: "We feel best about ourselves when we stop focusing obsessively on filling our own sense of deficit. Making others feel valued makes us feel more valued."[23] Instead of trying to better ourselves, we get far more satisfaction from trying to better others.

But many have pointed out the problems that result when people turn to benevolence and social activism as a way to find more fulfillment for themselves. This approach is ultimately, and ironically, extremely selfish. Your supposed generosity is really just building yourself up. The most famous of the critics is Nietzsche, who argued that modern people help the needy out of a sense of moral superiority.[24] They feel superior to their former, unenlightened selves, as well as to earlier times and societies which were not committed to equality as they are. In short, they are not serving others as much as serving themselves. They are using the needy and poor to achieve the self-worth they need. This not only can lead to paternalism but can also turn to disdain and contempt if their altruistic efforts are not met with respect and gratitude. Helping others in response to your own discontent will not work in the long run, either for others or for you.

Cynicism. By the time many sophisticated and urbane people in our culture reach middle age, they come to a position that could be expressed something like this: "Yes, when I was younger I thought fulfillment was out there. I thought sex and love and career success would be much more satisfying. But now, of course, I have grown up. I realize nobody is ever content and satisfied, but there's no need to obsess about this. I have stopped chasing rainbows; I have stopped crying after the moon. I have lowered my expectations of life and learned to enjoy what I have, and I'm getting by fine." As sensible as this sounds, it is problematic in at least two ways. One is that this stance almost always creates a certain amount of condescension toward anyone who is not as sophisticated and as ironic as you. This can make you as bigoted and self-righteous in your own way as the legalistic religionists you despise. But there is a more serious effect. As we heard from Martin Heidegger, what makes you a human being and not an animal is that you want joy, meaning, and fulfillment. If you decide that fulfillment, joy, and happiness are not there, and you harden your heart against hope, you can dehumanize yourself.

Detachment. We might ask why we don't revert to a purer form of the older "happiness hypothesis" of the Buddha and the Greek Stoics. Their counsel was not to love anything or hope for anything too much. Epictetus wrote, "What harm is there while you are kissing your child to murmur softly, 'Tomorrow you will die'?"[25] But here I must side with the modern research, which supports a deep human intuition, namely, that diminishing your love for others does not increase satisfaction but only undermines it. Even though ancient stoic detachment has a better philosophical pedigree than the jaded Western cynicism that sneers at everything, it ultimately also hardens your heart and dehumanizes you.

Understanding Our Discontent

We want something that nothing in this life can give us. If we keep pursuing it in this world, it can make us driven, resentful, or self-hating. If we try to harden our hearts so that it doesn't bother us, we harm our humanity and those around us. If, however, we don't harden ourselves, and fully feel the grief of desire's lost hope, we may find self-destructive ways of drowning it, as did the woman in Peggy Lee's song. All of these approaches look like dead ends.

What is the cause of this seemingly inescapable condition, of this enduring discontent?

One modern theory is summarized by Haidt as the "Progress Principle." People find more pleasure in working toward a goal than they experience when they actually attain it. Evolutionary psychologists opine that this is an adaptive mechanism. That is, they conjecture that our forebears who experienced postattainment disappointment were more likely to work harder to achieve higher goals. These people were then more likely to live longer and so, having more children, they passed down their genes to us. Therefore, the discontent—the feeling that nothing in the world fulfills our deepest longings—is actually a chemical response in the brain that helped our ancestors survive. The sense we have that "something is missing" is therefore an illusion, a trick played on us by our genes to get us to be more industrious. Haidt even briefly uses this evolutionary theory to explain the Peggy Lee song "Is That All There Is?" [26]

But the woman's life depicted in Peggy Lee's song undermines the theory. She finds the repeated disappointments of life not a motivation to work harder but rather a disincentive for doing anything but getting high at parties. And surely this is realistic. Though disappointment may, in the short term, drive some people to more attainment, it can just as likely undermine initiative and drive. And over time it usually will. Therefore, the feeling does not necessarily or even normally lead to survival behavior. The evolutionary explanation of our constant discontent doesn't seem to hold up.

A more time-tested explanation comes from the great Christian philosopher Augustine.

As a nineteen-year-old, Augustine read Cicero's dialogue *Hortensius*. This work considered the paradox that every person "sets out to be happy [but] the majority are thoroughly wretched."[27] Cicero concluded that the extreme scarcity of human contentment might be a judgment of divine providence for our sins. He counseled his readers not to seek happiness in the pursuit of material comfort, sex, or prosperity but rather to find it in philosophical contemplation. The book was electrifying to the young Augustine.[28] One of his lifelong projects became to discover why most people are so discontent and bereft of joy. He concluded that our discontent has both a functional cause and an ultimate source.

The functional cause of our discontent is that our loves are "out of order."

Augustine taught that we are most fundamentally shaped not as much by what we believe, or think, or even do, but by what we love. "For when we ask whether somebody is a good person, we are not asking what he believes or hopes for, but what he loves."[29] For Augustine, what we call human virtues are nothing more than forms of love. Courage is loving your neighbor's well-being more than your own safety. Honesty is loving your neighbor's interests more than your own, even when the truth will put you at a disadvantage. And because Jesus himself said that all God's law comes down to loving God and your neighbor (Matthew 22:36–40), Augustine believed all sin was ultimately a lack of love.[30] Look at injustice. You may say that you believe in social equality and justice and think that you do, but if you make business decisions that exploit others, it is because at the heart level you love your own prosperity more than your neighbor's. In short, what you love most at the moment is what controls your action at that moment. "A body by its weight tends to move toward its proper place. . . . My weight is my love: wherever I am carried, my love is carrying me."[31] You are what you love.

Augustine did not see our problems as stemming only from a lack of love. He also observed that the heart's loves have an order to them, and that we often love less important things more and the more important things less. Therefore, the unhappiness and disorder of our lives are caused by the disorder of our loves. A just and good person "is also a person who has [rightly] ordered his love, so that he does not love what it is wrong to love, or fail to love what should be loved, or love too much what should be loved less (or love too little what should be loved more)."[32] How does this work? There is nothing wrong with loving your work, but if you love it more than your family, then your loves are out of order and you may ruin your family. Or if you love making money more than you love justice, then you will exploit your employees, again, because your loves are disordered.

The Infinity of Our Discontent

The ultimate disordered love, however—and the ultimate source of our discontent—is failure to love *the* first thing first, the failure to love God supremely. In his *Confessions,* Augustine prays to God: "For there is a joy that is not given to those who do not love you, but only to those who love you for your own sake. . . . This is happiness and there is no other. Those who think that there is another kind of happiness look for joy elsewhere, but theirs is not true joy. Nevertheless their will remains drawn towards some image of the true joy."[33]

Augustine here distills the biblical view of humanity. Human beings were made in the image of a God who is tripersonal—Father, Son, and Holy Spirit. From all eternity those three divine persons have been loving one another in infinite degrees of joy and glory. We were created to know this joy by loving and glorifying God preeminently. Whether we acknowledge God or not, since we were created for it, we will always look for the infinite joy we were designed to find in loving communion with the Divine. We turn to things in the world to give it to us, but "[we] sin when, neglectful of order, we fix our love on the creature, instead of on Thee, the Creator."[34] The reason even the best possible worldly goods will not satisfy is because we were created for a degree of delight and fulfillment that they cannot produce. As Augustine famously says to God at the beginning of the *Confessions*: "You stir man to take pleasure in praising you, because you have made us for yourself, and our heart is restless until it rests in you."[35] We were made for God, and so nothing can give us the infinite joy that God can.

> All things are precious, because all are beautiful, but what is more beautiful than He? Strong they are, but what is stronger than He? . . . If you seek for anything better, you will do wrong to Him and harm to yourself, by preferring to Him that which He made, when he would willingly give Himself to you.[36]

You harm yourself when you love anything more than God. How does this work? If you love your children more than you love God, you will essentially rest your need for significance and security in them. You will need too much for them to succeed, be happy, and love you. That will either drive them away or crush them under the weight of your expectations, because they will be the ultimate source of your happiness, and no human being can measure up to that. If instead you love your spouse or romantic partner more than God, the same things occur. If you love your work and career more than God, you will necessarily also love them more than your family, your community, and your own health, and so that will lead to physical and relational breakdown and often, as we saw above, to social injustice.

If you love anything more than God, you harm the object of your love, you harm yourself, you harm the world around you, and you end up deeply dissatisfied and discontent. The most famous modern expression of Augustine's view was the ending of Lewis's radio talk:

> *Creatures are not born with desires unless satisfaction for those desires exists. A baby feels hunger: well, there is such a thing as food. A duckling wants to swim: well, there is such a thing as water. Men feel sexual desires: well, there is such a thing as sex. If I find in myself a desire which no experience in this world can satisfy, the most probable explanation is that I was made for another world.*[37]

The Augustinian analysis does justice to our experience. As we saw, the evolutionary explanation of our perennial discontent fails to account for it. The idea that "most people are basically happy" trivializes it, but it is not trivial at all. Some have, as it were, sought to fill the inner emptiness with billions of dollars and virtually unchecked power to gratify their impulses and appetites. Yet the testimony of the ages is that even goods on this scale cannot fill the vacuum. That is powerful evidence that the cavern in our soul is indeed infinitely deep.[38]

The Healing of Our Discontent

Here, then, is the conundrum we face. Our surprisingly deep discontent leads us to lock our hearts onto things with profound intensity. The ancients wisely taught that the only way to avoid unhappiness is to avoid this "love as attachment," that is, to attach ourselves so powerfully and exclusively to an object or person that we cannot imagine life without it or him or her.[39] Not only do such attachments lead to envy, resentment, anxiety, and even violence in order to defend our possession, but they also make us fragile and vulnerable to the inevitable changes and disruptions of life.

However, we have seen the dangers of finding contentment through *de*tachment. That not only brings about a selfishness and hardness but also weakens our love relationships, thus undermining the greatest source of joy we know. We need not only to receive love but also to give it.[40]

Augustine breaks through this logjam. He does a radical critique of love-as-attachment, and presents his own pre-Christian self as a case study. He had attached his happiness to a friend whom he loved intensely but who died suddenly. He later realized that he had "loved a person sure to die as if he would never die" (*Confessions*, book IV, chapter 8). This happens because our souls "become stuck and glued to these transient things," which "rend the soul with pestilential desires and torment" because "the soul loves . . . to take its repose" in them. Yet "in these things there is no point of rest, for they . . . flee away" (*Confessions*, book IV, chapter 10).[41]

However, after Augustine confirms the deadliness of love-as-attachment, he turns and says that such love is good, right, and essential when given to God. Though idolatrous attachment to earthly goods does indeed lead to unnecessary pain and grief, the solution was not to love the things of life less but to love God more. The problem is not that you love your family or job too much but that you love God too little in relationship to them. Intense attachment *and* detachment kill. Don't harden your heart against love, Augustine says, but don't give your heart ultimately to things that you can lose and cannot satisfy. Instead infuse your heart with a sense of God's love and incline your heart to love him in return. This will be transformative.

Consider this: If you live a long life, it will tear you up to see the people who matter most to you put into the ground one by one. If your greatest source of contentment and love is your family, that will be intolerable. But if you learn to love God even more than them, your greatest source of consolation, hope, joy, and value will not be diminished by grief. Indeed, the sorrow will drive you to drink deeper from it. You will not find yourself empty, and you won't always be hardening your heart in order to deal with how your losses tear you up. The love of God can never be taken from you, and in his love, the Bible says, you live with loved ones forever.[42]

Of course, not even the strongest believers love God perfectly, nor does anyone get close to doing so. Yet to the degree you move toward loving him supremely, things begin to fall into order, into their proper places in your life. Instead of looking to the things of the world as the deepest source of your contentment, you can enjoy them for what they are. Money and career, for example, become just what they are supposed to be. Work becomes work, a great way to use your gifts and be useful to others. Money becomes just money, a great way to support your family. But these things are not your source of safety and contentment. *He is.*

There is another powerful dimension to this reordering of loves. Paul Bloom, in his book *How Pleasure Works*, argues that what matters most for pleasure is not the simple impact on our senses but what it means in relationship to other persons who matter to us. A painting that we think is an original by an admired artist gives less pleasure when we find out it is not. A chair may be comfortable, but if it is our mother's favorite chair from her sitting room, it will give us even more pleasure. To use theological language, "we enjoy things most when we experience them as a sacrament—as carriers of the presence of another."[43] Some have charged that religion drains ordinary life of its joy by devaluing it in deference to "higher," more spiritual interests. This is not true—at least, it is not the case with Christianity, the faith that I know by far the best.

Christianity teaches that we are saved by God's free grace and pardon. Unlike some forms of religion, Christianity does not say that we merit blessing through depriving ourselves and turning our backs on the world in order to earn heaven. Once we know through faith in Christ's work for us that we are reconciled to God, and that the Creator is now not just our sovereign but our father, we can begin to have a more "sacramental" experience of the world. We see everything as a free gift from Father and a foretaste of the glory and goodness to come in our eternal inheritance. In short, as Miroslav Volf puts it, "Attachment to God amplifies and deepens enjoyment of the world."[44] It does not diminish it.

Here, then, is the message. Don't love anything less; instead learn to love God more, and you will love other things with far more satisfaction. You won't overprotect them, you won't overexpect things from them. You won't be constantly furious with them for not being what you hoped. Don't stifle passionate love for anything; rather, redirect your greatest love toward God by loving him with your whole heart and loving him for himself, not just for what he can give you.[45] Then, and only then, does the contentment start to come.

That is the Christian view of satisfaction. It avoids the pitfalls of both the ancient strategy of tranquillity through detachment and the modern strategy of happiness through acquisition. It both explains and resolves the deep conundrum of our seemingly irremediable discontent.

How to Love God

It may be that, reading this, you think Augustine's analysis and solution make good sense. The magnitude of our discontent points to something beyond this world. We harm ourselves if we try to satisfy our deepest longings in human love, and we also harm ourselves if we detach our hearts too much from love. Augustine's solution is that only the love of the immutable can bring tranquillity, and only an infinite love can satisfy our hunger for infinite joy.

Even if this all makes sense to us, how do we actually know that love? You can't just tell yourself "God loves me" and expect your heart to change. Nor can you just say, "From now on I will love God." Love cannot be generated simply by an act of the will. Children learn to speak only by responding to speech and learn to love only by reciprocating love. So we cannot love God just by thinking of an abstract deity who is loving in general. We must grasp and be gripped by the true story of God's actual sacrificial, saving love for us in Jesus.

In the Gospel of John, Jesus speaks to a crowd about the "bread of life," such that whoever eats it "will never go hungry" (John 6:35). He is talking metaphorically about something that gives both strength and delight, an image of fulfillment and satisfaction. He also observes that human beings seek this in the wrong places. He warns against "work[ing] for food that spoils," that does not in the end satisfy (John 6:27). But he does not just say, "I am the dispenser of the bread of life." Rather, he says, "I *am* the bread of life" (John 6:35) and "This is my body given for you" (Luke 22:19) and "This is my body, which is for you" (1 Corinthians 11:24).

The heart of the Christian faith is the simple Gospel message of sin and grace. Because we fail to love God and our neighbor, we sin, and for God to forgive our sin, the Son of God became mortal and graciously died in our place on the cross. This is an offensive idea to many people, but for the moment just consider the two ways this message can bring about the love relationship with God, which solves the human dilemma.

First, the knowledge of our sin softens our hearts. If you were to raise a child and work your fingers to the bone to send that child to college, and the child only occasionally sent you a Christmas card and never gave you the time of day, that would be wrong. It's wrong because the child owes not just deference but love. Now, if there is a God who created us and keeps us alive every minute, then the love we owe God would be infinitely greater. To not love him supremely would be infinitely worse. If you believe that, you begin to see how much we have wronged him. It begins to draw your heart outward toward him in humility and grief.

Second, the knowledge of his grace ignites our hearts. If you want to forgive someone who has wrongfully cost you a great deal of money and can't afford to pay you back, you must absorb and pay the debt your-self. If God was going to forgive us, he had to pay the debt we owed himself. And Jesus Christ pays it by going to the cross. Keep in mind that outside of salt and a couple of minerals, everything we eat has died so that we may live. If you are eating bread, not only did the grain die, but the bread has to be broken into pieces. If the bread stays whole, you starve and you fall apart. If the bread is broken into pieces and you take it in, then you live. When Jesus Christ says, "I am the bread of life. . . broken for you," (John 6:35; Luke 22:19) he is saying: "I am God be-come breakable, killable, vulnerable. I die that you might live. I am bro-ken so you can be whole."

Only if you see him doing this all for you—does that begin to change your heart. He suffered and died for your sake. Now out of joy we can love him just for his sake, just for the beauty of who he is and what he has done. You can't force your heart to love. A kind of vague god, a god of love, an abstract god will never change your heart. This is what will change it, draw it off its inordinate attachments to other things, and turn it away from the food that spoils. Someday, then, you will be able to say, "Because your love is better than life . . . I will be fully satisfied as with the richest of foods; with singing lips my mouth will praise you" (Psalm 63:3a,5). This is "it"—or at least its foretaste (1 John 3:1–3).

Five

Why Can't I Be Free to Live as I See Fit, as Long as I Don't Harm Anyone?

When "The Star-Spangled Banner" is sung at sporting events, the climactic phrase comes to an elongated high note: "O'er the land of the freeee . . ." The cheers begin here. Even though the song goes on to talk about "the brave," this is an afterthought. Both the melody line and our culture highlight freedom as *the* main theme and value of our society. It's our national anthem, and for good reason.

Certainly anyone in our society who seeks to measure "progress" will do so to a great degree by measuring increasing freedoms. Justice is done when marginalized and oppressed groups are given more political and economic freedom. Religions, as well as nonbelief, all flourish more when society gives individuals freedom to believe, live, and worship (or not worship) as their consciences lead them. In their landmark sociological study of American culture, Robert Bellah and other researchers discovered that "for Americans . . . freedom was perhaps the most important value."[1]

Human beings have always valued freedom, of course. There have been slave revolts back to at least Spartacus and the Third Servile War in the first century BC.[2] Aristotle and Plato called for freedom and democracy, though in a very limited way and for a very limited populace. But today, as Bellah and company discovered, freedom has become perhaps the only publicly shared and acknowledged moral value of our culture. In Alan Ehrenhalt's study of 1950s Chicago, he summarizes the modern attitude: "Most of us in America believe a few simple propositions that seem so clear and self-evident they scarcely need to be said. Choice is a good thing in life, and the more of it we have, the happier we are. Authority is inherently suspect; nobody should have the right to tell others what to think or how to behave."[3] Charles Taylor gives his own expression of the secular moral order: "Let each person do their own thing, and . . . one shouldn't criticize the others' values, because they have a right to live their own life as you do. The [only] sin which is not tolerated is intolerance."[4] As Ehrenhalt notes, these slogans about freedom are today considered self-evident givens, truths that everyone knows intuitively and that cannot be questioned.

The History of the Idea

How did freedom become not just one valuable thing among many but the ultimate good?

Older societies were much more religiously and culturally homogeneous. It was believed that a society could be cohesive only if it was built on the basis of commonly held moral and religious beliefs. But the wars between Catholic and Protestant in the sixteenth and seventeenth centuries produced a religion-fatigue reaction among the elites of Europe.[5] They began to theorize a new basis for society. All these early theorists expected that the citizens would be Christian, but they wanted a government whose laws were not tied to one Christian church or type of orthodoxy. Thinkers such as Hugo Grotius and John Locke conceived of a new political order based not on divine law but on the consent of the governed.[6] Government was seen as legitimate when it consisted of individuals coming together for common gain, providing each person the freedom to live in ways that satisfied his interest. In this conception of society, the only ethic required was "the ethic of freedom and mutual benefit."[7]

In the twentieth century, historical trends contributed further toward freedom's ascendancy to become the ultimate value. Both fascism in Germany and communism in Russia led to totalitarianism and violence on an unprecedented scale. Thinkers were aghast who had, both on the left and the right, thought that their respective political systems would ameliorate social problems and human suffering. Both Nazism and Stalinism were highly scientific and efficient. Both global capitalism *and* state socialism began to be seen as bringing about dehumanization and oppression, each in its own distinct way. This led many philosophers and thinkers to move toward making freedom *the* animating ideal and standard by which to judge all cultural organizations. They "refused to identify freedom with any institutional arrangement or fixed system of thought" and finally became "deeply skeptical of . . . all absolute claims."[8]

So in late-modern secularism (sometimes called postmodernism), we are no longer seen as free because we are God's creation, nor because of our rationality and free will, nor because of unfolding historical processes moving the human race toward inevitable progress. Those had been the bases of freedom in the past, argued by Aquinas, Kant, and Hegel, respectively.[9] Instead, for postmodern secular thinkers today, freedom is based on the discrediting of each of those very ideas.[10] We are considered to be free because there is no cosmic order, there is no essential human nature, and there are no truths or moral absolutes that we must kneel to. Today the view is that "there are no longer any foundations at all" because "the universe itself is arbitrary, contingent, aleatory."[11] Nothing, then, has any rightful claim on us, and we may live as we see fit.

It is only fair to observe that John Locke himself would have been astonished to see where we have come. He helped begin the process by championing political freedom and democratic self-determination, but he was a Christian who believed in moral truths and obligations that were independent of our minds and feelings and which limited our freedom. Today we hold to a new, unqualified kind of freedom (only and exclusively excepting the impingement on others' freedom). We understand freedom as the right of the individual to choose his or her own values altogether, something neither Locke nor his compatriots ever envisioned.[12]

The Enemy of Freedom?

Today as a culture we believe freedom is the highest good, that becoming free is the only heroic story we have left, and that giving individuals freedom is the main role of any institution and of society itself. It is, we could say, *the* baseline cultural narrative of our Western culture.[13] It has always been important, but now it is *ultimately* important. It is the one truth that relativizes all other doctrines and beliefs.

That includes, in the minds of many people, the doctrines of Christianity. In much of our society Christianity is seen as the archenemy of freedom. Columbia professor Mark Lilla writes in the *New York Times Magazine* of meeting a man who had graduated from the prestigious Wharton School of the University of Pennsylvania and discovering, to his shock, that the man had walked the aisle at a Billy Graham crusade and professed to have been "born again."

Lilla, as a teenager, had flirted with Christianity, but then he found the place in the Bible where Jesus tells Nicodemus, an accomplished scholar and leader, "You must be born again!" Lilla wrote: "Jesus seems to be telling Nicodemus that he must recognize his own insufficiency, that he will have to turn his back on his autonomous, seemingly happy life, and be reborn as a human being who understands his dependency on something greater. That seems like a radical challenge to our freedom. And it is." He goes on to say that this is the reason he couldn't follow suit.[14]

Is he right? Do we have to choose between freedom and faith in God? The answer is *yes* but *no*. By speaking in this way, I am not being indecisive. Rather, I want us to look more closely at our definitions. Brendan Gleeson, in the movie *Calvary*, plays a man who goes into the Catholic priesthood later in life. He has a daughter who recently failed in a suicide attempt. As he expresses his concern to her, she says assertively: "I belong to myself, not to anyone else." That, of course, is one expression of the cultural narrative of freedom. Her father answers, "True," but then, after a pause, he says, "False." He isn't changing his mind. He is saying, essentially, "There is some truth in what you are saying about freedom, but if you define it the way you do, it is ultimately false."[15]

His insight applies not just to this specific case but to the entire way our society understands freedom. True—the ideal of individual freedom in Western society has done incalculable good. It has led to a far more just and fair society for minorities and women. Indeed, there is a danger that a critique of the idea of freedom could be used to weaken or roll back these gains.

But false. Freedom has come to be defined as the absence of any limitations or constraints on us. By this definition, the fewer boundaries we have on our choices and actions, the freer we feel ourselves to be. Held in this form, I want to argue that the narrative has gone wrong and is doing damage.

It Is Practically Unworkable

Modern freedom is the freedom of self-assertion. I am free if I may do whatever I want. But defining freedom this way—as the absence of constraint on choices—is unworkable because it is an impossibility. Think of how freedom actually works.

Imagine a man in his sixties who likes to eat whatever he wants to eat. He also loves to spend time with his grandchildren. Both of these activities are an important part of what makes his daily life meaningful and satisfying. Then at his annual physical a doctor says to him, "Unless you severely restrict what you eat from now on, your heart problems will worsen and you will have a heart attack. You must completely stop eating all of your favorite foods."

The modern definition of freedom is the ability to do whatever we want. However, how does that definition work when your wants are in conflict with each other? He certainly does not want to be bedridden or to die, in which case his freedom to be with his grandchildren and see them grow up is curtailed. But, of course, he also wants to eat his favorite foods, eating being a major source of comfort and good feeling. This is the complexity of real life. He can accept either the limits on his eating or the limits on his health. It is impossible that he will have freedom in both areas. There is, then, not just one thing called "freedom" that we either have or do not have. At the level of lived life there are numerous *freedoms,* and no one can have them all. This man will have to decide which freedom to sacrifice for the other, because he will not be able to have both. The choice should not be hard in this case. If he wants the freedom of sustained loving relationships, he will give up the freedom to eat what he wants.

The question is not, then: How can this man live in complete freedom? The proper question is: Which freedom is the more important, the more truly liberating? Education and training is another obvious example. If you want the freedom that comes with having a good income, you need for years to sacrifice innumerable other freedoms of time and money in order to get the best education. You will not be able to live any way you like in school. For example, if you don't say no to most impulses to go out and hang out with friends and party, you will not get a degree. In the same way, if you want the varied set of freedoms that come with being a top performer in athletics or the arts, you will need to accept enormous constraints on your life. You will cede much control over your daily life to a coach. You won't even be able to choose where you live.

We see, then, that freedom is not what the culture tells us. Real freedom comes from a strategic loss of some freedoms in order to gain others. It is not the absence of constraints but it is choosing the right constraints and the right freedoms to lose. Some might object to this way of framing things. You may grant that freedom is the choosing of the right restraints. Then you may say, "But these restraints are the ones that *I* have chosen. So that still makes me free by today's definition, because I'm free as long as I am doing what *I* want."

That's too simplistic. You don't really freely choose most of these necessary limitations in life. You are just recognizing the limitations that are actually there in the world, that are independent of your desires and choices. For example, we have a body that is designed to do some things and not other things, and we only experience physical freedom when we submit our wills to the body's limits. When you eat right and exercise right, you gain the freedom to live in ways you could not do without the stamina and health that come from these regimens. This is not, however, anything like the postmodern ideal of "creating yourself." The liberating, "right" restraints we have spoken of, among many others, are not things you make up to please yourself. They are hard realities about the way we are and the way the world is. You don't choose them, you submit to them.

If you see a large sailboat out on the water moving swiftly, it is because the sailor is honoring the boat's design. If she tries to take it into water too shallow for it, the boat will be ruined. The sailor experiences the freedom of speed sailing only when she limits her boat to the proper depth of water and faces the wind at the proper angle.

In the same way, human beings thrive in certain environments and break down in others. Unless you honor the givens and limits of your physical nature, you will never know the freedom of health. Unless you honor the givens and limits of human relationships, you will never know the freedom of love and social peace. If you actually lived any way you wanted—never aligning your choices with these physical and social realities—you would quickly die, and die alone.

You are, then, not free to do whatever you choose. That is an impossible idea and not the way freedom actually works. You get the best freedoms only if you are willing to submit your choices to various realities, if you honor your own design.

It Is Unjust

The contemporary concept of freedom, which we could call absolute individual autonomy, is not only unworkable. It is also unfair because it denies what we owe others.

The Internet is filled with claims like "I am responsible only to myself. No one has the right to tell me how to live." These are always stated ex cathedra, as if they were self-evident truths. But they would be true only if no one had ever sacrificially invested in you, or if you were even now self-sufficient. Neither of those is the case. If we need other people—and we do—then there is some shared responsibility for and to others, and we don't really belong only to ourselves.

Dr. Atul Gawande, in *Being Mortal*, writes: "There are different concepts of autonomy. One is autonomy as free action, living completely independently, free of coercion and limitation. This kind of freedom is a common battle cry in our culture. But it is . . . a fantasy." It is an illusion that can be temporarily supported, he argues, when we are young and healthy adults. But as children we were dependent on the care of others, when we get old we will be again. If we ever become injured or sick, that can happen now. "Our lives are inherently dependent on others and subject to forces and circumstances beyond our control."[16]

As we saw in the movie *Calvary*, the priest's daughter attempted suicide and justified it by claiming autonomy: "I belong to myself, not to anybody else." He responds, "True . . . false," because her answer is unjust. "It's a tired old argument, I suppose," he says quietly, "but what about those you leave behind?"[17] Though Western people like to think of themselves as mainly the product of their own decisions and choices, such is not the case. You are the product of a family and a community of people who invested massive amounts of time, industry, and love in you, much of it happening before you could speak and before you can now remember. To commit suicide, the priest rightly says, is to strike a blow and inflict a pain on many that will never be healed. The question is, What right do you have to darken *their* lives permanently?

Here, then, we see a truth that is hard to deny but that does not fit well with the contemporary concept of individual freedom and autonomy. We unavoidably, to some degree, belong to one another. "No man is an island. . . . Any man's death diminishes me, because I am involved in mankind."[18]

It Cannot Stand Alone

Freedom is sometimes said to be the only unconditional good our society agrees on, and, it is argued, the only one we really need. Why try to impose a set of moral rights and wrongs on everyone? We don't want to be like the moralistic societies of the past. Instead, we should agree on just one thing, that everyone should be free to live as they desire as long as they do not harm anyone else.[19] This "harm principle" appears to make freedom of choice into a self-correcting absolute that gives us guidance for life together without the need for value judgments of any kind. Today, it is said, the only moral absolute should be freedom and the only sin should be intolerance or bigotry.

However, while the paragraph above describes the culturally dominant view, the harm principle is useless and even disingenuous as a guide. It works only if we are all agreed on what "harm" is—and we aren't. How can you know what hurts people unless you can define what a good and thriving human life is? One group may think no-fault divorce laws are very harmful while another believes they are not. The underlying problem is that the two groups have different understandings of the role of marriage in human life and what a good one looks like. Another example is obscenity laws. One man believes that strict laws violate free speech and that he is not harming anyone by consuming pornography in private. A second person responds that if the man watches pornography he is shaping himself in such a way that will be bad for male-female relationships and that affects society. Behind the disagreement about harm are two different ways of thinking how the individual relates to society and what healthy male-female relationships look like.

Of course we must avoid harming others, but any decision about what harms others will be rooted in (generally unacknowledged) views of human nature and purpose. These are beliefs—they are not self-evident, nor can they be proven empirically. That means that ultimately freedom of choice is not the "magic bullet" for society. Even in our supposedly relativistic culture, value judgments are made constantly, people and groups are daily lifted up in order to shame them, public moral umbrage is taken as much as ever. It is hypocritical to claim that today we grant people so much more freedom when we are actually all fighting to press our moral beliefs about harm on everyone.[20]

So freedom of choice cannot stand alone as a guide to behavior. We need some kind of moral norms and constraints on our actions if we are to live together.

It Is Corrosive of Community and Relationships

We are an "ultrasocial species,"[21] and so the culture's sacralization of individual autonomy not only is unjust to others but also can be tragic for you. Freedom, as it is widely conceived in our society, is corrosive to community in general and to enduring, committed love relationships in particular.

As we have seen, "happiness research" strongly confirms the importance of strong social relationships. Haidt writes: "Having [them] strengthens the immune system, extends life (more than does quitting smoking), speeds recovery from surgery, and reduces the risks of depression and anxiety disorders. . . . We need to interact and intertwine with others; we need the give *and* the take; we need to belong."[22] But then he adds,

> *An ideology of extreme personal freedom can be dangerous because it encourages people to leave homes, jobs, cities, and marriages in search of personal and professional fulfillment, thereby breaking the relationships that were probably their best hope for such fulfillment.*[23]

Here Haidt echoes Robert Bellah and, before him, the early-nineteenth-century social critic Alexis de Tocqueville in *Democracy in America*. Tocqueville saw a conundrum at the heart of American society. We are committed to individual freedom, but it can grow "cancerous" and so undermine the ties of family, neighborhood, and citizenship that it ironically "threatens the survival of freedom itself."[24] Tocqueville worried that self-absorbed individuals would not feel part of a community, would simply want to be free to pursue their own lives. This would lessen involvement in self-governing smaller communities such as families, neighborhood associations, churches, and synagogues, and other local civic organizations. The more personal individual freedom is emphasized, the more all these democratic institutions erode. This necessitates the "soft despotism" of a growing bureaucratic state, before which individuals are powerless. So ironically, the growth of freedom would lead to the loss of freedom.[25]

In their book Bellah and his colleagues show that much of the health of a society depends on voluntarily unselfish behavior. Being honest, generous, and public spirited—being faithful to your spouse and children—regularly infringes on your personal happiness and freedom. If people stop doing these things and (as Haidt says) put personal fulfillment above commitment and relationship, the only alternative is a more powerful and coercive government. Bellah and his colleagues made this case in their original 1985 study. Their case was that the culture's emphasis on personal freedom over commitment to community could undermine democratic institutions. In 1996 and 2008 the book was reissued with a new preface written by Bellah, and each time he pointed out that our situation was worsening.

Let's bring this down to a practical level. Just as a sailboat is not free to sail unless it confines itself in significant ways, so you will never know the freedom of love unless you limit your choices in significant ways. There is no greater feeling of liberation than to feel and be loved well. The affirmation that comes from love liberates you from fears and self-doubts. It frees you from having to face the world alone, with only your own ingenuity and resources. Your friend or mate will be crucial to helping you achieve many of your goals in life. In all these ways love is liberating—perhaps the most liberating thing. But the minute you get into a love relationship, and the deeper and the more intimate and the more wonderful it gets, the more you also have to give up your independence.

Let's say you get into a romantic relationship with someone who lives in the same city. Your independence is immediately curtailed in the most concrete ways. In the past you could simply leave town for the weekend if and when you wanted. Now if you do that, the other person calls you and says, "Where are you?" and can't believe you left without checking or informing. Now, you might respond by saying, "Well, I don't have to tell you where I am or where I'm going. I belong only to myself. No one has the right to determine for me how I live my life."

There will be a silence on the other end of the line. The person might say, "I think we need to break up!" and be quite right. Love relationships don't work that way. You can't be completely free in the contemporary sense of the word and simultaneously in a strong love relationship.

In a significant relationship, the loss of independence goes far beyond daily-life logistics. If the other person falls into sickness or difficulty, it will require an enormous expenditure of time and energy on your part. You cannot just go on your unimpeded way if the other person is in some kind of trouble or stress, nor would you want to if the relationship is not superficial. We should hasten to say that both persons must be mutually giving up their independence or the relationship will be exploitative. If one or both parties say, "Me first. My needs before yours," then the relationship will struggle and die. If, however, both parties habitually say and think, "You first. I will adjust for you. I will sacrifice my needs to meet yours," then there will be no exploitation and a relationship of great richness is in store. This mutual sacrifice of autonomy leads to the variegated, wonderful kind of liberation that only love can bring.

The limitation of the contemporary cultural freedom narrative comes through in an interview given some years ago in *Le Monde* with Françoise Sagan, the novelist. At one point the interviewer asked her, "Then you have had the freedom you wanted?" Sagan says: "I was obviously less free when I was in love with someone. . . . But one's not in love all the time. Apart from that . . . I'm free."[26] Sagan is here using the term "freedom' in the modern way of autonomy. And she is right to see love and autonomy as antithetical to each other. You can be in love or you can be free and autonomous—but never both at the same time. She acknowledges that you have to dip into love every so often to recharge your batteries in some way. But true to the culture, she sees freedom, not love, as the final nonnegotiable. It is the sole, ultimate value.

I believe she, and the culture that shaped her, is seriously wrong. Freedom is invoked as a means to happiness and fulfillment, but what is the environment in which you feel the most free, the most fulfilled? Isn't it in a love relationship, where people are not exploiting each other but serving the other's needs and giving themselves to the other? Here we see the cultural contradictions within the modern ideal of autonomous freedom.

It Is Incomplete

Philosophers have distinguished between positive and negative liberty. Negative liberty is freedom *from*—refusing any barriers or constraints on our choices. Positive liberty is freedom *for*—using your freedom to live in a particular way.[27] Our modern culture's idea of freedom is wholly negative. We are free as long as no one is constraining our choices. However, this concept is too thin to be adequate.

Dr. Atul Gawande discusses a cooperative in the Boston area that organizes affordable services to keep the elderly in their homes. This is to help them keep their "autonomy," their ability to live on their own. But Gawande wisely adds this doesn't really guarantee them a good quality of life. "Having more freedom seems better than having less. But to what end? The amount of freedom you have in your life is not the measure of the worth of your life. Just as safety is an empty and even self-defeating goal to live for, so ultimately is autonomy."[28]

Terry Eagleton says the contemporary idea of absolute negative freedom arises from the postmodern disbelief in any moral foundations or absolutes. But he questions whether absolute negative freedom—freedom not as a means to an end but as an end in itself—is really liberty. "It is hard to see that one can really speak of freedom here at all, any more than a particle of dust dancing in the sunlight is free." He insists that "freedom demands closure," that we want to land somewhere with our freedom.[29] Freedom cannot be the highest or the only value. We must use our freedom of choice to do something—but our culture is mortally afraid of saying what that should be or where we should land. Why? Because we fear that if we tell people, "You *ought* to be doing this," that will curtail people's freedom. So we just drift.

There is, then, one last great problem with our culture's concept of freedom. Freedom is a good only if it enables you to actually do something good. Negative freedom is an unresolved chord, an incomplete story. We aren't fully free if we refuse to commit ourselves—and diminish our negative freedom—in order to do something positive. By itself, autonomy is incomplete.[30]

The Slavery We Can't See in Ourselves

So our culture's main operating principle—freedom without any value judgments or constraints—has many serious problems. At this point readers may see Eagleton's point, that freedom should not become an excuse for selfishness. Freedom should be a means to an end, not an end in itself. You may, however, think this situation is not too hard to fix: "Okay, I'll use my freedom not for my own pleasure but to live a committed life. I will commit myself to my work, to my family, to my community." Yet you will not go far with this before you run up against a deep problem that we saw explicated by Augustine in the last chapter. He explained that we look to good but created things for our deepest satisfaction, rather than to God. However, this truth about the human heart explains not just our failure to find contentment, but also the human struggle to find freedom.

Françoise Sagan's claim was not wrong that when she was in love, she wasn't free. When you love someone, you lose control because you want so much to please the other person. His or her displeasure is unbearable, it is punishing, and it makes you a kind of slave. But what Sagan doesn't admit is that, even if you are not in a love relationship with a person, you have to live for *some* thing. Or, to connect to the last two chapters, everyone looks to *some* thing for their meaning in life and whatever that is becomes their supreme love. They may be living for their career, or a political cause, or a particular circle of friends and colleagues, or their family. And whatever is the object of your meaning and satisfaction ultimately controls you. You are never your own master, never actually free in the contemporary definition. Something else is always mastering you. Modern people are simply in denial about this.

You might protest, as perhaps Sagan would have, "No! I do not give my heart fully to anything—for this very reason. I sit loose to any relationship, to any enterprise. I do not wholly invest my satisfaction and meaning in anything. I travel light, as it were. I move often." But actually you *are* fully committed to something—your own independence. And it could be argued you are controlled by it, you are a slave to it, because it forces you to stay uncommitted and, probably, pretty lonely.

David Foster Wallace, the postmodern novelist, puts it like this:

> *In the day-to-day trenches of adult life, there is no such thing as . . . not worshipping. Everybody worships. The only choice we get is what to worship. And an outstanding reason for choosing some sort of god or spiritual thing to worship. . . . is that pretty much anything else you worship will eat you alive. If you worship money and things, if they are where you tap real meaning in life, then you will never have enough. Never feel you have enough. . . . Worship your own body and beauty and sexual allure, and you will always feel ugly, and when time and age start showing, you will die a million deaths before they finally plant you. . . . Worship power— you will end up feeling weak and afraid, and you will need ever more power over others to keep the fear at bay. Worship your intellect, being seen as smart—you will end up feeling stupid, a fraud, always on the verge of being found out.*

Finally, he adds that "the insidious thing" about these forms of worship is that they are not seen for what they are. "They are unconscious. They are default settings."[31] In other words, whatever is the source of your meaning and satisfaction in life is what you are worshipping, though you may not acknowledge it as such. You are not simply pursuing these things if they are what you are living for. If you are living for them, you *must* have them or you lose your purpose in life. If anything threatens them, you get uncontrollably anxious or angry. If anything takes them away, you can lose the very will to live. If you fail to achieve them you may fall into unending self-hatred. That is why they are "eating you alive." Put another way, you are enslaved to them. You *must* give yourself to something, or you have no meaning in life. Even if you try not to be in thrall to anything, you become Eagleton's dancing dust particle, in bondage to your own autonomy.

Wallace, of course, is not writing as a Christian and perhaps not as someone who believed in a personal God. He is merely reporting the facts of human experience, of human nature. And those facts show us that no one is free. Everyone needs love, meaning, and satisfaction in their lives, and so everyone is under the control of something.

Duty Becomes Choice

As we have noted, religion is popularly seen as the enemy of freedom. Instead of allowing religious authorities or tradition to dictate to us, we should be free to believe or live as we choose. But the reality is that we are none of us free agents. We are all worshipping and serving something. The better question is this: Which "master" will affirm, cherish, empower, and honor us, and which ones will exploit and abuse us? There is no such thing as freedom without constraints. What we should be looking for are the right, the liberating constraints that fit our nature and design. Which master is the right master for our hearts and lives and so brings those right constraints?

If there is no God, you will have to turn some created thing into a god to worship, and whatever that thing is, it will punish you with inner fears, resentment, guilt, and shame if you fail to achieve it. Tony Schwartz, who made a great deal of money early in his life, discovered that setting his heart on career and wealth for his inner satisfaction had made him a kind of addict, and an empty-hearted one at that. "The fact that so much external success didn't deliver what I had always imagined it would left me feeling empty and bewildered. . . . Any single-minded pursuit, unmoored to a deeper purpose, has the potential to take on the characteristics of an addiction. More and more is required to obtain the same high, and the compulsion of the pursuit prompts a growing sense of the despair . . . it is meant to solve."[32]

Schwartz discovered that to make "external success" into his main source of satisfaction was to turn it into a kind of master that enslaved him. It demanded increasing success and punished him internally if he failed to achieve it. What if, however, there is a true God, and if, as the New Testament declares, he came to earth to die for our sins on the cross? Then there is one Lord who, when we fail him, will *not* punish us but forgive us. If you serve your career, your career will never die for your sins. If you live for your career and you fail, it will crucify you inside with self-loathing. But Jesus was crucified for you.

This doesn't mean that the Christian God doesn't put any constraints on us. Everyone lives for something, and in every case our master constrains our behavior, telling us what we can do and what we cannot do. If we are living for Olympic gold, or for a successful career, or for our art or politics, or for a spouse, there are limits on our choices, things we can't do. So how do we know if we are taking on liberating, right constraints rather than restraints that will crush and abuse us? Christians answer that if we are living for the one who both created us and redeemed us, we are by definition taking on the liberating constraints.

First, if there is a God, he created us. This means there is what novelist Marilynne Robinson calls "the givenness of things."[33] As a Christian, Robinson argues that reality is not infinitely malleable. It imposes itself on us, and freedom comes only by living into that givenness. We were built to know, serve, and love God. If we try to live for anything else, it leads to slavery, but when we begin to live for God and follow his will, we find that we are actually becoming who we were meant to be, realizing our original design. We are a sailboat finally being put out into deep water. Someone may object that freedom should be doing what we really want to do. The Christian offer, however, includes this. It is not merely complying with the proper regulations of our creator; it also consists of a new, growing, inward passion to love and know our redeemer.

When you are falling in love, you take the initiative to discover a list of all the things that the loved one loves and hates. Then you go all out to say and do the things that delight him or her. You are "doing their will" rather than your own, but you gladly accept the new limits on your behavior. Why? It is because you have put your joy and happiness *into* the joy and happiness of the other. You are happy to the degree they are. You have come to discover the pleasure of giving pleasure. You don't follow their will as a means to get other things you want. Their love and joy *are* main things you want. They are ends in themselves.

This is how Christianity says our ultimate relationship works with God. When a Christian grasps how Jesus saved us at infinite cost to himself, how he emptied himself of his glory and took on a humble form to serve our best interests, it creates a grateful joy that inwardly moves us to want to please, know, and resemble him. Our happiness gets put into his happiness, and serving him becomes our perfect liberation.

Only this makes sense of how the Bible speaks of freedom. James 1:25 says God's law is the "law that gives freedom." Jesus says that following God's truth sets us free (John 8:31–32). The book of Hebrews says that when we put our faith in Christ, God's law is written on our hearts, not with chisel or ink but with the Spirit of God, and this creates freedom (Hebrews 8:10; cf. 2 Corinthians 3:2,3,17). All this means that Christians, like someone newly in love, are enabled to see the will of God not as a crushing, confining burden but as a list of God's loves and hates by which we can please him and come to be like him. To have the law "written on our hearts" means that we are freely doing what we most want to do. We are loving our redeemer through following his will.[34]

Our pleasure and our duty, though opposite before;

Since we have seen his beauty, are joined to part no more. . . .

To see the law by Christ fulfilled, and hear his pardoning voice

Changes a slave into a child, and duty into choice.[35]

"My Yoke Is Easy and My Burden Is Light"

As we follow God's will out of an inner desire to love our redeemer, we increasingly come to sense that we are also becoming who we were designed to be by our creator.

Imagine that you see a car being driven down the road. You look into it and see there is a five-year-old driving it. What will happen? It will be disintegration of some sort—the car is going to run into somebody, run into a tree, or destroy a fence. Why? Because although it is a good car, it is not designed to be driven by a five-year-old. When God says, "Here are the Commandments, the moral directives: Don't lie, don't be selfish, don't bear false witness," those directives come from your *designer*. And therefore they aren't busywork. To break them is to violate your own nature and to lose freedom, just like a person who eats the wrong foods and ends up in a hospital.

For example, the Bible says: Don't bear a grudge. Many years ago I was talking to a teenage girl in my church who was angry at her father for a number of very warranted reasons. She said, "I know that God says I *have* to forgive, but I don't want to." I began by agreeing that God requires forgiveness of his followers. "But," I said, "I want you to consider that God is our creator, and so his commands are never meaningless or arbitrary 'busywork.' His obligations are always in the end our liberation." If her father succeeded in making her bitter toward him, it would mean he would continue to shape and control her life. It would, perhaps, distort her view of men in general, it would make her more hard and cynical, and it might have many other effects. I said, "The best way to be free, to ensure that the wrong he has done to you does the least damage, is to forgive him." She later told me that the conversation had been a turning point for her.

If you are made in the image of God, who is a forgiver, then it is a directive—you *must* forgive. In the short run it can feel good to be angry at somebody who has wronged you, or to pay them back. But in the long run what is going to happen? Disintegration. It can hurt your body to be angry. It can certainly hurt all your relationships, making it harder to trust and commit. It can distort your whole life. Why? Because when you are disobeying a moral directive from God, you are going against the grain of your own nature, against the grain of the universe. You are like a five-year-old trying to drive a car, and it will not work. But when you begin to obey, you are "living into" your own design rather than working against it.

Christianity teaches that Jesus Christ is both your author and your redeemer. In Matthew 11 Jesus says, "Come to me, all you who are weary and burdened, and I will give you rest. Take my yoke upon you and learn from me, for I am gentle and humble in heart, and you will find rest for your souls. For my yoke is easy and my burden is light" (Matthew 11:28–30).

Jesus essentially says to us: "I call you only to do those things you were created to do, and you will find therefore that my yoke is easy. I put on you the burden of following me, but I have already paid the price, so that when you fail you will be forgiven. I've taken off you the burdens that other people have. I've removed the burden of earning your own salvation through your striving and effort. I've removed the burden of guilt or shame for past failures. I've taken off the burden of having to prove yourself worthy of love. I am therefore the only Lord and master who, if you find me, will satisfy you, and, if you fail me, will forgive you."

The claim is that Jesus is the only master, the only thing to live for that will not exploit you. And here is why. We observed that love relationships require the loss of independence but that both parties must give it up together. You must say to the other person: "You first. I will adjust for you, I will give up my freedom for you, I will sacrifice for you." However, both parties must say that. If only one person does that and not the other, that is exploitation.

Consider, then, what the Christian Gospel has to offer. For the moment, let's leave Jesus or Christianity out of the picture. What if you tried to just believe in God in general? What if you just tried to live a good life and pray to him? How would you get into a relationship with a God like that? Wouldn't that be exploitation? God wouldn't change—you would have to do all the submitting, all the repenting, make all the sacrifices.

But Christianity is different. Jesus Christ lost his glory and became mortal and died for us. In Jesus God says, "I will adjust to you. I will sacrifice for you. First I will give up my glory and immortality in becoming human in the Incarnation. Then I will give up all light and joy and my very life in the Atonement." He was nailed fast to the cross so he could not move. How is that for giving up your freedom?

Christianity is the only religion that claims God gave up his freedom so we could experience the ultimate freedom—from evil and death itself. Therefore, you can trust him. He sacrificed his independence for you, so you can sacrifice yours for him. And when you do, you will find that it is the ultimate, infinitely liberating constraint. "If the Son sets you free, you will be free indeed" (John 8:36).

Six

The Problem of the Self

W e have been looking at things—meaning, satisfaction, freedom— that human beings can't live without. Now we come to another such item known as *identity*, which is to answer the question Who am I?

What is your identity? It consists of at least two things. First, it consists of a *sense of self* that is durable. You live in many spheres at once. You are a family member at home, a colleague at work, a friend, and sometimes you are alone in solitude. To have an identity is to have something sustained that is true of you in every setting. Otherwise there would be no "you." There would be only masks for every occasion but no actual face behind them. What about you does *not* change from place to place? There needs to be a core understanding of who you are that is true from day to day, relationship to relationship, and situation to situation. Besides a sense of self, identity also includes a *sense of worth*, an assessment of your own value. "We each want desperately to matter, to feel a sense of worthiness."[1] Self-knowledge is one thing, but self-regard is another. It is one thing to know what you are like; it's another thing to appreciate it. What about you makes you feel your life is worthwhile, good, and of significance? The sense of self and of worth together compose your identity.[2]

Identity formation is a process that every culture pushes on its members so powerfully and pervasively that it is invisible to us. We may have no idea that other ways to get a sense of self and worth are available. In this chapter I am going to try to make the process in our secular culture a little more visible and then show you the radically different Christian resources for this fundamental dimension of living a human life.

In ancient cultures, as well as in many non-Western cultures today, the self was defined and shaped by both internal desires and external social roles and ties. Charles Taylor called the older concept the "porous" self, for it was seen as being inextricably connected not only to family and community but to cosmic, spiritual realities as well.[3] Your sense of self and of worth developed as you moved out toward others, assuming roles in your family and community. If you ask people in a traditional culture, "Who are you?" they will most likely say they are a son or a mother or a member of a particular tribe and people. And if they fulfill their duties and give up their individual desires for the good of the whole family, community, and their God, then their identity is secure as persons of honor.[4]

Modern Western identity formation is the very reverse of this. In place of the "porous" self we now have what has been called a "buffered," contained self.[5] This approach to identity formation has also been called "expressive individualism" in the classic *Habits of the Heart* by Robert Bellah and his sociologist colleagues. Our culture does not believe we learn or become who we are by sublimating our individual needs for those of the community or family. Rather, "each person has a unique core of feeling and intuition that should unfold or be expressed if individuality [or identity] is to be realized."[6] Unlike other societies, modern Western culture believes in "a socially unsituated self from which all [moral and meaning] judgments are supposed to flow."[7] In all former cultures, people developed a self by moving toward others, seeking their attachment. We found ourselves, as it were, in the faces of others. But modern secularism teaches that we can develop ourselves only by looking inward, by detaching and leaving home, religious communities, and all other requirements so that we can make our own choices and determine who we are for ourselves.[8]

The cultural message is: Don't try to get affirmation from others. Affirm yourself because you are doing what you want to do. Be who you want to be, and it doesn't matter what anybody else thinks. That is the heart of modern Western expressive individualism.

Two Different Ways with Identity

The contrast could not be starker. In traditional cultures the heroic narrative is *self-sacrifice*. You are your duties, and your self-worth depends on the honor that is bestowed upon you by your community for discharging them. In Western cultures the new heroic narrative is *self-assertion*. You are your individual dreams and desires, and your self-worth depends on the dignity you bestow on yourself, because you have asserted your dreams and desires regardless of the opposition you may have had from the community.

Anyone who reads older literature cannot fail to see the sea change between the two ways with the self. The examples are innumerable. There is the tenth-century Anglo-Saxon poem "The Battle of Maldon." It becomes clear to the surviving English warriors that they have lost their battle with the Danes. But they believe the glory of their people is more important and would be better served if they took a last stand rather than retreat to save their lives. They are ready, even eager, to die bravely and happy that the privilege is theirs. So Birhtwold shakes his spear of ash wood over his dead captain and says to his companions: "Purpose shall be the firmer, heart the keener, courage shall be the more, as our might lessens. Here lies our lord all hewn down, good man on the ground. . . . From here I will not turn, but by my lord's side, by the man I loved, I intend to lie."[9] Birhtwold was pursuing not his own safety or happiness but the honor of his people.

Contrast this with the song sung to Maria in *The Sound of Music*:

Climb every mountain,
Ford every stream,
Follow every rainbow,
'Til you find your dream.[10]

In no way do I draw this contrast in order to hint that Maria's decision to leave the convent was wrong. (She was not actually a nun under vows but a postulant, considering entering the abbey.) But the advice given to her in the form of the song is an archetype of modern thinking and is now applied almost universally to all situations. We must detach, leave the community, and go out in order to find ourselves. A more recent and famous example is Elsa, one of the main characters in the Walt Disney movie *Frozen*. She sings:

> It's time to see what I can do
> To test the limits and break through
> No right, no wrong, no rules for me,
> I'm free![11]

Rather than connecting with "some source outside us," with family and people, with "God or the some other cosmic Good . . . now the source we have to connect with is [not outside us but] deep within us. . . . We come to think of ourselves as beings with inner depths."[12] I find myself not by self-giving to something outside but through self-expression of something inside.

The Great Goods of Modern Identity

Before addressing what is wrong with Western identity formation, we must acknowledge the great positives. In the past vast numbers of people were locked into a given social status in extremely hierarchical societies where peasants were to stay forever poor simply because it was thought that one's identity *was* one's role in society. These hierarchies were justified as reflecting some cosmic order of spiritual and moral absolutes. As we will see in chapter 10 the Christian church has often ignored the implications of its own teachings about every person being created in God's image, about the importance of justice for the poor, and about the kingdom of God being hard for the rich and powerful to enter. Despite these biblical themes and doctrines, the church largely supported the rigid stratification of society.

Secular thinkers, however, attacked the very idea of a cosmic, normative moral order, and this created major problems we will address immediately below. Yet we must give credit where credit is due and appreciate the good that modern individualism has wrought. For example, while the American civil rights movement was led by the African American church and was justified with biblical vocabulary and categories, it has been argued that the broader society was willing to embrace the movement and implement changes because of American culture's growing emphasis on the individualistic values of self-determination, personal freedom, and equality.[13]

My grandfather was born in Italy in 1880. He lived in a small town outside of Naples. His father was a potter, and his grandfather and his great-grandfather were all potters. In his teenage years he said to my great-grandfather, "I don't want to do pottery. I want to do something else." His father said, "There are only three things you can do: You can be a priest, you can go into the military, or you can be a potter. That is it." When he asked why, he was told that his family made pottery. That was who they were. Nobody was going to give him any other job. That was his place. If he tried to move to another town, the people there were likely to say, "What are you doing over here? You are from over there. That's who you are. Go back." In response he emigrated to America.

This rigid, exploitative social stratification stemmed from the traditional understanding of identity. You *were* your rung in the socially stratified culture; you related to the world not as an individual but through your family and class. Your mission in life was to "know your place" and fulfill your assigned role. There was no way out; there was no mobility at all. So we can be grateful for the ways that the modern Western view of identity has helped so many people escape. And yet modern Western culture's identity formation in very different ways is every bit as crushing, if not more so. How?

Modern Identity Is Incoherent

First of all, our contemporary approach is incoherent. If you look into your heart to find your deep desires, you certainly will discover many of them. And you will discover something else—that they contradict one another. You may very much want a certain career, but then you fall in love with someone whom you also want very much. Because of the particular nature of both the career and the relationship, you realize you won't be able to have both. What are you going to do? You might insist that one of these desires—for career or love—must be deeper and more "you," but that's naive. Why assume that your internal desires are arranged in such an orderly way? Francis Spufford writes that you are "a being whose wants make no sense, don't harmonise: whose desires, deep down, are discordantly arranged, so that you truly want to possess and you truly want not to, at the very same time. You're equipped . . . for farce or even tragedy more than you are for happy endings."[14]

Sigmund Freud is perhaps the most trenchant critic of the idea that our inner desires are coherent and positive. Freud believed that each individual had deep desires that were essentially and unstoppably selfish. He called the inmost instincts the "id." This is the part of the self that "never says *No*."[15] Freud believed that our inmost being was filled with "unsociable chaos" of desires for power, love, comfort, and control, which vie with one another and would trample on others to reach their goals, if they could. Our conscience (or "superego") is society's inner policeman, punishing us with inward pain, shame, and guilt when we transgress cultural moral norms. Freud taught that although we can make some adjustments and navigate better trade-offs and compromises between our desires and our conscience, in general, guilt and shame are the price we pay in order to have civilization or an orderly society at all.[16] "Guilt may be denied . . . [but] it is the secret agent of public order."[17]

Freud was, as Philip Rieff puts it, a pessimist and a "moralist," because he saw human beings as irremediably selfish and largely unable to admit the depth of that selfishness and the cruelty of which they are capable. Freud would have shaken his head at many of his descendants in modern psychotherapy who have lost his realism about the inner darkness, incoherence, and destructiveness of the inmost desires. "We are not happy because we are frustrated. . . . We are frustrated because we are, first of all, unhappy combinations of conflicting desires. Civilization can, at best, reach a balance of discontents."[18]

Not only do your desires contradict, but they also are elusive. "What *are* the wants of the self?" Bellah asks. "For all its unmistakable presence and intensity on occasion, the experience of feeling good, like being in love, is so highly subjective that its distinguishing characteristics remain ineffable."[19]

And besides being contradictory and elusive, our desires constantly change. As I have said, part of having an identity is having a stable, core sense of who you are, day in and day out, in different settings and times. That is why the traditional way of forging an identity through connection with something solid outside the individual self made sense. But if your identity is just your desires, they are going to be changing all the time. If in every situation you seek your own self-interest, responding in ways that get the approval and control you want at the moment, then identity essentially disappears. "In the work of Erving Goffman . . . [comes the view that] there is no self at all. What seems to be a self is merely a series of social masks that change with each successive situation."[20] Ironically, the emphasis on "being yourself" apart from fixed social roles results in there being no sustained "you" left, which is common to all situations.

Modern Identity Is Illusory

Our culture tells us that you must look inside to discover your deepest desires and dreams and to express them. You must do this yourself, and must not rely on anyone outside to affirm and tell you who you are.[21] A classic description of this understanding can be found in Gail Sheehy's 1970s best seller *Passages*. There she speaks to a person who is heeding her guidance on finding an authentic self:

You are moving away . . . away from institutional claims and other people's agenda. Away from external valuations and accreditations, in search of an inner validation. You are moving out of [social] roles and into the self. . . . Whatever counterfeit safety we hold from overinvestments in people and institutions must be given up. The inner custodian [i.e., conscience] must be unseated from the controls. No foreign [external] power can direct our journey from now on. It is for each of us to find a course that is valid by our own reckoning.[22]

In short, do not look to anyone else to validate you. Use no standards from the outside. *You* bestow the verdict of significance on yourself.

But this is an impossibility.[23] You cannot get an identity through self-recognition; it must come in a great measure from others. Theologian Philip Ryken quotes from a contemporary novel about a young single woman. She writes a New Year's resolution: "Develop inner poise and authority and sense of self as woman of substance, complete *without* boyfriend, as best way to obtain boyfriend." However, she sees a problem. "My sense of self comes not from other people but from . . . myself? That can't be right."[24] Yes, it isn't right. In fact, it can't be done.

In the end, we can't say to ourselves, "I don't care that literally everyone else in the world thinks I'm a monster. I love myself and that is all that matters." That would not convince us of our worth, unless we are mentally unsound. We need someone from outside to say we are of great worth, and the greater the worth of that someone or someones, the more power they have to instill a sense of self and of worth. Only if we are approved and loved by someone whom we esteem can we achieve any self-esteem. To use biblical terms, we need someone to bless us because we can't bless ourselves. We are irreducibly social and relational beings. We need someone we respect to respect us. We need someone we admire to admire us. Even when modern people claim to be validating themselves, the reality is always that they are socializing themselves into a new community of peers, of "cheerleaders," of people whose approval they crave.

Years ago I was watching an episode of the science-fiction TV show

Star Trek: The Next Generation. The captain, Jean-Luc Picard, was talking to a young man who was trying to get into the Starfleet Academy. He professed that one of his reasons for doing so was so that the captain would be proud of him. Picard's response was perfectly in line with Gail Sheehy: "Wesley—you have to measure your successes and your failures within, not by anything that I or anyone else might think."[25] I remembered it because I had recently counseled a man who had parents who always answered him in the same way. He told me: "They never said, 'I would be proud of you if you did this or that.' When I asked them for guidance, they always said, 'We just want you to do what *you* truly want to do—what*ever* that is, it will be all right with us.'" The man complained that this made him feel unloved and rudderless. He doubted that they would be equally happy with any of his life choices, but he could not get them to reveal the kind of life for which they would admire him. He knew they meant well and that they thought they were being open-minded and modern. However, he said, "No one can tell yourself, 'I'm okay.' I needed somebody to tell me, 'That's the right thing to do. I'm proud of you!' I had to go look for other kinds of family, because my family wouldn't be the family I needed."

So, contrary to our cultural narrative, we must look outside ourselves and connect to something else first, before we can descend into ourselves and make any assessment.

Let's conduct a thought experiment to serve as evidence of this. Imagine an Anglo-Saxon warrior in Britain in AD 800. He looks into his heart and sees two strong inner impulses and feelings. One is aggression. When people show him any disrespect, his natural response is to respond violently, either to harm or to kill. He enjoys battle. Now, living in a shame-and-honor culture with a warrior ethic, he will identify with that feeling. He will feel no shame or regret over it. He will say, "That's me! That's who I am! I will express that." But let's say that the other impulse he sees in his heart is same-sex attraction. He wishes that were not there. He will look at that feeling and say, "That's not me. I will control and suppress that."

Now come forward to today. Imagine a young man walking around

Manhattan. He has the same two inward impulses, both equally strong. What will he say to himself? He will look at the aggression and say, "This is not who I am," and will go to therapy or to some anger-management programs. He will look at his sexual desire, however, and conclude, "That is who I am. That's me."

This illustration demonstrates several things. First, it shows it's an illusion to think identity is simply an expression of inward desires and feelings. You have many strong feelings, and in one sense they are all part of "you," but just because they are there does not mean you must or can express them all. No one identifies with all strong inward desires. Rather, we use some kind of filter—a set of beliefs and values—to sift through our hearts and determine which emotions and sensibilities we will value and incorporate into our core identity and which we will not. It is this value-laden filter that forms our identity, rather than our feelings themselves. And where do we get this filter? We get it from some community, some people whom we trust. Then we take this set of values into ourselves and we make sense of our insides. We prioritize some things we find there and reject others. It is misleading to the point of dishonesty to say, "I just have to be myself, no matter what anyone else says." Your "self" is defined by what one set of "anyones" has to say. Our inner depths on their own are insufficient to guide us. To put it another way, identity is determined not by our feelings and desires but rather by our beliefs *about* our varied, contradictory, changing feelings and desires.

Also this comparison of the warrior and the young man shows us that modern people are ultimately no more liberated to be themselves than ancient people were. Why, in the example, does the contemporary person believe that his particular sexual feelings are "who he is," whereas the Anglo-Saxon would think of them as more extraneous or even hostile to his identity? It is because in each case their society is telling them what to believe. We must get our beliefs from somewhere, and most are picked up unconsciously from our culture or our community—whether ethnic or academic or professional or familial. Every community has "a set of understandings and evaluations [about life] that it has worked out over time." This set of beliefs is "an inherent dimension of all human action" and it is usually invisible to us.[26] So many today say, "This is who I am—I don't care what society thinks; I only care what I think." But then on social media we see what has really happened. One community and set of cheerleaders has been rejected, and new ones adopted. And the person is thinking about him or herself the way that has been dictated.

Robert Bellah says strikingly, "The irony is that here, too, just where we [modern people] think we are most free, we are most coerced by the dominant beliefs of our own culture. For it is a powerful cultural fiction that we not only can, but must, make up our deepest beliefs in the isolation of our private selves."[27] He goes on to say that modern people simply cannot see how much their identities owe to others. "Insofar as they are limited to a language of radical autonomy" and "cannot think about themselves or others except as arbitrary centers of volition," it means "they cannot express the fullness of being that is actually theirs."[28]

Our identity, then, is not, after all, something we can bestow on ourselves. We cannot discover or create an identity in isolation, merely through some kind of internal monologue. Rather, it is negotiated through dialogue with the moral values and beliefs of some community. We find ourselves in and through others. "We never get to the bottom of ourselves on our own. We discover who we are face to face and side by side with others in work, love, and learning."[29] In the end the contemporary identity—simply expressing your inner feelings, with a valuation bestowed on yourself independently—is impossible.

Modern Identity Is Crushing

Ironically, the apparent freedom of secular identity brings crushing burdens with it. In former times, when our self-regard was more rooted in social roles, there was much less value placed on competitive achievement. Rising from rags to riches was nice but rare and optional. It was quite sufficient to be a good father or mother, son or daughter, and to be conscientious and diligent in all your work and duties. Today, as Alain de Botton has written, we believe in the meritocracy, that anyone who is of humble means is so only because of a lack of ambition and savvy. It is an embarrassment now to be merely faithful and not successful.[30] This is a new weight on the soul, put there by modernity. Success or failure is now seen as the individual's responsibility alone. Our culture tells us that we have the power to create ourselves, and that puts the emphasis on independence and self-reliance. But it also means that society adulates winners and despises losers, showing contempt for weakness.[31]

All this produces a pressure and anxiety beyond what our ancestors knew. We have to decide our look and style, our stance and ethos. We then have to promote ourselves and be accepted in the new space— professional, social, aesthetic—in which we have chosen to create ourselves. As a result, "new modes of conformity arise" as people turn themselves into "brands" through the consumer goods they buy.[32] The irony is that the conception of a "nonsocial . . . conception of reality"[33] actually leaves the person more dependent than ever on outside validation and more vulnerable to outside manipulation. This is why we are far more dependent on consumption of fashion and electronics and other goods and products in order to "feel good about ourselves."

The self-made identity, based on our own performance and achievement in ways that older identities were not, makes our self-worth far more fragile in the face of failure and difficulty. While we claim to have a new freedom from social norms, we now look not to our family for our validation but to our chosen arenas of achievement, where we need the acceptance and applause of others who are already within those circles. This makes us, more than ever, "vulnerable to the recognition given or withheld by significant others."[34] You have got to be brilliant. You have got to be beautiful. You have got to be hip. You have got to be accomplished. And *they* have to think so. It is all up to you, in a way that, in traditional cultures, just wasn't the case.

In Arthur Miller's play *After the Fall*, the narrator sees modern life as a "series of proofs"—arguing and proving your smarts, your sexual prowess, your abilities, your sophistication—all in the pursuit of some kind of "verdict."[35] But this is a trap, because you will have to fixate on some good thing—like work or career or romance or love—and it will become no longer just another good thing to enjoy. It will become *you*—the basis of your identity. And that makes you radically vulnerable and fragile.

In the *New York Times* Benjamin Nugent writes about the struggles he had when he was a full-time novelist. He says: "When good writing was my only goal in life, I made the quality of my work the measure of my worth. For this reason, I wasn't able to read my own writing well. I couldn't tell whether something I had just written was good or bad, because I needed it to be good in order to feel sane. I lost the ability to cheerfully interrogate how much I liked what I had written, to see what was actually on the page rather than what I wanted to see or what I feared to see." When his identity was based in being a good writer, it made him a worse writer. He announces at the end of the article that he doesn't base his self on writing anymore because he "fell in love, an overpowering diversion."[36] But is the love of someone else a better basis for an identity?

Ernest Becker, in *The Denial of Death*, wrote presciently about the sweeping changes that secularism was bringing to the issue of identity. At one time people got their self-image and self-regard from connecting to something more important than their individual interests—to God, or family, or nation, or some cultural configuration of all three. Now we have to go get our own identity. Some do it through love and romance. He calls this the "romantic solution": "The self-glorification we now need to achieve in our innermost being, we now look for in our love partner. . . . Modern man fulfills his urge to self-expansion in the love object just as it was once fulfilled in God."[37]

Becker goes on to say that this is a doomed project. He explains in detail all the ways that our overdependence enslaves us to the other person so either we end up overly controlling them or they us. "If your partner is your 'All' then any shortcoming in him becomes a major threat to *you*. . . . We see that our gods have clay feet, and so we must hack away at them in order to save ourselves, to deflate the unreal over-investment that we have made in them in order to secure our own apotheosis. . . . But not everyone can do this because many of us need the lie in order to live. We may have no other God and we may prefer to deflate ourselves in order to keep the relationship, even though we glimpse the impossibility of it and the slavishness to which it reduces us."[38]

Finally, he concludes: "After all, what is it that we want when we elevate the love partner to the position of God? We want redemption—nothing less. We want to be rid of our faults, our feeling of nothingness. We want to be justified, to know that our creation has not been in vain. . . . Needless to say, human partners cannot do this."[39]

If we base our identity on love we come to the same cul-de-sac that we saw with the novelist who got his identity from work. Just as he could not bear poor work, so we will not be able to handle the problems in our love relationships. The writer *had* to believe he is a great writer in order to be *sane*. We will *have* to believe our love relationship is okay—if it goes off the rails, we lose our sanity. Why? If our very identity is wrapped up in something and we lose it, we lose our very sense of self. If you are getting your identity from the love of a person—you won't be able to give them criticism because their anger will devastate you. Nor will you be able to bear their personal sorrows and difficulties. If they have a problem and start to get self-absorbed and are not giving you the affirmation you want, you won't be able to take it. It will become a destructive relationship. The Western understanding of identity formation is a crushing burden, both for individuals and society as a whole.

Modern Identity Is Fracturing

In the last chapter we talked about how the secular view of freedom as the absence of restrictions undermines community. Taylor argues (and Bellah demonstrates) that the secular view of identity and self does the same thing. "This view," argues Taylor, reduces relationships and community to things "purely instrumental in their significance."[40] In traditional cultures our most crucial relationships are more important than our individual self-interest, because our identity depends on honoring the relationships. Therefore they are inviolate and we are solidly embedded in them. A traditional human community, according to Bellah, was "an inclusive whole, celebrating the interdependence of public and private life."[41] Your private life—whom you have sex with, how you spend your income, how you spend leisure time—was of public significance. It mattered to the rest of your family, neighborhood, and community, because it was incumbent upon you to conduct your whole life in a way that supported the common good and the health of the social whole.

But when, as in the modern approach, you bestow significance on yourself, then your individual interests are more important than any social tie. If a relationship is satisfying to you, you keep it only so long as it pleases you. "It fosters a view of relationships in which these ought to subserve personal fulfillment. The relationship is secondary to the self-realization of the partners. On this view, unconditional ties, meant to last for life, make little sense."[42] Human communities become thinned out into "lifestyle enclaves" or "social networks" in which people connect, flexibly and transiently, only to people like themselves. They relate to one another around similar tastes in music or food or common wealth status (such as in a gated housing development), but their private and public lives are no one else's business. It is well documented that under the conditions of the modern, individualistic self, social ties and institutions are eroding, marriage and family are weakening, society is fragmenting into warring factions, and economic inequality is growing.[43]

The problems of the secular, individualist self are well documented by some of the leading thinkers of our time.[44] We cannot take any longer to explore its impact on our society and culture. But we can compare the modern self with the Christian teaching about identity and imagine the difference it can make. We will do that in the next chapter.

Seven

An Identity That Doesn't Crush You
or Exclude Others

W hat are the alternatives to the modern identity with all its problems? Isak Dinesen, in *Out of Africa*, can help us begin to see a different way forward. She writes: "Pride is faith in the idea God had, when he made us." A person who has grasped this "is conscious of the idea, and aspires to realize it. He does not aspire to happiness or comfort, which may be irrelevant to God's idea for him. His success is the idea of God, successfully followed through, and he is in love with his destiny." In other words, the believer in God takes hold of the divine design and calling and finds him- or herself in it, just "as the good citizen finds his happiness in the fulfillment of duty to the community." But, she writes, many people "are not aware of any idea of God in the making of them, and sometimes they make you doubt that there ever has been much of an idea, or else it has been lost, and who shall find it again? They have to accept as success what others warrant it to be so, and to take their happiness, and even their own selves, at the quotation of the day. They tremble, with reason, before their fate."[1]

In this remarkable passage Dinesen recognizes three paths toward identity, each taken by a different group of people. First there are those looking outward. These are the traditional people who look to their duty and role in the community to find a self. Then there are those who look inward. They do not believe in any cosmic order but, as we have seen, this means they must rely on competition and shifting fashions to find self-esteem. They are no freer than members of traditional society, for they must take "their happiness, and even their own selves, at the quotation of the day." No wonder they "tremble, with reason, before their fate."

But there is a third option—there are people who, as it were, look neither outward nor inward but upward. Dinesen proposes something neither traditional nor modern. What if we were created by a personal God and given a personal mission and calling? Then neither does the individual take precedence over the group (which can lead to social fragmentation), nor does the community take precedence over the individual (which can lead to oppression). What matters is not what society says about me, nor what I think of myself, but what God does.

Dinesen follows another great Danish writer Søren Kierkegaard, who said:

> *In fact, what is called the secular mentality consists simply of such men who, so to speak, mortgage themselves to the world. They use their capacities, amass money, carry on enterprises . . . perhaps [to] make a name in history, but themselves they are not. Spiritually speaking, they have no self, no self for whose sake they could venture everything, no self before God, however self-seeking they are otherwise.*[2]

The modern self is crushing. It must base itself on success or achievement or some human love relationship, and if any of these things is jeopardized or lost, you lose your very identity. However, Dinesen and Kierkegaard are not simply calling on modern people to adopt religion in general. The traditional self is suffocating, captive to what your family and tribe tell you that you must do. Adding some religion and moral strictures only aggravates the problem. Both the traditional and modern "selves" are inherently insecure. They can never be either fully at peace or bold enough to "venture everything" for the good and right. They are always in danger of dissolution, being so conditioned by what others think and say of you.

This is why Kierkegaard looks to a different way to gain a self, one not based on our performance, one based not on the desires of either the individual or the community but on God. As we have seen, nobody can affirm or bless themselves. You have to have a word from outside. But who will be that ultimate source of recognition? If you look to your parents, what if you disappoint them and they reject you? Even if you do not disappoint them, they will die. The same is true of a love partner or spouse or any human being. If, on the other hand, you look to professional acclaim or some other kind of accomplishment, you are vulnerable to your own failure or the failure of others to rightly value your work.

Some adults look mainly to their own children for this deep affirmation. This too is unworkable. I once knew a mother who had a brilliant and beautiful daughter and who wanted her admiration and love above all things. Whenever the girl didn't obey her or show respect and affection, however, it triggered explosive anger. The woman experienced what she should have seen as normal childish resistance to authority as a profound rejection. This led her daughter to first mistrust and then despise her. As soon as the girl was able, she put distance between them, leaving her mother with a seemingly unfillable hole in her life.

As we said in the last chapter, there has to be somebody whom you adore who adores you. Someone whom you cannot but praise who praises and loves you—that is the foundation of identity. *The praise of the praiseworthy is above all rewards.*[3] However, if we put this power in the hands of a fallible, changeable person, it can be devastating. And if this person's regard is based on your fallible and changeable life efforts, your self-regard will be just as fleeting and fragile. Nor can this person be someone you can lose, because then you will have lost your very self. Obviously, no human love can meet these standards. Only love of the immutable can bring tranquillity. Only the unconditional love of God will do.

What We Are Offered

The New Testament recognizes the same range of options for identity that Dinesen sketches. Paul writes: "I care very little if I am judged by you or by any human court; indeed, I do not even judge myself. My conscience is clear, but that does not make me innocent. It is the Lord who judges me" (1 Corinthians 4:3–4). Here Paul says, "I don't care what you or any organized social structure thinks of me," rejecting traditional identity, yet then, remarkably, he says he doesn't look within to his own sensibility for an evaluation either. Just because his conscience is clear, he does not assume that he is in the right. Supporting Paul are the histories of innumerable war criminals who insisted, "My conscience is clear; I was just following orders." In this move Paul is denying both traditional identity that gives all power to the social *and* modern identity that gives all power to the personal, to our own limited, individual perspective. He wants neither the tyranny of the group nor the dictatorship of his own insatiable desires and incoherent impulses. He refuses to let either society or his own inner consciousness define him. He looks to some other bar for judgment. He says, in effect, "I don't care what anyone else thinks, but I don't care what I think either. All I care about is what God thinks of me."

And here we see the richness, complexity, and startling distinctiveness of the Christian approach to identity. Paul can say, "God judges me," not with alarm but with confidence. Why? Because unlike either traditional or secular culture, a Christian's identity is *not achieved but received*. When we ask God the Father to accept us, adopt us, unite with us, not on the basis of our performance and moral efforts but because of Christ's, we receive a relationship with God that is a gift. It is not based on our past, present, or future attainments but on Christ's spiritual attainments. In the Christian understanding, Jesus did not come primarily to teach or show us how to live (though he did that too) but to actually live the life we should have lived, and die in our place the death—the penalty for our moral failures—we should have died. When we rest in him alone for our salvation, he becomes a substitute and representative for us. On the cross Jesus was treated as we deserved, so that when we believe in him, we are treated as he deserves.

Here we come to the heart of the Christian Gospel, and we see the sharp difference between this faith and many religions, in which individuals are expected to achieve their own salvation through moral effort and religious observances. In contrast, St. Paul says that Christians are "found" in Christ, a term that means God regards us not on the basis of our own record and character but "in Christ." Socrates may cry, "Know thyself!" and that is good advice, but St. Paul cries that in addition it is crucial to be *"knowing Christ,* and . . . be found in him, not having a righteousness of my own that comes from the law, but that which is through faith in Christ—the righteousness that comes from God on the basis of faith" (Philippians 3:8, 9).

And now in Christ it is literally true that the person we adore most in the universe adores us. In the eyes of God, in the opinion of the only one in the universe whose opinion ultimately counts, we are more valuable than all the jewels that lie beneath the earth.

How do Christians know this is true? Jesus Christ, the Son of God, who had the highest honor and name, the loftiest identity possible, emptied himself of his glory and went to the cross, where he died an ignominious death so that we could have an everlasting name and identity that last forever (Philippians 2:1–11). That's how much he valued us.

A New Motivation

This is neither the traditional nor the modern way with the self. Ordinary moralistic religion operates on this principle: "I live a good and moral life; therefore God accepts me." Gospel Christianity operates in the opposite way: "God accepts me unconditionally in Jesus Christ; therefore I live a good and moral life." In the first case you live a good life out of the hope of a reward, with all the insecurity and self-doubts that go with it. Will you ever be good enough for the reward? How will you know if you are, and how will you keep it up even if you are? In the Christian approach the motivation is one not of fear but of grateful joy. You live to please and resemble the one who saved you at infinite cost to himself by going to the cross. You serve him not in order to coerce him to love you but because he already does.

Now, for example, you pursue your career not to get a self and achieve self-worth. You do it to serve God and the common good. Your work is still part of your identity, as are your family, your nationality, and so on. But they are all relieved of the terrible burden of being the ultimate source of your self and value. They no longer can distort your life as they do when they are forced into that role. They are, as it were, demoted to being just good things. Work is no longer something you use desperately to feel good about yourself. It becomes just another good gift from God that you can use to serve others. The internal psychological and motivational dynamics of the personality are profoundly transformed by faith in Christ.

Some years ago there were two young men attending my church, exploring Christianity and also trying to make it in acting. I'll call them Sam and Jim. Sam was moving toward faith in Christ while Jim was moving away. As Jesus became more real to Sam, he stopped looking to his stage career as the measure of his worth. Then Sam and Jim found themselves auditioning for the same role. It was a very big part in a very big production. If either of them had gotten the job, it would have propelled him to great heights.

So they performed at the audition, but neither of them was chosen. They both were turned down. Jim, the one whom most people would have considered the more self-confident, was simply devastated, while Sam was just disappointed. Sam went out and got a job in business, and after that he kept one foot in acting. Over the years he became very active in the church and was reasonably successful in business. Opportunities for stage or screen acting occurred occasionally, but he engaged in them only as an avocation. His life thrived. Jim, however, went into a tailspin. He was angry at himself and the industry and left acting altogether, but he hated any other job he took. He seldom remained in a job for more than a year, drifting from place to place.

What happened? Originally, both men had acting as the core of their identity. It was the main factor in their self-regard. But then Sam had an identity shift. Acting became a good thing but not an ultimate thing. His love of the stage was not evicted from his life, but its stranglehold on his self-image and worth was broken. It became part of who he was but not the essence of who he was. That's why the rejection of not getting the role could not get at his identity. It was safe, impervious, hidden in Jesus Christ (Colossians 3:1–3). Jim, however, had a highly vulnerable modern identity. His failure was an ax blow to his psychological tree. The rejection went right to the root of what made him feel he counted, what made him significant.

If you believe the Gospel and all its remarkable claims about Jesus and what he has done for you and who you are in him, then nothing that happens in this world can actually get at your identity. Imagine, for a moment, what it would be like to believe this. Consider what a sweeping difference it would make.

A New Kind of Identity

The sense of worth or value that comes through faith in Christ is arguably more secure than any other. It has several facets to it. First, there is the worth we have as God's creations. All human beings are made in God's image (Genesis 1:26–27), made to reflect many of God's own qualities and character. The implication is that no matter who they are, where they are from, or what they have done or failed to do in life, there is an irreducible glory and significance about every single human being.[4]

In addition, for Christians there is the inestimable worth we have through what the Bible calls our *adoption*. Through faith in Christ we become God's loved children (Galatians 3:26–4:7). God is not simply a boss or sovereign who serves us only as long as we meet the conditions of good behavior. Rather, God is a now a perfect Father to us, giving us the unchanging security that only a parent-child relationship can give. He delights in us, singing over us in joy (Zephaniah 3:14–17). He will never leave or forsake us even if we fall or sin (Hebrews 13:5; Hosea 11:8). Why? Has he no standards? Yes, he is perfectly just and holy, but Jesus has fulfilled them for us. He has absorbed and paid our penalty, being pierced for our transgressions and crushed for our iniquities (Isaiah 53:-5–6). Therefore now God is not our judge but our Father who will never condemn us (Romans 8:1).

In Isaiah 49:15 God speaks to his people and makes this astonishing comparison: "Can a mother forget the baby at her breast and have no compassion on the child she has borne? Though she may forget, I will not forget you!" The bond between a mother and her nursing infant could not be stronger physically and emotionally, yet God says it is only an infinitely weaker analogy of his unbreakable love for us and joy in us.[5] This is the very opposite of a fragile, thin, and insecure identity, based on our own performance, whiplashed by endless "market gyrations" of popularity and rejection, of accomplishment and failure.[6]

The Christian faith not only provides a uniquely durable and unbreakable sense of worth but also is a dynamic resource for a durable and integrating core sense of self in every situation. Philosophers have puzzled over the question of "personal identity over time." What makes it the case that the person you were five years ago is still "you," or that the persons you are at work and in the home and with your friends are all, at bottom, "you"?[7] Sociologist Erving Goffman, as we have noted, believed there is no essential self that endures in all circumstances but rather only a series of roles that we play.[8] The modern view of identity, based as it is solely on internal, changing desires and cost-benefit calculations, makes it difficult to imagine any unchanging core of characteristics that integrate all the various roles we play.

But the Christian answer, as Kierkegaard puts it, is that our true self is the self we are before God. "I am God Almighty," said the Lord to Abraham in Genesis 17:1, "walk before me faithfully." To walk with someone, in Hebrew idiom, meant to befriend someone and to journey with him or her face to face. Walking before someone entails both accountability, because the one you walk with can see you, as well as security and intimacy, because you never face trouble alone. To walk with God means that his eyes and opinion alone matter. If others say either overly negative things or overly positive things about you, you are neither decimated or puffed up (2 Corinthians 12:10). You know yourself as a sinner full of weakness but also as a citizen of the heavenly city, a child of the king of the universe, and an intimate friend of the one who made you (2 Corinthians 4:17–18).

You are now liberated from cultural categories as you look into your heart to understand yourself. There are many things that are true of you—how do you know which ones are "you" and should be affirmed and which ones are not? Do we (like the Anglo-Saxon warrior) follow the dictates of a shame-and-honor culture or those of our contemporary, highly individualistic society? Christianity says "neither" because it does not see either the individual or the society as having the ability to reveal who you are. God, your creator and designer, alone has the right and the wisdom to show you those things in your heart that, if they are embraced and enhanced, will help you become the person you were made to be.

Passages like Romans 7:14–25 realistically describe warring desires and deep conflicts within, but progress can be made. Ephesians tells how to "put off [the] old self," which is distorted by inordinate, enslaving desires, and "put on [the] new self, created to be like God" (Ephesians 4:22,24). When we stop building our identity on career, or our race, or our family, or any other created thing and rest in God, the fears and drives that enslaved us recede, and we experience a new freedom and security.

Walking with God, who always sees us and loves us, brings a new integrity and sense of self. We cannot and do not simply blend into each new setting, saying the things we need to say to get the most benefit out of the situation. We are not merely a set of dramatic roles, changing every time we play to a new set of spectators, because God is our primary audience every moment.

So who am I? If I am a Christian, I am who I am before God. Those things God affirms are the true me; those things he prohibits are the intrusions of the foreign matter of sin and not part of the person I was made to be and the Spirit is bringing about. Even as I age and sense some physical deterioration, I sense my true identity becoming clearer and my true self becoming stronger. "Though outwardly we are wasting away, yet inwardly we are being renewed day by day. For our light and momentary troubles are achieving for us an eternal glory that far outweighs them all" (2 Corinthians 4:16–17). There is nothing more valuable than this new identity. "What does a man gain by winning the whole world,"

Jesus said, "at the cost of his true self? What can he give to buy that self back?" (Mark 8:36–37)[9]

The great paradox is that we "find" our selves, this unconquerable identity and confidence, only through humbling ourselves, giving up the right to self-determination, and following Christ. "Whoever finds their life will lose it, and whoever loses their life for my sake will find it" (Matthew 10:39). That is, when we stop trying to find and serve ourselves and instead give ourselves in service to God and others as we put our faith in Christ, we will find ourselves. This is, of course, the path of Jesus, who had the greatest glory and honor but gave it away in order to save and serve us (Philippians 2:1–11) and, as a result, now has an even greater glory and honor than before.

The Christian Gospel offers us the most invincible, confident assurance of our own worth and yet at the same time requires humble service and the loss of our autonomous independence. Therefore it creates a culture neither of self-realization and promotion nor of self-abnegation and denial. It brings neither and yet in the best senses fulfills both. It neither inflates nor crushes the ego. Neither the society nor my own feelings control me and tell me who I am. "It is the Lord who judges me" (1 Corinthians 4:4). So C. S. Lewis can write:

> *The same principle holds . . . for more everyday matters. Even in social life, you will never make a good impression on other people until you stop thinking about what sort of impression you are making. Even in literature and art, no man who bothers about originality will ever be original whereas if you simply try to tell the truth (without caring twopence how often it has been told before) you will, nine times out of ten, become original without ever having noticed it. The principle runs through all life from top to bottom, Give up yourself, and you will find your real self. Lose your life and you will save it. . . . Nothing that you have not given away will be really yours. Nothing in you that has not died will ever be raised from the dead. Look for*

yourself, and you will find in the long run only hatred, loneliness, despair, rage, ruin, and decay. But look for Christ and you will find Him, and with Him everything else thrown in.[10]

The Dynamics of Exclusion

Much philosophy, sociology, and literary theory today recognizes that identity ordinarily is created through the "exclusion of the Other."[11] We can't create "Us" without also creating "Them." Social belonging happens only as some other contrasting group is labeled as the Different or the Other. We bolster our identity by seeing others in a negative light and by excluding them in some way.[12] A seminal description of this understanding of identity is in Zygmunt Bauman's *Modernity and Ambivalence*. He argues that identity in society depends on creating dichotomies or "binaries." I can feel I am one of the good people because I know I am not one of the bad people. This is, Bauman says, always an exercise of power, but that power disguises itself by denouncing the Other, which is "degraded, suppressed, exiled." Ironically, this means that the self-esteem and identities of those in power are actually dependent on the people being looked down upon and disdained.

Theologian Miroslav Volf summarizes the four ways that we can assert and bolster our self-worth by excluding others. We can literally kill or drive the Other out of our living space. A more subtle and common way is exclusion by assimilation. We can demand that they conform completely to our own patterns and standards, not allowing them to express any difference at all. "We will refrain from vomiting you out . . . if you let us swallow you up."[13] A third form of exclusion could be called "dominance." We will let you live among us and maintain your identity, but only if you assume an inferior place—not getting certain jobs, attaining particular levels of pay, or living in certain neighborhoods. The fourth kind of exclusion is abandonment. That is, we exclude the Other by disdaining and ignoring them, taking no thought for their needs.[14] The reason we indulge in these attitudes and practices is that by denouncing and blaming the Other it gives us "the illusion of sinlessness and strength."[15]

Many people conclude, therefore, that disdaining and excluding others is inevitable in the modern quest of gaining an identity and self-esteem. Much postmodern theory has argued strongly against any binary accounts of human life. Many tell us to get beyond dichotomies of normal and abnormal, law-abiding and deviant, civilized and barbaric, reasonable and emotional, good and evil, ignorant and expert, male and female, orthodox and heretical, citizen and foreigner.[16] Postmodern thinkers call us to stop thinking in binaries and avoid all value judgments. "We should flee both universal values and particular identities and seek refuge from oppression in . . . radical autonomy. . . . We should create spaces in which persons can keep . . . acquiring new and losing old identities . . . ambivalent and fragmented, always on the move and never doing much more than making moves."[17] This, it is thought, is the only way to stop oppressing others. We should refuse to identify ourselves with any social structures or systems of "truth." We should assume that identity is endlessly fluid, changing, and multifarious.

But Terry Eagleton, in *The Illusions of Postmodernism*, shows that dichotomies in identity making are impossible to avoid. "For all its talk of difference, plurality, heterogeneity, postmodern theory often operates with quite rigid binary oppositions, with 'difference,' 'plurality' and allied terms bravely up on one side of the theoretical fence as unequivocally positive, and whatever their antitheses might be (unity, identity, totality, universality) ranged balefully on the other."[18] So the effort to blur all distinctions and erase moral value judgments creates a new "good guys and bad guys" binary, in which the postmodernist is the hero and all who hold on to outdated views of identity and morality are the villains, the Other. "For all its vaunted openness to the Other, postmodernism can be quite as exclusive and censorious as the orthodoxies it opposes . . ." needing "its bogeymen and straw targets to stay in business."[19] Ironically, even an effort to avoid these distinctions becomes a way to construct our own selves at the expense of others.

A New Openness to Difference

We seem to be at an impasse. Traditional identity, with its emphasis on family, tribe, and blood, has a well-known history of violence and oppression. But modernity and even postmodernism also create dichotomies that lead to exclusion. It seems at the psychological level this is impossible to avoid. If I find my identity in working for liberal political and social causes, it is inevitable that I will scorn conservatives, and the same goes for conservatives regarding liberals. In fact, if the feelings of loathing toward the opposition are not there, it might be concluded that my political position is not very close to the core of who I am. If my identity rests to a great degree in being moral and religious, then I will disdain those people I think of as immoral. If my self-worth is bound up with being a hardworking person, I will look down on those whom I consider lazy. As the postmodernists rightly point out, this condescending attitude toward the Other is part of how identity works, how we feel good and significant.

So the question is, as Volf puts it, "*What kind of selves [do] we need to be* in order to live in harmony with others?" What kind of identity is "capable of envisioning and creating just, truthful, and peaceful societies"?[20] Both Volf and an older British Anglican statesman, John Stott, answer that the unique identity with "the Cross at the center" is the way forward.[21] How so?

According to Volf, the two constituent aspects of exclusion are, paradoxically, overbinding and overseparating. We overseparate from the Other when we fail to recognize what we have in common. We refuse to admit that we are to a great degree like them. But we overbind the Other when we refuse to grant them their difference, when we insist that they really are, or should be, just like us. Ordinary identity—whether traditional, modern, or postmodern—makes both of these moves, since they both bolster our fragile self-respect.[22]

As an example, Volf explains how the ordinary identity responds to wrongs and injustices with exclusion rather than forgiveness. "Forgiveness flounders because I exclude the [Other] from the community of humans even as I exclude myself from the community of sinners."[23] We say to ourselves, "*I* would never do what they did. I am nothing like them." To forgive and embrace, rather than to exclude or subjugate, requires a self-image that does not strengthen itself through drawing such contrasts. To forgive those who have wronged us and to treat warmly those who are deeply different from us requires a combination of two things. We need a radical humility that in no way can assert superiority over the Other. We must not see ourselves as qualitatively better. But at the same time there can be no insecurity, for insecurity compels us to find fault and to demonize the other, to shore up our own sense of self. So that humility must proceed not from our own emptiness and value-lessness but from a deeply secure and confirmed sense of our own worth. Only then will I not *need* to think of others as worse than they are or myself as better than I am. Only then can I accept them as they are.

But how can such confidence and humility exist in the same heart? Ordinary identity formation makes them mutually exclusive because self-worth is achieved through self-effort. When I am succeeding and meeting my standards, then I may feel confident and secure, but it will make it harder to understand or be sympathetic to those who do not meet my criteria. Or if I am failing to reach my own life goals, I may be more empathetic to others, but then I will lack that confidence. We may have humility or we may have confidence, but we cannot have both at the same time.

What will create a different kind of identity in which humility and confidence grow jointly? Volf answers: "No one can be in the presence of the God of the crucified Messiah for long . . . without transposing the enemy from the sphere of monstrous humanity into the sphere of shared humanity and herself from the sphere of proud innocence into the sphere of common sinfulness."[24] Christians are *simul justus et peccator*— simultaneously perfectly righteous in Christ and in the Father's eyes yet in ourselves very flawed and sinful. This leads to a security and humility that live together.

John Stott argues that this is a cross-shaped identity, one that leads to self-affirmation and self-denial at once. Jesus went to the cross to die for our salvation. That is, at the same moment, a profound statement of our sin, telling us that we are so flawed and guilty that nothing less than the death of the Son of God can save us. But it is at the same time the highest and strongest expression of his love for us and our value to him.[25] Volf describes the cross-centered identity as having a "de-centered center," a self that is so humbled by the cost of its salvation yet so affirmed by it that it cannot exclude others, nor does it need to. An experience of Christ's grace strikes a fatal blow to our egocentricity. The sight of Jesus dying for us out of love destroys both pride and self-hatred at the same time.[26]

At the heart of Christian faith is a man dying for his enemies, praying for their forgiveness rather than retaliating. The cross reveals a God who is so committed to justice that the cross was necessary. Sin and evil cannot be overlooked—they must be judged. Yet at the same time it shows us a God so loving that he was willing to bear the cost and take the judgment himself. He refuses to choose between truth and love—he will have both, and the only way for that to happen is if he pays the price for forgiveness himself. This becomes the Christian model of self-donation, of sacrificial love and forgiveness. But the cross doesn't simply give us an inspiring example. Through faith in the cross we get a new foundation for an identity that both humbles us out of our egoism yet is so infallibly secure in love that we are enabled to embrace rather than exclude those who are different.

The Cultural Flexibility of Christianity

It is only fair for the reader to wonder about the evidence that Christian identity is so unique. There are some remarkable examples of Christians using their spiritual resources to reach out to those whom most people would hate and exclude. Consider the Amish community that forgave the killer of five of its schoolchildren in 2006. Look at the families of the victims of the Charleston, South Carolina, shootings at Mother Emanuel AME Church, who more recently openly loved and forgave the killer of their loved ones.[27] When the nation looked on in amazement at how the Amish gathered around the family of the shooter and provided help and support without bitterness, many public voices opined that this was America at its best. A book by sociologists analyzing the event argued against this sanguine assessment. It explained that modern American society is now a culture of "self-assertion" in which all people are encouraged to express themselves and assert their rights. The Amish Christian community, by contrast, is a culture of self-renunciation, strongly based on the cross, on nonretaliation, on *uffgeva*, which means the renunciation of one's rights in the service of others.[28] In other words, the modern view of the self and expressive individualism does not give us the cultural resources for forgiveness and reconciliation, and therefore it is not surprising that such vivid examples of it at Nickel Mines, Pennsylvania, and Charleston, South Carolina, arise from Christian communities.

Nevertheless, it is possible to come up with competing lists. For every individual example of Christians who forgive enemies and are open to the Other, it is possible to make other citations of oppression and injustice done by believers. However, it could be helpful to look at the big picture of Christianity's cultural flexibility.

One of the unique things about Christianity is that it is the only truly worldwide religion. Over 90 percent of Muslims live in a band from Southeast Asia to the Middle East and Northern Africa. Over 95 percent of all Hindus are in India and immediate environs. Some 88 percent of Buddhists are in East Asia. However, about 25 percent of Christians live in Europe, 25 percent in Central and South America, 22 percent in Africa, 15 percent (and growing fast) in Asia, and 12 percent in North America.[29] Professor Richard Bauckham writes: "Almost certainly Christianity exhibits more cultural diversity than any other religion, and that must say something about it."[30] As we have seen, Christianity has been growing explosively in Asia and Africa for over a century now. It is no longer a Western religion (nor was it originally). It is truly a world religion.

What is fueling this remarkable spread of Christianity? A contemporary African writer has an intriguing answer. Lamin Sanneh writes that Christianity is less culturally imperialistic than secularism. How so? At the core of Africanness is the conviction that the world is full of spirits—good and evil. The problem, however, how can we be protected from the evil forces? If an African were to go to one of the great secular universities of the world, the professors would tell her that the solution to her fears was to see that there are no spirits, evil or good, that everything has a scientific explanation. Not only that, but all moral standards are person specific and relative to culture, and all moral values have to be self-authorizing. Ironically, her professors would say they wanted to affirm her culture and hear her "voice," yet at the same time they would be taking the very heart of her Africanness out of her.

Christianity, Sanneh says, took a very different approach. It answered the challenge so that the existing African "framework was reconfigured without being overthrown." A reading of the Bible shows that it respects the African belief that there is a vast supernatural realm, full of evil and good spirits, but it also tells us that there is one who by the cross has "defeated the principalities and powers," because he has procured forgiveness and the favor of God (Colossians 2:12–25), and by the Resurrection he has "[broken] the power of him who holds the power of death—that is, the devil—and free[d] those who all their lives were held in slavery by their fear of death" (Hebrews 2:14–15). So Christianity honors the African understanding of the condition and problem of human life, but it offers a solution—an invincible Savior. Sanneh concludes:

> *People sensed in their hearts that Jesus did not mock their respect for the sacred [as secularism does] or their clamor for an invincible Savior, and so they beat their sacred drums for him. . . . Christianity helped Africans to become renewed Africans, not remade Europeans.*[31]

What makes Christianity less culturally imperialistic than many other great worldviews? The crucial reason is that Christians are saved by grace alone. They do not enter their salvation by obedience to moral law, nor do they keep themselves saved that way. Therefore, unlike many religions, the New Testament has no book of Leviticus, no detailed set of laws and rules about behavior that tend to remove its adherents from their local cultures.[32] The Christian who makes Christ and his love the core of his or her identity, then, discovers that we need not completely reject other identity factors. Our race and national identity, our work and profession, our family and politics and community ties can all remain intact. They are no longer the ultimate basis for our significance and security, but that does not mean they are flattened or eliminated. Rather we are free to enjoy them as God's gifts to us, but we are no longer enslaved to them as our saviors.

For these reasons, those who have been given a Christian identity have the resources to become more open to difference and to become more culturally flexible than they would ever have been otherwise.

The Humble Will Be Exalted

Jesus contrasted the ordinary, exclusionary identity with that of a life based on his grace. He told a parable "to some who were confident of their own righteousness and looked down on everyone else" (Luke 18:9). There were "'two men [who] went up to the temple to pray, one a Pharisee and the other a tax collector.'" Tax collectors were despised in society as greedy and as collaborators with the Roman imperial power.

> *The Pharisee stood by himself and prayed: "God, I thank you that I am not like other people—robbers, evildoers, adulterers—or even like this tax collector. I fast twice a week and give a tenth of all I get." But the tax collector stood at a distance. He would not even look up to heaven, but beat his breast and said, "God, have mercy on me, a sinner." (Luke 18:10–13)*

Here is one identity based on moral self-effort and entailing exclusion to strengthen itself. The other man is seeking a wholly different route, one that acknowledges sin and need but also the reality of God's free mercy and grace. Jesus's conclusion: "'I tell you that this man, rather than the other, went home justified before God. For all those who exalt themselves will be humbled, and those who humble themselves will be exalted'" (Luke 18:14).

If you believe in Jesus's message, you believe in a truth, but not a truth that leads to exclusion. Many voices argue that it is exclusionary to claim that you have the truth, but as we have seen, that view itself sets up a dichotomy with you as the heroically tolerant and others as villainously or pathetically bigoted. You cannot avoid truth claims and binaries. The real issue is, then, which kind of truth—and which kind of identity that the truth produces—leads you to embrace people who are deeply different from you? Which truth claims lead you to scorn people who oppose you as fools? Which truth claims lead to community? Which truth claims both humble and affirm you so that you're not afraid of people who are different than you are, nor can you despise them? If I build my identity on what Jesus Christ did for me and the fact I have an everlasting name in him by grace, I can't, on the one hand, feel superior to anybody, nor do I have to fear anybody else. I don't have to compare myself with them at all. My identity is based on somebody who was excluded for me, who was cast out for me, who loved his enemies, and that is going to turn me into someone who embraces the Different.

Christians, of course, so often fail to realize and live out of the resources they have. But the world needs millions of people who have the capacity to do what the Gospel compels and empowers them to do.

Eight

A Hope That Can Face Anything

U.S. suicide rate surges to 30-year high, said the headline on an April 2016, *New York Times* front-page article. The overall suicide rate rose 24 percent from 1999 to 2014, with the rise over the last eight years double the annual rises the first seven years. It tripled for girls ages ten to fourteen and rose for every racial and gender category except African American men. Various experts were, of course, consulted within the article for explanations. One attributed the trend to diminishing job and economic prospects, yet the suicide rate of black men, perhaps the most economically excluded population of all, was not rising. Robert Putnam, professor of public policy at Harvard, was the only expert cited in the article who mentioned the word "hopelessness."[1] Why should modern people feel more hopeless when, arguably, our lives are more comfortable and we are living longer than ever before?

This ennui is reflected in our literature as well. Just a few days earlier, the *New York Times Book Review* selected two authors and asked them this question: "Which subjects are underrepresented in contemporary fiction?" One, Ayana Mathis, said that today writers are "flummoxed by joy." Instead, they "seem to have decided that despair, alienation and bleakness are the most meaningful, and interesting, descriptors of the human condition. In our ennui and end-of-days malaise, we . . . are suspicious of the . . . fullness of life."[2] A quick survey of the most popular movies and TV shows alone bears this out. Blockbuster films are filled with end-of-the-world nuclear and environmental disasters, zombie invasions, and other dystopias. The "high-quality" TV dramas, such as *Breaking Bad*, *House of Cards*, and *Mad Men* are all characterized by antiheroes.[3]

Innumerable polls in the United States and Europe show declining confidence about the future. No matter how all this is analyzed, it adds up to a loss of hope. No one can live without hope, but in this chapter we will look at the resources that Christianity gives us for a future hope unlike any other.

Imagine you have two women of the same age, the same socioeconomic status, the same educational level, and even the same temperament. You hire both of them and say to each, "You are part of an assembly line, and I want you to put part A into slot B and then hand what you have assembled to someone else. I want you to do that over and over for eight hours a day." You put them in identical rooms with identical lighting, temperature, and ventilation. You give them the very same number of breaks in a day. It is very boring work. Their conditions are the same in every way—except for one difference. You tell the first woman that at the end of the year you will pay her thirty thousand dollars, and you tell the second woman that at the end of the year you will pay her thirty *million*.

After a couple of weeks the first woman will be saying, "Isn't this tedious? Isn't it driving you insane? Aren't you thinking about quitting?" And the second woman will say, "No. This is perfectly acceptable. In fact, I whistle while I work." What is going on? You have two human beings who are experiencing identical circumstances in radically different ways. What makes the difference? It is their expectation of the future. This illustration is not intended to say that all we need is a good income. It does, however, show that what we believe about our future completely controls how we are experiencing our present. We are irreducibly *hope-based* creatures.

What we need, however, is not just a general "hopefulness." In fact, there are scientific studies showing that a sunny disposition and optimistic personality do not necessarily produce a better life.[4] The kind of hope we need is something deeper.

How Hope Became Optimism

Andrew Delbanco, in his penetrating analysis of American history, *The Real American Dream: A Meditation on Hope*, writes that human beings need to organize the sequence of individual sensations and life experiences into a particular story.[5] "When that story leads somewhere . . . it gives us hope."[6] We cannot, Delbanco argues, bear life by living only in the present, facing one disconnected event after another, pursuing only "instant desire."[7] We are future-oriented beings, and so we must understand ourselves as being in a story that "leads somewhere."[8] We cannot live without at least an implicit set of beliefs that our lives are building toward some end, some hope, to which our actions are contributing. "We must imagine some end to life that transcends our own tiny allotment of days and hours," writes Delbanco, "if we are to keep at bay the dim back-of-the-mind suspicion that we are adrift in an absurd world."[9]

Delbanco's cultural history of the United States has three chapters, three different hopes or stories that our society has given its people over the years. He names them "God," "Nation," and "Self." For the first phase of American history, "hope was chiefly expressed through a Christian story that gave meaning to suffering and pleasure alike and promised deliverance from death." But then, under the influence of Enlightenment rationality, belief in God and the supernatural began to weaken among cultural elites. Instead of finding ultimate hope in the kingdom of God, Americans began to believe in the sacred calling of being the "greatest nation on earth," one that would show the rest of the world the way to a better future for the human race. It essentially substituted a "deified nation" for God. There was no more vivid example of this sacralization of nationhood and citizenship than "The Battle Hymn of the Republic": "As [Jesus] died to make men holy, let us die to make men free."

Robert Nisbet, in *History of the Idea of Progress*, also explains how the older Christian idea of the coming kingdom of God became secularized into a narrative of historical advancement. He shows that ancient peoples generally saw time and history as cyclical, but especially Christianity gave humanity the idea of progress.[10] Christian theology understood history to be linear, sovereignly controlled by God, moving toward a day of judgment, justice, and the establishment of the peaceable divine kingdom. By modern times, however, the Christian idea had been secularized into "the Story of Progress, or Reason and Freedom, or Civilization . . . or Human Rights." So deeply is this idea of human progress etched in our thinking that it is embodied in vocabulary that describes good trends as "progressive," bad ones as "regressive" or "backward," and some thinkers as "ahead of their time."[11]

The Decline of Secular Optimism

Today, however, this idea of progress is beginning to crumble. Some of the attacks on it are philosophical. If in our secular society we no longer have moral absolutes—no agreed-upon understanding of right and wrong—then how can we even define what progress (and regress) is? Isn't every claim that such and such is "progressive" a value judgment that is neither self-evident to all nor empirically provable? Therefore, every declaration of progress is an imposition of one group's values on the rest of us.

Another critique of the idea of progress is that it assumes endless economic expansion. The modern narrative of historical development has been defined largely in terms of greater material prosperity, physical comfort, and technological control over nature. But today we seem to be coming up on a time in which, as Christopher Lasch put it, "an awareness" of "the natural limits of human power and freedom . . . has become inescapable."[12] Lasch was writing in 1991, so this critique was prescient. Today the threat of environmental decline or disaster calls into question the economic models used by the more "advanced" nations for the last two hundred years, models that require exponential growth in consumption.

There has been a remarkable cultural shift away from older optimism about history. Younger Americans today are perhaps the first generation to be certain that they are and will be "worse off" than their parents.[13] The interconnected nature of the world makes nightmare scenarios—pandemics, global economic collapse, climate-change disaster, cyberattacks, terrorism—all seem like genuine possibilities, even probabilities. Another proof of this loss of cultural hope is the hoarding of trillions of dollars by U.S. companies. A *New Yorker* article tells us that this is unprecedented in economic history, as businesses usually borrow and spend rather than save. To hold such sums is "economically absurd" because interest rates are so low on savings that almost any investment is likely to earn greater profit. Google alone has $80 billion sitting in bank accounts or short-term investments, enough to go out and buy Goldman Sachs if it wanted to.

When economic experts were consulted about this unparalleled situation, the answer was that people no longer have the same confidence that the future will see the same kind of progress we have been used to in the past.[14] Our modern belief that the new is usually better is vanishing.

Lasch argues that secular optimism in progress is doomed. The "more extravagant versions of progressive faith" have already begun to fade. At the beginning of the twentieth century a future was envisioned where the problems of society were solved. This was "premised on the perfectibility of human nature" through science, education, and social policy. These more grand beliefs began to collapse in stages after each of the World Wars. But a latter version—of belief in greater economic prosperity, comfort, and individual freedom—has persisted.[15] Only now is it beginning to fail as we begin to see the limits, within the environment of our planet, of growth. The secular concept of progress requires "an indefinite expansion of desires, a steady rise in the general standard of comfort" through unlimited, constant economic growth. This material prosperity is necessary if the secular social ideal—individuals becoming more and more free to pursue happiness according to their own private definitions of good—is to be realized.[16] But that kind of economic growth cannot be sustained.

Why Optimism Must Become Hope

Lasch argues that secular optimism has been a disaster not only for the environment but also for the human spirit. It weakens our ability as people to face difficulties and suffering, and it cannot move people to sacrifice immediate pleasures for a larger purpose. "Progressive ideology weakens the spirit of sacrifice," Lasch writes. It cannot provide any effective antidote to despair, because the immediate pleasures *are* the whole point of history.[17] Eric Kaufmann fears that his own secularist view "cannot inspire a commitment to generations past and sacrifices for those yet to come."[18]

The alternative to secular optimism in progress is hope. Real hope, as Lasch defines it, "does not demand a belief in progress" at all. "The disposition properly described as hope, trust, or wonder . . . three names for the same state of heart and mind—asserts the goodness of life in the face of its limits. It cannot be defeated by adversity."[19] Why not? Elsewhere Lasch points to the example of African slaves in America. How did they keep hope alive? As Eugene D. Genovese and other historians of slavery have made clear, "it would be absurd to attribute to slaves a belief in progress." It was Christianity, Genovese showed, that gave them "a firm yardstick" with which to measure and judge the behavior of their masters and "to articulate a promise of deliverance as a people in this world as well as the next."[20] Hope does not require a belief in progress, only a belief "in justice, a conviction that the wicked will suffer, that wrongs will be made right, [that] the underlying order of things is not flouted with impunity."[21] Hope that stands up to and enables us to face the worst depends on faith in something that transcends this world and life and is not available to those living within a worldview that denies the supernatural.

Howard Thurman, an African American scholar at Boston University in the midtwentieth century, gave a famous lecture at Harvard in 1947 on the meaning of "Negro spirituals."[22] He engaged the criticism that the African American spirituals were too otherworldly, too filled with references to heaven, to crowns and thrones and the robes the singers would wear when Jesus returned. The argument was that such beliefs made people docile and submissive. On the contrary, Thurman argued, this sung faith served to deepen the slaves' capacity for endurance. The spirituals encompassed the Christian belief in a final judgment, a day on which all wrongs would be made right. It also included a belief in personal immortality and the reunion with loved ones forever. Out of these doctrines "the conviction grew that this is the kind of universe that cannot deny ultimately the demands of love and longing. . . . Uniting with loved ones turned finally on the hope of immortality and the issue of immortality turned on God. Therefore God would make it right."[23]

Thurman denied that this Christian hope weakened the slaves' self-respect or ability to face their captors. Rather, "it taught a people how to ride high in life, to look squarely in the face those facts that argue most dramatically against all hope, and to use those facts as a raw material out of which they fashioned a hope that their environment, with all its cruelty, could not crush. . . . This . . . enabled them to reject annihilation and to affirm a terrible right to live."[24] Why could nothing destroy their hope? It was because it *was* otherworldly, it was not based on any circumstance within the walls of this world. It lay in the future of God. This hope enabled them to "affirm a terrible right to live."

At one point in his lecture, Thurman answers the objection "But we can't take all this sort of thing literally. Surely all this talk of crowns and heaven is symbolic." He retorts that if such things were seen as mere symbols and not real, they could never have served to provide a life of hope to slaves when the prospects for improvement were so small. Imagine how ludicrous it would have been to sit down with a group of early nineteenth-century slaves and say, "There will never be a judgment day in which wrongdoing will be put right. There is no future world and life in which your desires will ever be satisfied. This life is all there is. When you die, you simply cease to exist. Our only real hope for a better world lies in improved social policy. Now, with these things in mind, go out there, keep your head high, and live a life of courage and love. Don't give in to despair."

Such a thought experiment reveals how much more power Christian hope has for sufferers than a mere optimism in historical progress. Thurman points to the simple fact of history that hope in eternal justice and divine blessing sustained the African American people.

Nothing to Be Frightened Of?

However, the great challenge to human hope is not just the question of where history is going but of where *we* are going. The great problem is how to have a human hope that can make sense of death, stand up to death, and help us face the fear of death and even triumph over it.

Delbanco, as we have seen, titles the last chapter of American cultural history "Self." In colonial days "the self expanded toward . . . the vastness of God. [Then,] from the early republic to the Great Society, it remained implicated in a national ideal lesser than God but larger and more enduring than any individual citizen. Today hope has narrowed to the vanishing point of the self alone."[25] In our current phase of American history we have lost belief in God and salvation, or in any shared sense of national greatness and destiny. We do not see serving God or the nation as being more important than self-actualization. We do not consider the claims of religion or national loyalty to ever overrule our pursuit of individual freedom and happiness. Our hope now is for individual freedom to pursue our own private ideas of good and to discover our authentic selves.[26]

The great trouble with that story, however, is that it does not do what every other worldview and cultural narrative has sought to do in the past. It cannot incorporate into itself and render meaningful the single most immutable and certain fact of human life—death. One of the crucial parts of the Christian story has always been "deliverance from death" through Christ. And death also had a meaningful place in the cultural era of nation and patriotism. There was no higher glory than to give one's life in the service of one's country, to "die to make men free." So in both of the older forms of hope there was some way to triumph over death and make it serve our highest aspirations. Dying well could actually propel you toward your great life goal, whether salvation or the glory of your people and country. But in the contemporary, individualistic, secular understanding of things, death simply interrupts and stops the story. It does not enhance progress toward your goals but destroys it.

One of the most common secular responses to this is to do something fairly new in human history. Rather than see death as a terror that must be overcome with some sort of religious hope, many contemporary thinkers counter that it is nothing to fear and that it can indeed be seen as part of the living story of the world.

The title of British writer Julian Barnes's memoir, *Nothing to Be Frightened Of*, refers to death.[27] He argues that it is a perfectly natural phenomenon and not to be feared. Here Barnes follows in the footsteps of thinkers such as Epicurus, who reasoned that there are only two possible situations to be in with regard to death. Either you are alive and death is elsewhere, or death has come upon you, and you are not here to know it. When you are dead, you simply don't exist, so there's no suffering or anything at all. Why, then, worry about death?[28] Death, then, is nothing to fear.

Another example of this approach is the article "It's Silly to Be Frightened of Being Dead," by legendary British editor Diana Athill, who is now in her late nineties. In this essay and her book *Alive, Alive Oh!* Athill insists that death is a perfectly "natural process." She refuses to call it the "'end of life' because it is part of life," part of the life cycle of the earth. Living beings arise from the earth and then go back to it, making the earth capable of nurturing new lives. She learned from Montaigne that death is inevitable and that "something inevitable is natural and can't be too bad." She explains how her meditating on death's naturalness "caused belief in an afterlife to melt away" as wholly unnecessary. Death is merely "sliding down into nothingness," and so it is silly to fear it.[29] At the end of her book of essays on this topic, she writes a poem, "Why Want Anything More Marvelous Than What Is?"[30]

This view now runs through innumerable books and articles on how to understand death and how to explain it to children. Perhaps the most famous popular-culture expression of this account is put forth in the movie *The Lion King*, in which a young lion is told that, though lions eat the antelope, they eventually die and fertilize the grass, and the antelopes eat the grass, "and so we are all connected in the great Circle of Life."[31] Death, then, is a part of life and nothing to be feared.

The Fear of Death

But the reality is that the great majority of people fear death quite a lot despite knowing all these biological realities.

Philosopher Peter Kreeft recounts the story of a seven-year-old boy whose cousin died at the age of three. He asked his mother, "Where is my cousin now?" She did not believe in God or the afterlife, and so she could not with integrity talk to him about heaven. Instead she followed the modern secular narrative. "Your cousin has gone back to the earth," she said, "from which we all come. Death is a natural part of the cycle of life. And so when you see the earth put forth new flowers next spring, you can know that it is your cousin's life that is fertilizing those flowers."

How did the little boy respond? He screamed, "I don't want him to be fertilizer!" and ran away.[32] Kreeft argues that the mother had let the modern narrative suppress the natural human intuition that death is *not* natural at all. Kreeft elsewhere argues that to tell people they must accept death as just another "stage of growth" is like telling a quadriplegic that paralysis is another stage of exercise.[33]

Statements like Diana Athill's—that we should not want anything other than what is, or that nothing inevitable can be bad—can't hold up either to rational scrutiny or to our deepest moral convictions. Scientists will all agree that there is nothing more inevitable and natural than violence—evolution and natural selection are based on it. Yet we believe it is bad. And everyone can easily imagine—and want—a world more marvelous than the one we have. Nor is "sliding down" into nonconsciousness a pleasant prospect for most people. In Samuel Johnson's famous biography he recounts how a Miss Seward told him that death was only a "pleasing sleep without a dream." Johnson vehemently denied it, snorting that it was *"neither pleasing, nor sleep."*[34] Unconsciousness, violently imposed on someone, is considered a crime. So should we consider death a thief and murderer.

All ancient myths and legends that deal with death depict it as an intrusion, an aberration, and a monstrosity. It always appears because something has gone wrong.[35] You will not find the accumulated wisdom of the ages insisting that death is perfectly natural. Death is not the way it is supposed to be. "Death does not *feel* natural, however biologically necessary it may be. This feeling . . . cannot be put to death by reasonable considerations about the cycles of nature. [We simply do] not *feel* like recycled fertilizer."[36] Dylan Thomas is far closer to the hearts of most when he counsels us to *"not* go gentle" into the night of death, that we should "rage, rage against the dying of the light."[37]

As one writer puts it, "The fact of death is the great human repression, the universal 'complex.' . . . Death is muffled up in illusions."[38] To insist that death is nothing to be frightened of is simply another illusion muffling the obscenity of death. We live in denial of it, but like all repressed facts, it keeps disturbing us, haunting us, and quietly (or not so quietly) draining our hope.

Why do we fear?

Why do we fear death? Why does it make us rage? The first reason is because of what it does to our relationships. Epicurus and others spoke of permanent nonconsciousness as nothing to fear, but indeed it is. It means the end of love. Carl Jung says bluntly:

> *Death is indeed a fearful piece of brutality: there is no sense pretending otherwise. It is brutal not only as a physical event,*

but far more so psychically: a human being is torn away from us,
and what remains is the icy stillness of death. There no longer
exists any hope of a relationship, for all the bridges have been
smashed at one blow.[39]

Jung shows the hole in the argument of Epicurus and Barnes. Above all, the things that make life meaningful are love relationships. Death removes them one at a time over the years, stripping you down and down. Finally, it comes for you and removes you from the loved ones remaining. Almost by definition, real love wants to last; it never wants to part from those we love. Death strips us of everything that makes life meaningful—so how can it be nothing to fear? On the contrary, it is our ultimate enemy (1 Corinthians 15:26). There is no more terrible experience than seeing a loved one dead. Nothing within this life can ever heal you of it.

There is at least one more reason that we fear death. The death-is-natural approach assumes that after death there is nothing—no existence or consciousness. But that cannot be proven, and to be certain of it requires a leap of faith. "What men fear," wrote Epicurus, "is not the fact that death is annihilation but that it is not." It is not the fact of death per se but the gnawing uncertainty of what lies beyond it that cannot but disturb us.[40] Shakespeare, through Hamlet's mouth, tells us that the dread of something after death, "that undiscovered country from whose bourn no traveller returns," leads us to "bear those ills we have, than fly to others that we know not of," because "conscience doth make cowards of us all."[41] The poet John Dryden wrote: "Death, in itself, is nothing; but we fear to be we know not what, we know not where."[42] Rousseau agrees: "He who pretends to face death without fear is a liar."[43]

As a minister I have spent decades visiting the sick and dying. In hospitals the seriously ill are, not surprisingly, quite willing to talk to the clergy. Even those who have no belief in God or the afterlife feel compelled to examine themselves, to ask, "Have I been loving enough to my friends and family? Have I been generous enough with my money? Have I continually postponed changes I knew should be made in my life?" In the shadow of death something makes us ask if we have lived as we should, and the answer to that is almost inevitably "no." No wonder that conscience, combined with the inability to be sure of what happens after death, "makes cowards" of so many as death approaches.

A man who was dying of cancer once quoted T. S. Eliot to me: "Not what we call death, but what beyond death is not death, / We fear, we fear."[44] I asked him what he thought was beyond death. He answered that he had no idea, but he couldn't understand how his secular friends could be so completely sure that there was simple nonexistence. "It's crazy," he continued. "They mock people for betting their lives on the existence of God by sheer faith, but then they bet the ranch that afterwards there will be nothing, no judgment, *nada*. How can they be sure of that?" There was a pause and I said, "So you are having some regrets?" He nodded emphatically and said that he had wronged many people and he had strong intuitions that somehow deeds of injustice and evil "follow us." He knew there was no way to "put things right" before he died. Helplessness before inexorable death finally revealed his heart to him, and he was without hope.

If you were driving a car sixty miles per hour, but unable to see out the windows, it would be frightening. And if you are driving toward death without the ability to see what is coming, it will also make you afraid.

Jesus, Our Champion

So what is the Christian hope, which not only explains why we feel death is so unnatural but also gives us the ability to face and even triumph over it?

In John 11 Jesus comes to the tomb of his friend Lazarus, who has recently died. Both verses 33 and 38 say that while he was weeping with grief he was also snorting with anger. Jesus could not have been weeping for Lazarus because he knew he was about to raise him from the dead.

What, then, was he so grieved and angry about? He was furious at the sin and death that had ruined the creation and people he loved.[45]

The book of John makes it clear that Jesus claimed to be God, and so it is significant that he could be angry at death without being angry at himself. The book of Genesis explains how this could be so. Death was not part of God's original design. We were not created to age, weaken, fade, and die. We were not created for love relationships that end in death. Death is an intrusion, a result of sin and our human race's turning away from God. Our sense even now that we were made to last, that we were made for love without parting, is a memory trace of our divine origins. We are trapped in a world of death, a world for which we were not designed.

The solution to our dilemma is classically expressed in the New Testament letter to the Hebrews. It teaches that the immortal Son of God was sent into the world, sharing in our humanity, becoming subject to weakness and death. But then through death he broke its power, in order to "free those who all their lives were held in slavery by their fear of death" (Hebrews 2:14–15). How did he do this? He did so as our "champion." "[God] made the champion of their salvation perfect through what he suffered" (Hebrews 2:10).[46] In ancient times a "champion" meant one who engaged in representational combat, as when David fought Goliath on behalf of Israel (1 Samuel 17). So Jesus stood engaged in mortal combat with death, fighting on our behalf. At first sight, he did not win, because on the cross he died. Yet in the biblical account death is not simply our enemy but our executioner. "The wages of sin is death" (Romans 6:23). It is the punishment for turning away from God. And just as a creditor's power over us is broken when someone pays our debt fully, so death's claim and power over us was broken when Jesus died in our place, paying our penalty.

That is why Jesus's death destroys the power of death. "God raised him from the dead, . . . because it was impossible for death to keep its hold on him" (Acts 2:24). Put another way, the darkness of death swallowed Jesus, he entered it, but then he blew a hole out the back of it. It had no right to him, because he was innocent. Now, however, it also has no ultimate right to those who by faith rest in him (1 Thessalonians

4:13–18). He has paid for our sins. We may physically die, but death now becomes only an entryway to eternal life with him.

This is why believers in Christ are no longer enslaved to the fear of death. They can sing the hymn:

> *Jesus lives! And death is now*
> *But my entrance into glory.*
> *Courage then, my soul, for thou*
> *Hast a crown of life before thee.*[47]

So Hamlet was wrong. There *is* one traveler who has returned from death, the undiscovered country. He has gone there and come out through it again into life, and all who follow him can walk the same path. George Herbert addresses death, telling it that it once was "an executioner at best," but

> *Thou art a gard'ner now, and more,*
> *An usher to convey our souls*
> *Beyond the utmost starres and poles.*[48]

All death can now do to Christians is to make their lives infinitely better.

In John Updike's memoir, *Self-Consciousness*, he addresses those "who scoff at the Christian hope of an afterlife . . . [with] a certain moral superiority." They argue that it is selfish and egocentric to want what Christianity promises, "to hope for more than our animal walk in the sun." Shouldn't we rather "submit to eternal sleep gratefully" as all other living creatures must do?[49] Richard Dawkins and others have critiqued the idea of a heavenly reward as a cosmic bribe.[50] It seems shallow and mercenary to live a moral life mainly so it will pay off in eternal bliss.

These common objections reveal popular misunderstandings about the character of Christian hope. While secularism offers no hope for any life after death, most religions do. Nevertheless, there are several ways in which the Christian understanding is distinct, even unique.

The Christian Hope Is Personal

As we have seen, secular thinkers often speak of how we continue to exist after death in that the matter of our bodies takes new form and replenishes the earth. Eastern religions today teach that after death our souls merge with the All-Soul of the universe. Just as a drop of water returning to the ocean loses its individual nature in the whole, so we become an impersonal part of the impersonal spiritual life force knitting all things together. But if after death there is nonexistence, impersonal existence, or in any case nonconsciousness, that means there is no *love*, because only persons can love. If we are not a self after death, then we have lost everything, because what we most want in life is love.

Love between persons is the heart and core of the Christian hope, and this is the reason that heaven is not a bribe. C. S. Lewis argues that it is right to condemn a man who marries a woman for the sake of her money. The reason is because "money is not the natural reward of love." But, he adds, "marriage *is* the proper reward for a real lover, and he is not mercenary for desiring it."[51] The same thing could be said, then, about the Christian promise of heaven. It is possible, of course, that an individual might indeed see heaven in a mercenary way. Updike, who worked at the *New Yorker* for many years, notes how the cartoons so often mocked the belief in heaven by depicting white-robed people on clouds with harps "and haloes thrown in for added risibility."[52] Even as satire this shows an understanding of heaven as consumer paradise, where all the pleasures and comforts you sought to buy on earth are now free for the asking. And indeed, as a minister who has talked to people for over forty years about these matters, the popular religious imagination does tend to think of heaven as simply a trouble-free place of ease. But this is to miss the essence of what is promised in the Bible. What if you want heaven the way a lover wants marriage? That would be different.

Eighteenth-century philosopher and preacher Jonathan Edwards wrote a famous sermon titled "Heaven Is a World of Love," which conveys the Christian hope with power.[53] Edwards understands the ultimate Christian hope not to be in abstractions such as radiance and immortality but in *relationship*. At the center of heaven is not merely a generic God but the triune Christian God, one God in three persons, Father, Son, and Holy Spirit, "who are united in infinitely dear and incomprehensible mutual love."[54] There is "an . . . eternal mutual holy energy between the Father and the Son, a pure holy act whereby the Deity becomes nothing but an infinite and unchangeable act of love."[55] Pouring love into one another in degrees of unimaginable power and joy makes this three-in-one God into a "fountain of love." In heaven this fountain "is set open without any obstacle to hinder access to it," and so it "overflows in streams and rivers of love and delight, enough for all to drink at, and to swim in, yea, so as to overflow the world as it were with a deluge of love."[56]

Although we all have found remarkable joy in love, Edwards characterizes all earthly relationships as being highly "clogged."[57] Imagine a water pipe that is almost completely clogged with clay and mud, so that only a tiny amount of polluted water comes through. That is what all human experience of love is like. Even the best human relationships in this life, because of our weaknesses, let as little love through as a clogged pipe allows water. But in heaven love flows unspeakably more fully and cleanly. We can therefore get a tiny hint of the joy of that place by reflecting on the factors that sully and weaken all love here, or that make it painful, and on what it would be like if they were removed.

In this world, for example, we seldom love another person equally to their love for us. Usually there is pain because some love us more than we love them or we love them more than they love us. But in heaven all love will be "answerable" and perfectly mutual.[58] Also, love "disposes us to praise" and creates an overwhelming need to give voice and articulation to itself, but here we feel "clogged . . . in the exercises . . . of love." However, in heaven we will have no such difficulty. Our tongues and voices will utter our love in perfect expression, and so it will complete the joy of love in a way we have never known before.[59]

Edwards also reasons that our love here is always mightily diminished by envy and selfishness. We are attracted to and love people who we think can make us happy and affirm us. If they fail to do this, we become angry. If they prosper more than we do, we can become jealous. In short, we don't love God or others for their own sakes, to serve them and their joy. Rather we love others for our sake, to serve us, so "most of the love which there is in this world . . . proceeds . . . from selfish motives, and to mean and vile purposes." But in heaven "love is a pure flame" where all will "love God for his own sake, and each other for God's sake . . . [for] the image of God that is upon them. . . . Having no pride or selfishness to interrupt or hinder its exercises, their hearts shall be full of love."[60] Filled with God's love, and therefore no longer having any emptiness or need within, we will "put our happiness *in* to the loved one's happiness." That is, their joy will become our joy. "If the love be perfect, the greater the prosperity of the beloved is, the more the lover is pleased and delighted. For the prosperity of the beloved is, as it were, the food of love, and therefore the greater that prosperity the more richly is love feasted." Envy will be impossible. The happier we are, the happier we will make each other. And that means that in heaven our joy and glory will multiply exponentially forever, "with inconceivable ardor of heart."[61]

In addition, we will never again fear separation from those we love. Disrupted love, the greatest sadness that earthly life contains, will be gone forever. In heaven "they shall know that they shall forever be continued in the perfect enjoyment of each other's love." All things there "shall flourish in an eternal youth. Age will not diminish anyone's beauty or vigor, and there love shall flourish . . . as a living spring perpetually springing . . . as a river which ever runs and is always clear and full."[62]

Most important of all, "then Christ will open to their view the great fountain of love in his heart far beyond what they ever before saw . . . and they shall know that he has loved them with dying love."[63] There is nothing more transforming than when someone makes a powerful declaration and expression of love toward us. So what will this be like? In response to this ultimate experience of divine love every person in heaven will become "a note in a concert of music which sweetly harmonizes with every other note . . . and so all helping one another to their utmost to express their love and . . . to pour back love into the fountain of love, whence they are supplied and filled with love and with glory. And thus they will live and thus reign in love, and in that godlike joy which is the blessed fruit of it, such as eye hath not seen, nor ear heard, nor hath ever entered into the heart of any in this world to conceive" (1 Corinthians 2:9).[64]

None of this is possible if when we die we simply become part of the earth, or even an impersonal part of the impersonal All-Soul of the world, as in many Eastern religions. Love is possible only between persons, and Christianity promises that through Christ you can (in Updike's phrase) "be a Self forever." The Gospel accounts relate that the risen Christ was both the same and yet different, so that his disciples did not at first recognize him yet did so eventually (Luke 24:16,31; John 20:14,16). An analogy would be knowing a ten-year-old girl and then not meeting her again until she was a beautiful, intelligent woman of twenty-five. You would not likely recognize her at first, but it would become clear that it was still her. Our future, glorified selves will be continuous with who we are now, but the growth into wisdom, goodness, and power will be infinitely greater.

Christianity denies the modern secular belief that "we are insignificant accidents within a vast uncaused churning." Rather, it declares that "our life is a story" and that "the universe has a personal structure." Updike, for all his skeptical temperament, comes down on the side of Christian belief. "I have the persistent sensation," he writes, "that in my life and art, I am just beginning."[65]

The Christian Hope Is Concrete

Updike observed that many believe the desire for the afterlife is selfish. He counters that the yearning that Christianity fulfills "is the opposite of selfish: it is love and praise for the world. . . . It is not for some *other* world but for *this* world."[66]

Here Updike touches on one of the unique aspects of the Christian hope. The Bible's promise is not simply that we will live on forever in an immaterial, spiritual paradise removed from this world. At the end of history, described in images that overflow and swamp all our categories, we do not ascend to heaven, but God's heavenly glory and purifying beauty and power descend to renew this material world, so that evil, suffering, aging, disease, poverty, injustice, and pain are removed forever (Revelation 21:1–5; 22:1–4). Christians do not merely look forward to the redemption of their souls but also of their bodies (Romans 8:23). Like Jesus, we will be resurrected (1 Thessalonians 4:14–17). This is why one Christian preacher from Sri Lanka, when asked, "Don't you think salvation comes through other faiths too?" answers, "What salvation are you talking about?" Not this one! No other religion even claims to hold out hope for the salvation of this world along with our souls and bodies.[67]

Suffering, evil, and death have ruined life in this world. Even our brightest moments are painful because they are taken from us too soon. Edgar Allan Poe's strange, famous, and dark poem "The Raven" gives us a black raven saying, "Nevermore. Nevermore."[68] Some have understood Poe to be speaking of the irretrievability of life. The longer you are alive the more you sense that the things you are losing, at least within the walls of this world, will never come back to you. Sometimes they are opportunities that you have missed. There are beloved places that have literally been torn down, wonderful groupings and relationships that have unraveled and can never be restored. As time goes on, you realize the irretrievability of it all, a constant kind of death in the midst of life.

But Christians are not merely hoping for some consolation for the life we have lost. They look toward the restoration of the life we wanted but never had. The resurrected Jesus was not a phantom, and neither shall we be. He received a new body, and so shall we. "Touch me and see; a ghost does not have flesh and bones," he said to his astonished disciples, "as you see I have" (Luke 24:39). You will not simply get your life back, but you will get the life you always longed for but never were able to achieve. The Resurrection says "No!" to nevermore. You will not miss out on anything, because this is not just a consolation but a restoration.

Updike is right—to love this world that much, to want to see it as all that it was created to be, is not selfish. Many secular, liberal people also long to see nature unsullied, no longer warped by human exploitation. They want to see the end of hunger and disease and people freed from poverty and oppression. They want the same thing as Christian believers at this point. They may refuse to believe the Christian hope, but their reason for doubting should not be that it is a bribe but that it is too good to be true.

If we recall the argument of Howard Thurman, we see how important it is that Christian hope is so concrete. Why have so many of the poor and downtrodden been attracted to Christianity? There are many who say that we can't take the Resurrection literally—it is merely a symbol. But a symbol of what? Is it a symbol that somehow even in the darkest times we can see things getting better? Real life is not like that. Sometimes light comes after darkness, but often there is none at all. So the Resurrection as merely a symbol that "things will get better eventually" will let you down, but if we believe in the Resurrection as a historical fact, then real justice will be done on the earth someday. All wrongs will be made right.

If we believe that the Resurrection really happened, then Jesus Christ has, as it were, made an opening in the barrier between the ideal and the real. The downtrodden of the world can say, "Now I have got something. I have a hope. I have a hope for the future." Middle-class people can get excited about philosophy and ethical principles, but not the masses, not the people who are really stuck in the darkness of this world. The Resurrection, not taken as a symbol but believed as a concrete fact, will lift up the downtrodden, and will change the world. Belief in a final judgment gives us enough hope so that we will neither resort to violence to bring in justice nor give in and collaborate with injustice.[69]

The Christian Hope Is Unimaginably Wonderful

The promise of the Resurrection, however, promises much more than justice, as great as that is.

In his great essay "On Fairy-Stories," J. R. R. Tolkien explains why people spend so much money and energy to consume movies, plays, and books that are fairy tales. The audience for what we call "fantasy" literature is vastly larger than that for realistic fiction and other works favored by the critics—to the great irritation of the literati of the world. But why?

In the essay Tolkien says there are a number of "primordial human desires" that modernity has not been able to extinguish.[70] Those things include the desire to "survey the depths of space and time" and, if possible, to escape death itself, "the oldest and deepest desire."[71] We desire also to hold communion with other, nonhuman living things, to connect to the birds, beasts, and trees from which we feel now alienated, and perhaps to know other intelligences as well.[72] We want to live long enough to realize our artistic and creative dreams, we want love without parting, and we desire to see the final triumph of good over evil.[73] Even though we know the tales are fiction, we have such a deep longing for these things that we get a unique satisfaction from immersing ourselves in the stories, particularly if they are well told.

As a Christian, Tolkien believed that these stories resonate because they bear witness to an underlying reality. We have intuitions of the plotline of the Bible, namely, that the world was made to be a paradise but it has been lost. The tales bring us joy, because deep down we sense that they describe the world as it *ought* to be and what we were made for. Tolkien says realistic fiction will never quench the thirst for these things. Even if we repress this knowledge intellectually, we know it imaginatively, and the tales stir our hearts.

In the epilogue to his essay, Tolkien makes a full disclosure of his belief that the Gospel of Jesus Christ is "a story of a larger kind which embraces all the essence of fairy-stories."[74] By likening the Gospel to a fairy tale he does not at all mean that it is merely a legend. On the contrary, "this story [alone] has entered History and the primary world."[75] It is *the* story to which all the other joy-bringing, spell-casting, heart-shaping old stories only point. Why? This is the one story that satisfies all these longings yet is historically *true*. It happened. If the Gospel and all it means and offers is understood, "there is no tale ever told that men would rather find was true, and none which so many skeptical men have accepted as true on its own merits."[76] Every well-told story, according to Tolkien, gives us a taste of the Gospel, the *evangelium*, when there is a "sudden and miraculous grace" and "the joy of deliverance." It gives us a "fleeting glimpse of Joy, Joy beyond the walls of the world, poignant as grief."[77] But in the Gospel we get far more than a glimpse. The death and Resurrection of Jesus Christ actually happened. "Because this story is supreme; and it is true, [a]rt is verified."[78]

If Jesus Christ was really raised from the dead—if he is really the Son of God and you believe in him—all these things that you long for most desperately will come true at last. We *will* escape time and death. We will know love without parting, we will even communicate with non-human beings (think angels), and we will see evil defeated forever. In fairy stories, especially the best and most well-told ones, we get a temporary emotional reprieve from a "real world" in which our deepest desires are all violently rebuffed. But if we believe the Gospel, we are assured that all those longings will be fulfilled in real time, space, and history.

The Christian Hope Is Assured

Most religious systems teach an afterlife, but ordinarily it is conditioned on your living a morally good and religiously observant life. Christianity, as we have seen, on the contrary offers salvation as a gift. It does not belong to the good people but to the people who will admit that they are not good enough and that they need a savior. And so Christians do not approach death uncertain whether they will be found worthy of eternal life. They believe in Jesus, who alone has a record worthy of eternal life, and they are secure in him.

And how can we be sure that faith in Christ will usher us into this future? One ground of our assurance is the Resurrection of Christ himself, the historical evidence for which is formidable, as demonstrated by scholars such as Wolfhart Pannenberg, N. T. Wright, and others.[79] (We will look further at this evidence in chapter 12.) Another ground of our hope is the foretaste of the future we get now, as we receive intoxicating if fleeting experiences of God's love through prayer. "And hope does not put us to shame, because God's love has been poured out into our hearts through the Holy Spirit, who has been given to us" (Romans 5:5).

These are the reasons that from his prison cell, awaiting his execution for plotting against Hitler, Dietrich Bonhoeffer was able to call the death of a Christian "the supreme festival on the road to freedom."[80] Likewise, fifty years earlier an American minister wrote his own epitaph: "Some day you will read in the papers that D.L. Moody, of East Northfield, is dead. Don't you believe a word of it. At that moment I will be more alive than I am now."[81] This is no fist of defiance, shaken at the unending darkness. This is hearing Christ say, as did the thief on the cross when all seemed lost, "Truly I tell you, today you will be with me in paradise" (Luke 23:43). There is a joy that sorrow can only enrich and deepen until it completely gives way to it. This is hope indeed.

Nine

The Problem of Morals

A. N. Wilson graduated from Oxford in the early 1970s and considered going into the Anglican ministry, but by the 1980s he had lost all faith, called himself an atheist, and wrote a short book, *Against Religion: Why We Should Try to Live Without It*.[1] He became an award-winning biographical author and scholar. He met up with his old colleague Richard Dawkins and had dinner with Christopher Hitchens, two of the most prominent "New Atheists." They were glad to hear of his nonbelief. "So—absolutely no God?" Hitchens asked. "Nope," said Wilson confidently.[2] Yet years later he startled many by announcing his return to faith in God with two long articles in the British magazine the *New Statesman* and in the *Daily Mail*. What led him to believe? As with any conversion or reconversion, it came with the cumulative weight of both existential and rational evidence. However, the various forms of evidence he found compelling had primarily to do with the problem modern secularism has with the establishment of a moral compass.

The "existential" evidence included the strength of moral character he saw in Christians. He particularly singled out those who were "not the famous, not saints" but whom he had seen face evil and death with calm and courage he found inexplicable. He saw Christianity's "palpable and remarkable power to transform human life."[3]

However, he also felt the force of reason. "Materialist atheism is . . . totally irrational," he said bluntly, and went on to explain that it could not account for the significance of love, beauty in art, or morality.[4] Morality was a particular problem, he felt, for the strictly secular point of view. He wrote that one of the last pieces of evidence that moved him out of nonbelief in God was "writing a book about the Wagner family and Nazi Germany, and realizing how utterly incoherent were Hitler's neo-Darwinian ravings, and how potent was the opposition, much of it from Christians; paid for, not with clear intellectual victory, but in blood. Read Pastor Bonhoeffer's book Ethics, and ask yourself what sort of mad world is created by those who think that ethics are a purely human construct."[5]

Dostoyevsky's Challenge

Wilson was essentially feeling the challenge of Fyodor Dostoyevsky, who famously wrote: "Without God and the future life . . . everything is permitted, one can do anything."[6] This quotation usually makes secular people bristle, with some warrant, because many use it to imply that people without faith in God are necessarily less good and moral than those who believe.

This is not true. Anyone who tries to claim that atheists are either individually or as a whole less moral than others will run up against common sense and experience. Christians have additional reasons to doubt such a statement, because the New Testament teaches on the one hand that all persons, regardless of belief, are created by God with a moral conscience (Romans 2:14–15). On the other hand, the same text tells them that all people, including believers, are flawed sinners (Romans 3:9–12). So even on the premises of Christian doctrine, it is wrong to declare or imply that you can't be good without God.[7]

However, neither Wilson nor Dostoyevsky is claiming that atheists are less good and moral than believers, and to read them that way is to miss the force of the challenge. Dostoyevsky does not say that without God there can be no moral feelings or moral behavior. He says that without God there can be no moral *obligation*, that everything is "permitted," allowed. What does this mean?

Anyone can say, "I feel this is right to do, and so that is how I will act." The "moral source" in this case is a feeling within. However, on the secular view of reality, how can anyone ever say to anyone else, "This is right (or wrong) for you to do, whether you feel it or not"? You can never say that to someone else unless there is a moral source outside them that they must honor. If there is an omniscient, omnipotent, infinitely good God, he himself, or his law, could be that moral source. If there is no God, however, it creates a great problem in that there doesn't appear to be an alternative moral source that exists outside of our inner feelings and intuitions. Therefore, while there can be moral feelings and convictions without God, it doesn't appear that there can be moral obligation—objective, moral "facts" that exist whether you feel them or not.

Atheist author Julian Baggini is willing to concede the difficulty. He writes that "atheists are quite rightly keen to counter the accusation that life without God cannot be moral." However, he goes on to admit that "for the religious, at least there is some bedrock belief that gives a reason to believe that morality is real and will prevail. In an atheist universe, morality can be rejected . . . without a clear, compelling reason to believe in its reality, [and] that's exactly what will sometimes happen."[8]

This would not be a difficulty, of course, if secular people were to grant that there is no moral obligation, that all moral intuitions are subjective, and that there is nothing that is objectively wrong and evil to do whether you feel like it is or not. However, there is virtually no one who truly believes that, who thinks that there are no moral facts. Morality is, therefore, a significant rational difficulty for the secular viewpoint.

However, it is only fair to admit that morality is also a problem for believers, although in a much different way. Someone has said that while the secular sources for morality are too weak, for religious people they seem often to be too strong. Religious people have proclaimed divinely sanctioned moral truth but then have used it to be harsh and exclusive toward others, or downright abusive. Morality can be a fearsome thing in the hands of a religious believer.

In this chapter we will turn first to and explore the problem that morals pose for secular people. In chapter 10 we will look more at the particular problem for believers, of how belief in moral absolutes rooted in God often makes religion into an oppressive force.

The Schizophrenia of Modern Morals

It could be claimed that secular Western society is one of the most moral cultures in history. Compared with the past, every human life is more highly valued today. "Our age makes higher demands of solidarity and benevolence on people today than ever before. Never before have people been asked to stretch out so far, and so consistently, so systematically, so as a matter of course, to the stranger outside the gates." And to the demand for universal benevolence is added the demand for universal justice. "We are asked to maintain standards of equality which cover wider and wider classes of people, bridge more and more kinds of difference, and impinge more and more on our lives."[9]

Yet if today we ask, "*Why* should we live in these ways? Why should we support equality and guard rights and sacrifice to help the poor?" our cultural institutions can give no answer. All previous societies could point to some shared, outside ethical source—whether sacred writings or ancient tradition or wisdom of the sages—all of which expressed what was understood to be the moral order of the universe. In contrast, the morality of modern secular people is "self-authorizing."[10] All morals, we believe, should be chosen by us individually or perhaps by our culture collectively. In either case, it is said, there are no objective, moral facts "out there" that we must discover and embrace. One way or another we create our moral commitments. We must be our own "legislators of meaning," as Charles Taylor says. In this we are unique. "The claim to issue the norms we live by on our own authority" has never happened before in history across a whole society.[11]

This has led to a kind of intellectual schizophrenia. As we have observed, if we create our own values individually, on what basis could we urge anyone else to accept them? Or if we create those values collectively, how then can we recommend them to any other culture? Yet we do, unavoidably, and forcibly. For example, Mari Ruti, a professor at the University of Toronto, writes: "Although I believe that values are socially constructed rather than God given . . . I do not believe that gender inequality is any more defensible than racial inequality, despite repeated efforts to pass it off as culture-specific 'custom' rather than an instance of injustice."[12] Notice that first she says what she must say as a modern, secular person, namely, that all moral values are socially constructed by human beings, not grounded in God. But then she hears some say that therefore they do not have to listen to her call for gender equality, because it is nothing but a Western, culturally constructed custom. On the contrary, she strongly retorts, it is not—gender equality is a universal moral norm that must be honored by all cultures. But how could that be? If all morality is person specific or socially constructed, how can any statement of right and wrong be true for all? In essence, Ruti is saying: "Your moral values are just socially constructed, but mine are not, and so are true for everyone." This self-justifying, self-contradictory stance is pervasive in our secular culture today.

This is a signal example of what Taylor calls the "extraordinary inarticulacy . . . of modern culture," which comes from the view that "moral positions are not in any way grounded in reason or the nature of things but are ultimately just adopted by each of us because we find ourselves drawn to them."[13] Today there is no way to justify or even to have a conversation about a moral claim with someone who disagrees. All we can do is shout the other person down.

This schizophrenia does not exist only in academic circles.[14] It is now pervasive, especially in the day-to-day lives of younger adults. Sociologist Christian Smith found that younger American adults held two views of morality in sharp tension, even contradiction. Most are relativistic, not believing in abiding moral absolutes.[15] And yet they have many very strong moral convictions, which they insist others should honor. When asked how they knew if an action was moral or not, most said that they "automatically know . . . what is right and wrong in any situation."[16] When asked how they would explain to someone else why they should do or not do some action, they repeatedly insisted that "everybody already knows" what is right and wrong.[17] But there is no set of moral values that is self-evident to all people.

Again, this leaves modern, secular people in the position of insisting that other people's morals are constructed yet acting toward others as if theirs are not. In theory we are relativists, but in practice and interaction with those who disagree with us we are absolutists. This schizophrenia is a major source of the increasing polarization we see in our culture.

A woman in my church who was a public-school teacher told me of her great frustration with the various "character education" curricula that she was given to teach to her children. They taught moral values such as justice, unselfishness with possessions, and truth telling. However, she told me, the teacher's material strictly forbade her to bring in religious justifications for any of the particular values being taught. That seemed at first glance to be sensible. Yet the practical result, she said, was that she could never offer any answer at all when her students asked, "Why?" Whatever answer she might give would get her into the forbidden realm. If she answered, "Because some things are just right to do and other things are evil," it would lead to the question "Who is to say what those things are?" If she answered instead, "It's just practical for society, because there are no moral absolutes, really," that would also be getting into a religious or philosophical realm. She concluded that the only way to teach moral values without bringing in matters of belief about God, human nature, morals, and meaning was simply to teach a set of values without any grounding at all. "I could never answer the most basic of the students' questions—'Why?' I had to keep the values groundless, floating in space."[18]

The Failure of the Social Sciences

Where can we turn in a secular society to find shared moral sources we can agree on? Can we look to the social sciences? No, we can't.

Yale sociologist Philip Gorski recently wrote of the "failure of the social sciences to develop a satisfactory theory of ethical life . . . that could explain why humans are constantly judging and evaluating." He notes that there are two main theories put forward by social scientists to explain morality without recourse to religion.

First there are those who believe that our moral convictions are the product of evolution. Those human ancestors who felt that loving self-sacrifice was right survived at greater rates than those who did not have those same moral feelings. And so today we all feel that way. Gorski dismisses this theory as inadequate. He wonders, as do many others, how our current admiration for self-sacrifice—particularly for sacrificing yourself for someone *out*side of your family, tribe, or race—could have been a trait that led to greater rates of survival. Even beyond that, Gorski points out, the theory fails to explain why any of our ancestors would have had "moral feelings [the sense of "oughtness" around certain behaviors] in the first place."[19]

He then considers the more influential theory of "cultural relativism and social constructionism." It goes like this: "Once upon a time, we thought there were moral universals. . . . Then, we discovered . . . [that] what is forbidden in one culture may be enjoined in another. . . . We realized that there is no [cosmic] moral law within us, much less in the starry skies above us. . . . We concluded that all [moral] laws are ultimately arbitrary. They are the product of power, not reason, be it human or divine."[20]

Gorski admits that this theory is the most "intellectually satisfying." It fits with our secular view of a material-only world. It makes us feel more in control of our morals than does the evolutionary theory. But in the end both theories tell us that the feeling we have that "moral facts" exist—that some actions are simply wrong, no matter what your genes or your culture or your emotions say or whether they are practical for survival or society or not—is just an illusion. It is a trick that our biology or society has played on us. For the sake of argument, let's say that loving, altruistic behavior helped our ancestors survive, and so the brain chemistry that makes us feel that is good behavior to do is with us today. Does the fact that this behavior was practical in the past constitute a moral obligation (not just a feeling) that we *must* do it now? Of course not.

Therefore, neither the evolutionary nor the constructivist theory allows that there is such a thing as an objective moral absolute, fact, or obligation. It means that though we may feel that murder and rape are wrong, we feel that way only because they are impractical to our selfish interests—either to our physical survival or our social well-being. They are not truly "wrong," as if there were some moral source outside of our biologically or socially imposed feelings. Some thinkers argue that internal moral intuitions coming from evolution or culture *do* create obligation, but that isn't true. David Bentley Hart writes that, though it may be difficult to resist genetically instilled desires, there is nothing that generates a *duty* to do so. After all, "what has been generally beneficial to the species over the ages may not be particularly beneficial to an individual in the present," and "if morality is really a matter of benefit rather than of spiritual obligation transcending personal concerns," then any set of ethical guidelines "can, like any other useful instrument, be taken up or laid down as one chooses."[21]

On either view, the evolutionist or the constructivist, there is no reason not to act in any way we desire, if we can get away with it practically. There's simply no way to tell right from wrong, so we shouldn't try.[22]

However, Gorski notes wryly, the problem with both theories is that no one can actually believe them, not even those who insist that they do. "Our own relativism is rarely as radical as [our] theory requires," he writes. "Who would now deny that the Holocaust was evil?"[23] Nicholas Wolterstorff agrees, adding that "almost always those who think and talk [of morals as relative] are living comfortable, privileged lives. . . . Imagine you were being tortured: would you be tempted by any of these views?"[24] Neither the evolutionary nor the constructivist view allows for the category of "evil" behavior that is wrong regardless of inbred feelings or cultural norms. Yet no holders of these theories can actually live as if that is true.

Gorski concludes, "We can't be complete relativists in our everyday lives."[25] He gives the example of academic social scientists, thoroughgoing relativists in their theory who nonetheless get moralistic and furious over "data fudging" by other scientists. Just as Mari Ruti did, they insist that other people's values are socially constructed but then they unavoidably act as if their own values are not.

Morality in the secular view could be given, with warrant, the same title as the fairy tale "The Emperor Has No Clothes." Yale law professor Arthur Leff points to how Robert Nozick begins his influential book *Anarchy, State, and Utopia*: "Individuals have rights, and there are some things no person or group can do to them."[26] This opening sentence is widely applauded. Yet as Leff points out, this is mere assertion, not argument. If all morality is culturally relative or just the product of evolutionary biology—and these are the only two secular explanations of moral value available—how can such a categorical declaration be made? Why should non-Westerners, for example, accept the Western view of human rights?

Gorski is right to see this as evidence of theory failure. Even the people who say they believe that there are no objective moral facts show the next moment that at the deepest level of their intuition they know that they do exist. So neither the evolutionist nor the constructivist theory can account for the most ordinary daily way that people live and make judgments. Therefore, neither have succeeded, and secularism continues to lack even a rudimentary explanation of why moral obligation exists if there is no God.

So our contemporary culture has a schizophrenia about moral commitments, has no good way to impart them to our children, and does not even have a good explanation about why we have such convictions. Modern people say they do not believe in absolute moral values but can't function without practically assuming them. And they won't admit they are doing it. How did this unprecedented situation come about?

How We Got Here

In 1958 Oxford philosopher Elizabeth Anscombe wrote the highly influential essay "Modern Moral Philosophy."[27] In the past, she wrote, the "oughtness" of moral statements was grounded in the will of God or in some cosmic order. Because we thought we were created or at least were emanations of that spiritual order, we had a duty to honor it. But today we no longer want to base morality on God or universal moral absolutes.

Where, then, does the duty to live in a certain way come from now? Why should someone else have a duty to follow my moral feeling if he or she doesn't share it? Anscombe looked at the various secular proposals but finds them all wanting.[28]

Anscombe concluded, strikingly, that modern people should stop using the word "ought" altogether because there is now no way to justify it. When we use the word in a conversation with another we give the impression that there is a moral standard outside of us to which we both have a duty. But if you do not believe there is any such law or norm, then you really mean "I have a feeling that this is wrong and I want you to follow my feelings rather than yours."[29] That statement, of course, has far less power and authority than "you ought." However, Anscombe shows us, it is the only honest way to speak today. "The concepts of . . . *moral* obligation and *moral* duty," she writes, "and of what is *morally* right and wrong, and of the *moral* sense of 'ought,' ought to be jettisoned . . . because they are survivals, or derivatives from survivals, from an earlier conception of ethics which no longer generally survives, and are only harmful without it."[30]

Building on Anscombe's work, philosopher Alasdair MacIntyre discerned the historical process that brought us to the place today that she describes.[31] He observes that Greek philosophers in ancient times and Christian thinkers in the medieval age understood morals as guiding human beings toward an end state. "The whole point of ethics . . . is to enable man to pass from his present state to his true end."[32] This is the concept of *telos*. To describe humanity's *telos* is to answer the questions "What are we *for*?" and "What is our purpose?" Eighteenth-century Enlightenment thinkers, however, were committed to the belief that human reason and science, apart from ancient tradition or divine revelation, were sufficient to give us the knowledge we needed to understand our world and live rightly. To answer the question "What are humans *for*?" required some belief in God or divine creation or a spiritual cosmic order. And because that could not be confirmed by science or reason alone, the Enlightenment rejected "any notion of essential human nature" or of a *telos* for human beings.[33]

Modern thinkers therefore set out to determine some basis for morals and ethical rules without reference to any idea of a *telos* or purpose for the human race. Hume, Kant, Kierkegaard, and others sought to provide justification for objective moral claims. But they all failed, and this is why our society today is riven by polarized, irreconcilable, alternate universes of moral discourse, none of which can convince the others in the slightest.[34]

MacIntyre does not merely argue that the Enlightenment project of morality failed but that it *had* to fail. Why? Because a moral judgment about something can never be made apart from an examination of its given purpose.[35] To make his case MacIntyre uses the illustration of a pocket watch. If we complain that the watch "is grossly inaccurate and irregular in time-keeping" we are justified in concluding that "this is a bad watch."[36] Most people, however, would not say that a watch is bad if you throw it at the cat and it doesn't hit it.[37] Why? Because we know what a watch is made for—to tell time, not to hit cats or anything else. If the watch realizes its *telos*, it is good; if it fails to do so, it is bad. If, for the sake of argument, some people came upon a watch and had absolutely no idea of what it was or what it was made for, they would have no way to determine if it was good or bad.

All judgments that something or someone is good or bad do so based on an awareness of purpose. If you know what that purpose is, then your moral evaluation of something can be a factual statement, a truth that exists apart from your personal likes and dislikes. You may not like watches for some reason, but if it is a good one, you will have to acknowledge it to be so. If you know the purpose of a farmer is to get a crop out of a piece of land, but she does not get any yield at all, year after year, then you know she is a bad farmer, however much you may like her personally. If, however, you have no idea of the purpose of an object, then any description of it as "good" or "bad" is wholly subjective, completely based on inner preferences.

How, then, can we tell if a human being is good or bad? Only if we know our purpose, what human life is *for*. If you don't know the answer to that, then you can never determine "good" and "bad" human behavior. If, as in the secular view, we have not been made for a purpose, then it is futile to even try to talk about moral good and evil.[38]

We see, then, the great problem of morals within the secular point of view. Since we can't know anything about human purpose, all statements about some action being "good" or "bad" are subjective, never statements of fact. So there can be no arguing to a conclusion, only endless fighting.

Is There a Way Forward?

Many readers at this point might counter that things are not so bleak as I have painted them. They might argue that moral obligation does not create such insurmountable problems for the secular view as I have said. There are two ways that secular thinkers have made their case for this claim.

The first approach is to insist that moral obligation simply does not exist and that, despite the reluctance of most people to face this, there really is no right or wrong, good or evil. Though Gorski has said that few people want to hold this, Christian Smith discovered in his survey of young American adults that this is not so rare. Thirty percent, Smith found, are marked by "strong moral relativism," the claim that there are no definite rights and wrongs that are true for everyone.[39] One young woman was asked if there were any terrorist acts that she would say were "final," absolute wrongs. She answered that there were not. She said:

> *I don't know that people, like terrorists, what they do? It's not wrong to them . . . they're doing the thing that they think is the best thing they could possibly do and so they're doing good. I had this discussion with a friend recently and she's like, "But they're still murdering tons of people, that just has to be wrong." And I was like, "But do we have any idea if it is actually wrong to murder tons of people?" Like what does that even mean? So you*

could say that people who are terrorists . . . are born into cul-
tures where it is taught that it's all right and necessary and re-
ally important for them to kill a bunch of people.[40]

The most famous thinker who took this path was Nietzsche, who said that because there is no God there can be "no moral facts whatsoever."[41] He looks at Kant's categorical imperative, namely, that human beings must never be treated as means but as ends in themselves, and (rightly) denies that this is either self-evident or a logical conclusion. It is smuggling in a Christian view.[42] He likewise mocks utilitarianism, which holds that an action is moral if it brings "the greatest happiness for the greatest number." How can you inspire people to unselfish, loving behavior by appealing ultimately to selfish motives, that it will pay off for them?[43]

Nietzsche has contemporary allies in the belief that there are no moral facts and therefore ultimately no good or evil. J. L. Mackie, in his book *Ethics: Inventing Right and Wrong*, concludes that because science cannot prove the existence of objective moral facts, they don't exist, or at least we should not believe in them.[44]

So, this group of thinkers concludes, what is the problem with just saying there is no good or evil? Just say it and get on with life. Yet there really is a problem. Mackie ends up by recognizing the need for morality if society is to work. He also concedes that morality motivates only if we believe, wrongly, that objective moral facts exist, which he calls the "error theory of morality." His final conclusion is that people will function best if they don't believe that what Mackie teaches is true![45] It is hard, then, to see this as a viable worldview for people to adopt.

Responsible to Whom?

The second approach that secular thinkers take is to simply see moral obligation as a "brute fact." One evening after one of our church's meetings for skeptics, a man approached me and said, "I'm an atheist, but I'm no relativist—not at all. Murder, racism, exploiting the poor, lying and cheating, these are all wrong, anytime, anywhere, regardless of who is doing them." I asked him why, if there was no God, he thought that. "I see a tree and I know it's a tree. It's just there, and that doesn't prove there's a God. I see good and evil and I know them too. They are just there, and that doesn't prove there is a God."

This man was taking the path of a number of secular thinkers who agree that there is real moral obligation and that obligation cannot simply be the feelings instilled in us by evolution or culture to enable survival. Neither would create any true duty to do good and avoid evil. "There simply are," they say, "objective moral facts. Just as there are forests and mountains. Nevertheless, this doesn't prove that there is a God."

One well-known proponent of this view was the late Ronald Dworkin. In an essay Dworkin pressed readers to see that "we have a *responsibility* to live well and believe that living well means creating a life that is not simply pleasurable but good."[46] Dworkin rejected the idea that morality is relative or just a matter of practical self-interest. However, then he rightly asks, "You might ask, responsibility to whom?" He searches for an answer. "It is misleading to answer: responsibility to ourselves," he argues, because the people to whom responsibility is owed can release those who are responsible, but "we cannot release ourselves" from the obligation to live good, moral lives. But again, then, responsibility to whom? Dworkin finally answers that we are "charged" to live good lives "by the bare fact of our existence as self-conscious creatures."[47]

Dworkin's honest wrestling with the problem of morals is admirable, but ultimately it only deepens the mystery. He himself admits that duty or responsibility only makes sense within a personal relationship. That is why he asked not "Responsible to what?" but "Responsible to *whom*?" If there is no *one* with the right and authority to demand we live in a certain way, then how can there can be moral obligation? Yet there is. So maybe there is a Person, whom we are sensing in our heart of hearts, to whom we owe a moral life.

That is how I replied to the man who had approached me. I argued that with the tree he was sensing an object, but with the obligation to do good and not do evil he was sensing a relationship. "You perceive a responsibility not to do evil, but a responsibility to whom?" He responded that we are responsible to others or to ourselves, but I gave his Dworkin's refutation of those answers, which he said he would think about. I went on to say that obligations arise only in relation to persons, not to things. An absolute morality above our culture and biology implies an absolute Person behind all things. "You sensed the tree with your eyes, but I'd like you to consider that your moral intuition is sensing a relationship and responsibility to your Maker."

David Bentley Hart goes so far as to argue, "It is certainly not the case that one needs to believe in God in any explicit way in order to be good; but it is certainly *is* the case . . . that to seek the good is already to believe in God, whether one wishes to do so or not."[48]

The Moral Argument for God

We have been tracing out the lines of what has been called the "moral argument for the existence of God." Like all the classic arguments for God, this one has had many forms and versions.[49] However, its most basic form can be presented in two premises and a conclusion:

1. *If there are objectively binding moral obligations, then God exists.*

2. *There are objectively binding moral obligations.*

3. *Therefore, God exists.*[50]

Is this an inescapable, watertight proof of God's existence? No, it is not. Why? As we have seen, the second premise can be denied, as Mackie has, and the first premise can be denied, as Dworkin has. Yet we see the severe difficulties of both positions. In the end, why would we unavoidably sense not only the reality of an objective good and evil but also an abiding, overarching personal obligation to do one and turn from the other, when there is no Person to whom we are responsible?

Philosopher George Mavrodes says that the reality of moral obligation may not prove the existence of God, yet it is very strong evidence for it. He outlines three kinds of universes: the secular one; the Platonic universe, in which there is a supernatural realm of Ideas; and the traditional universe, with a morally good creator God. Then he asks, in which kind of world would we expect moral facts or obligations? The answer is that the secular universe would not lead us to expect them, while the Platonic or Christian world would. Now, in theoretical physics, if you hold a theory and you observe a new phenomenon that your theory would not lead you to expect, you don't say, "I don't care about the fact—I'm going to hold tight to my theory." No, you at least open your mind to the possibility that your theory is wrong and another theory is more true to reality.[51]

Mavrodes concludes that the secular thinkers should admit that if they believe in moral facts and obligation, these make much more sense in a world with God and a transcendent realm than in one without them.[52] They should consider that their theory of the world cannot account for one of the most indelible and central aspects of human life— morality—and therefore they should be open to the possibility that another theory of the world is more true to reality.[53]

Over the years it has probably been at this very point that many of my secular friends and conversation partners have felt some unease with their own point of view. Most of the skeptics whom I have seen move toward faith later told me that it was around this issue of moral obligation that they first began to wonder whether their views really fit the actual world they lived in.

One reason for the power of the moral argument is that it brings together both the rational and the personal evidence that we saw come together in the life of A. N. Wilson. If there is a God of goodness and truth, and we enter into a relationship with him, shouldn't this goodness and truth also manifest themselves in human life? Wilson insists that they do.

The Gospel would still be true even if no one believed it. The hopeful thing is that, where it is tried—where it is imperfectly and hesitantly followed—as it was in Northern Ireland [and South Africa] during the peace process[es], as it is in many a Salvation Army hostel this Christmas, as it flickers in countless unseen Christian lives, it works. And its palpable and remarkable power to transform human life takes us to the position of believing that something very wonderful indeed began with the birth of Christ into the world.[54]

Ten

A Justice That Does Not Create New Oppressors

I n one of the first years I was working as a minister in Manhattan, I was on a panel discussion at a local university. There I had a conversation with a prominent faculty member who told me that he was a secular man but that he held strongly to various humanistic values. "That's why I avoid churches," he added. I told him I didn't follow him. "There are only two kinds of churches," he said, "the legalistic and the relativistic. Both are bad news. I want open-mindedness but real, solid values. Can't get that combination in church." He told me some harrowing tales of his experience in some very narrow, abusive, doctrinaire churches, but then of his disgust with the "You can believe anything you like" denominations as well. "These churches are filled with people like me fleeing the legalists, but what they have created is nothing much more than a social club."

He was quite wrong that there is no alternative to these two kinds of churches. However, we must start by fully admitting and addressing the problem. There are indeed many of both kinds of congregations. For every one person I've met who turned away from faith because of reasoning and an apparent lack of evidence, there are many more who have left because of church people who are proud, self-righteous, and imperious. There is no excuse at all for this, and therefore Christians should be very quick to listen to these objections.

Secular people may have trouble getting a firm hold on the slippery concepts of morality and truth. But though religious people may have a strong grip on these things, they also often use them as bludgeons to intimidate and control those who share them and to condemn and punish those who do not. To think, "We are on the side of truth," can give people internal warrant to be abusive to those they believe have heretical opinions. Put another way, while secular people struggle with the problems that come with relativism, religious people wrestle with moralism.

If we ask the question "Is religion a force for justice and good in the world, or is it a force for injustice?" an enormous number of concrete, well-attested historical events and movements can be brought out to support *either* a negative or a positive answer to the question. One of the most obvious cases in point is the African slave trade and the abolition of slavery. Christians led the way to abolish slavery, for Christian motives and moral reasons. And yet the creators and defenders of the trade were also Christians, who had theologians and Bible scholars to support the practice with sacred proof texts.

Today we have plenty of attestation to abuses of women and children in many countries dominated by religion and also within religious institutions in our own Western societies. Yet sociological studies also reveal that in almost any city or community in the United States the amount of charitable giving, volunteer hours, and nonprofit service to needy groups generated by churches and religious bodies could never be replaced by government services without a massive increase in taxes. One study by a University of Pennsylvania professor selected eleven churches and one synagogue and showed that the average economic worth of each to its Philadelphia neighborhood was over $4 million a year.[1]

Also, shared religious faith and religious institutions create "social capital," the deeper associational trust that creates social and economic cooperation in neighborhoods and communities. Social capital lowers the cost of economic transactions and fosters social ties that lower crime rates, homelessness, and school dropout rates. Government policy and programs cannot create social capital.[2] In addition, students of community organizing among the poor testify to the need for religious institutions, and in particular churches. Grassroots organizing that confronts both unresponsive government and big business with the needs of marginalized groups relies heavily on the churches to do this.[3]

Nicholas Kristof, a columnist for the *New York Times,* wrote an article titled "A Little Respect for Dr. Foster" about an unknown evangelical Christian doctor who ran a rural hospital in Angola, where the child mortality rate was the highest in the world. He had raised his family in one of the most dangerous places possible. Kristof wrote:

> *Most evangelicals are not, of course, following such a harrowing path, and it's also true that there are plenty of secular doctors doing heroic work. . . . But I must say that a disproportionate share of the aid workers I've met in the wildest places over the years, long after anyone sensible had evacuated, have been evangelicals, nuns, or priests.*[4]

In the end, the relationship of religion to justice cannot be answered simply by adding up religious abuses and injustices on one side of the sheet against a list of religious benevolences and goods on the other. The goods may outnumber the abuses, even by far, but wrongdoings lodge more deeply in the memory and consciousness. In the end, it would be better to look for other grounds on which to explore the relationship between religious faith and justice.

Justice and Rights

We could begin by asking whether religion or secularism is a better support for human rights.

What are "human rights"? Philosopher Nicholas Wolterstorff says a human right is an obligation or claim that a person has on you when she enters your presence. She has the right not to be killed, tortured, defrauded, or abducted, and she may have other rights as well. And she has these rights not by virtue of being a particular race or gender, or being of a certain moral character, or being able to contribute to society and the economy. She has these rights simply by being a human being. Some may be far better human beings than others in various respects, but all are equally human and therefore share these rights equally.[5] This basic account of human rights is a belief of most Western, secular people, many of whom believe that religion is one of the great hindrances in the world to the pursuit of rights.

The question is, however, *why* do people have such rights? The United Nations' Universal Declaration of Human Rights does not answer the question but simply lists them.[6] Is that enough? Is it sufficient to say that "human rights simply exist, they are there, and we don't know why"? That is the secular approach, as the UN declaration attests. Most would say that human rights are simply obvious. But there are growing problems with that approach.

Michael Ignatieff, in *Human Rights as Politics and Idolatry*, shows that the advance of human rights in the world is under attack outside the West as just the latest form of Western imperialism, while on the inside of our culture it is losing confidence in its own theoretical foundations. Though the human-rights movement appears to be moving ahead, Ignatieff argues, it is actually in crisis.[7] Similarly, in his essay "Conditions of an Unforced Consensus on Human Rights" Charles Taylor explains the Western dilemma in the face of resistance from Asian and Middle Eastern nations. Taylor writes, "An obstacle in the path to . . . mutual understanding comes from the inability of many Westerners to see their culture as one among many."[8] Western secularists insist that their view of human rights is simply obvious to any rational person, but non-Western cultures respond that they are "far from self-evident."[9] This leaves human-rights activists quite vulnerable to charges of imperialism. If human rights and equality exist "just because we say so," then activists are not able to persuade, only to coerce. They can force cultures to adopt Western, individualistic ideas of rights and equality by using money, political power, or even military force. But, the charge goes, all this is just the latest stage in the West's inveterate bent to domination and colonialism. Western nations are now doing what they've always done, but disingenuously now, under the banner of "human rights."

Are we reduced to saying, "We smart and good people can see

them—why can't you?" Or is there some way to justify human rights? Some secular thinkers have tried to explain why human rights exist. Wolterstorff writes: "Almost all secular proposals concerning the ground of human rights . . . are what one might call *capacity accounts*. They hold that the worth that grounds human rights supervenes on a certain capacity that human beings have . . . either the capacity for rational agency in general, or some specific form of that capacity, such as . . . the capacity for acting on an apprehension of the good."[10] In other words, it is argued that human beings have rights because of their capacity for rational choice, or some other aptitude. The problems with this view are serious. For example, "newborn infants do not yet have the capacit[ies]" mentioned, nor do those in a coma, those mentally impaired in other ways, nor even many of the very elderly. So on the main secular theory defining and grounding human rights, the very young and old have none. Yet virtually all would agree that these persons without capacities still have the right "not to be shot and have their bodies tossed into a dumpster."[11]

But if we don't base human rights on capacities, what do we base them on? Wolterstorff, summarizing much recent historical scholarship, argues that individual human rights developed not for the first time in the Enlightenment but out of medieval Christendom, based on theological themes in the Bible.[12] In addition, he contends that there is no plausible or better alternative grounding for human rights than the original, religious basis. All this means that, in the long run, religious belief in God is a better support and grounding for human rights. Here is a comparison of two thinkers that illustrate Wolterstorff's point.

Two Case Studies

In the twentieth century there have been two well-known proponents of human rights and democracy, one an academic and one an activist.

The academic was Harvard philosopher John Rawls. He proposed a famous thought experiment. Imagine people coming together to decide the kind of society they want to create but doing so behind a "veil of ignorance." They don't know what race, age, level of intelligence or talent, gender, or education level they will be or occupy in this new society. So they should create the kind of society they would want to live in whatever place in society they would inhabit. Rawls believed that if people simply used reasonable self-interest, creating the kind of society they'd want if they knew they might be poor or in some other position weak in social power, then a society would develop that honored human rights.[13] And this would not require any moral values or religious beliefs, all of which should remain private.

But there are real problems with this approach. It is not true that you could complete this exercise and design a society using only some kind of neutral, objective reason. Each of us will also be deeply affected by our particular convictions about what a good human life is, what a good human being is, and what human life is *for*. For example, if you have a more individualistic view of human nature then, however poor you might be, you would want a society with all the emphasis on personal initiative and a free market, with no impediments to free enterprise. A different view of things might lead you to design a much greater role for government in help of the poor and the regulation of markets. Your preference for one or the other goes beyond rational self-interest to beliefs about human nature.

So even behind a "veil of ignorance" people will not choose the same kind of society because, as Harvard political philosopher Michael Sandel insists, all notions of justice are "inescapably judgmental." The idea that "we should not bring moral or religious convictions to bear on public discussions about justice" is frankly impossible. Sandel writes: "Whether we're arguing about financial bailouts . . . surrogate motherhood or same-sex marriage, affirmative action or . . . CEO pay . . . questions of justice are bound up with competing notions of honor and virtue, pride and recognition."[14] Alasdair MacIntyre's book *Whose Justice? Which Rationality?* has a title that summarizes Sandel's thesis. There is no simple, single way to reason or to understand justice. Our rationality and understanding of justice depend on our beliefs about right and wrong, the nature of virtue, the relationship of the individual to the group, and many other things.[15]

So Rawls's hopes of a new social unity based on keeping our religious and moral views private must be dashed. And, of course, they have been dashed. This approach has been used for a generation and has not worked. Our culture is split and fractured by warring factions with fundamentally different visions of justice and social good. The appeal to human rights strictly on the basis of "reasonable self-interest" is uncompelling.[16]

By contrast, Dr. Martin Luther King Jr. sought a just society on a considerably stronger footing. He argued that segregation was not simply impractical for the overall good of a society but that it was a sin. He knew that human rights have no power if they are simply created by a majority or imposed by judicial fiat. They have power only if they are really "there," existing on their own, dependent only on the fact that the wronged person before you making the claim against you is a human being. Drawing on the biblical teaching that every human being is created in the image of God (Genesis 1:26–27), he wrote that God's image in us gives every person

> *a uniqueness, it gives him worth, it gives him a dignity. And we must never forget this as a nation: there are no gradations in the image of God. Every man from a treble white to a bass black is significant on God's keyboard, precisely because every man is made in the image of God.*[17]

The Bible gives us the strongest possible foundation for the idea of human rights. Your neighbor comes into your presence with an inherent worth, an inviolable dignity (Genesis 9:6). Martin Luther King Jr. did not ask white America to make African Americans free to pursue rational self-interest, their own individual definitions of a fulfilling life. Rather, quoting Amos 5:24, he called them to not be satisfied until "justice rolls down like waters, and righteousness like a mighty stream."[18] The secular approach of Rawls pales before the Christian foundation for justice used by Dr. King.

The Oppression of Modernity

Though many people think that a commitment to rights is part of a secular view of things, the reality is that human rights have a troubled relationship both with phases of secularism, the first of which is called modernity, and the second often called postmodernism.

As we saw earlier, the leaders of the Frankfurt School, Max Horkheimer and Theodor Adorno, came to see how both capitalism and socialism, both Right and Left, could be oppressive. Both fascism and communism lost their moral bearings as they defined "the greater good" in such a way as to justify violence and used bureaucratic and scientific methods to do it efficiently. Each ideology found ways to make its respective social ideal so totalitarian as to exclude and exploit any opposed to it. This led to Adorno's "negative dialectic" against systems of thought that were "totalizing," that is, that claimed to be able to explain all of reality, to fix and improve all reality, and that crushed and marginalized all dissent to their account.[19]

This critique that grew out of the Frankfurt School became what is now called postmodernism and poststructuralism.[20] Philosopher Jean-François Lyotard famously defined postmodernism as "incredulity toward metanarratives."[21] A grand narrative or metanarrative is "a totalizing [as in totalitarian] theory that aims to subsume all events, all perspectives, and all forms of knowledge in a comprehensive explanation."[22] Lyotard was following on from Adorno in identifying these "grand theories" that tended not only to be utopian but also, in the name of their high, positive vision of their own power, to destroy all disagreement.

Lyotard would include Marxism in this group, with its belief in the inevitable triumph of the working class, and so postmodernism is not popular with many on the Left.[23] But he and those following him also opposed the claims of capitalism, of Adam Smith's "invisible hand" of the market. That metanarrative dictates that people can best be understood as rational actors and consumers, and that only free enterprise will inevitably lead human beings to the most rational and efficient allocation of all assets. The market, not government, is the way to bring about prosperity and peace in the world. A third metanarrative in this category is neo-Darwinism, which purports to be a comprehensive explanation of all of human behavior and history. Everything about us can be understood in terms of evolutionary biology and neuroscience. If Lyotard were alive, he would undoubtedly view the claims of Silicon Valley to also be a totalizing metanarrative—both its day-to-day claims to be "changing the world" to the predictions that technology will solve poverty, racism, disease, aging, and even overcome death.[24]

Postmodern thinkers argue that modern metanarratives are inherently authoritarian because they suppress difference. Dissent against any of them is seen not as merely a different point of view but rather as anti-rational or antisocial, a form of primitive barbarism. To oppose these modern grand narratives, postmodernism denied any universally true values, any ability of reason to penetrate and comprehend all of reality. Rulers use truth as a form of "social control."[25] So all claims of "truth" are now perceived as being a rhetorical move by those in power to marginalize and dominate those whose criticism might diminish their hold on power. In place of "truth" (a word that they always put within scare quotes) postmodernists promote a crowd of contradictory and contending "micronarratives." People can live within their own self-created narratives of life. In popular parlance, "what is true for me is not true for you." We should recognize a host of personal and social "truths" that are fine for individuals but do not necessarily fit into a coherent whole. Any attempt at all to reach consensus and peace in society was seen by Lyotard and his heirs as always oppressive to someone or some group.

The great irony is that postmodernism creates its own metanarrative. As Terry Eagleton has pointed out, postmodernism is just as prone to divide the world into a binary of "white hats"—those promoting plurality, multiple, local, changeable micronarratives—and "black hats"—those espousing universal values, absolutes, and metanarratives.[26] Postmodern advocates are just as "exclusive and censorious," just as quick to demonize and marginalize opposing points of view, as the orthodoxies it opposes.[27] The difference is that modern metanarratives silence and marginalize opposition by calling them antirational, whereas the postmodern metanarrative marginalizes opponents by insisting that anyone making a claim of universal value is sitting in the seat of the oppressor. Argument is silenced by the claim that all debate is a ruse of the privileged to keep their privilege.

This, of course, is just as totalitarian and stifling as the older modern metanarratives. In "sacrificing the notion of truth altogether," postmodernism ends up being just one more tool for the use of oppression. By "insisting that truth is a function of power and desire, they sail hair-raisingly close to what their rulers hold in practice."[28] In other words, if it is true that claims of truth are just ways to get power, then claims of there-is-no-truth-only-power are *also* nothing but ways to get power.

And ultimately this strategy against oppression must fail. If there is no truth, on what basis can the weak say to the strong that what they are doing is wrong? If there is no truth but only power, why shouldn't the strong merely hold on to their power and use it as they wish? One academic writes: "If 'truth' is an illusion employed by the powerful to subordinate the weak, will the weak be better off if the powerful were to accept that proposition and proceed to subordinate the weak by direct exercise of power?"[29]

The Failure of Postmodernism

All of this has led many to claim that postmodernism is now waning. In 2011 the Victoria and Albert Museum produced "the first comprehensive retrospective on postmodernism," titled "Postmodernism: Style and Subversion, 1970–1990." The museum was speaking mainly of postmodernism as a movement in the arts, but in an important article Edward Docx observed that the exhibit signaled that the philosophical movement of the deconstruction of all truth claims and master narratives had also begun to wane in its influence.[30]

Docx explains why it has faded in the arts. At first "the supremacy of western capitalism seemed best challenged by deploying the ironic tactics of postmodernism." But "because postmodernism attacks everything," there was no way to establish any aesthetic criteria—no one had the right to say that this art was good or this was bad. This meant that the only way to assess artworks was by the money they made. Ironically, "by removing all criteria, we are left with nothing but the market, the opposite of what postmodernism originally intended."[31]

He says that in the realms of philosophy and politics, the chilling effects of postmodernity have been similar. Because it attacks all claims and rejects any criteria for judging anything, "a mood of confusion and uncertainty began to grow and flourish until, in recent years, it became ubiquitous." The problem comes whenever we seek to establish a social movement or any program of justice. "If we de-privilege all positions, we can assert no position, we cannot therefore participate in society or the collective and so, in effect, an aggressive postmodernism becomes, in the real world, indistinguishable from an odd species of inert conservatism. Looked at in this way, it's easier to see why its power has been diminishing."[32] Richard Bauckham adds that "postmodern relativism offers no cogent resistance" to the narrative of fulfillment through "consumer lifestyle choices," which only shores up the market and capitalism, the very thing postmodernists originally wanted not to do.[33]

Perhaps it has been the recognition of postmodernism's cul-de-sac, as well as of the totalizing tendencies of modern science and rationality, that has led to the surprising recent move of many traditionally secular intellectuals on the left to admit the importance of religion for doing justice in the world. Philosopher Simon Critchley, who is not a religious believer, has written a book titled *The Faith of the Faithless*.[34] In it he asks, "Is politics conceivable without religion?" and he answers yes, because there are many secular political theories, including Rawls's.

However, then he asks, "Is politics *practicable* without religion . . . without any appeal to transcendence? . . . Can a political collectivity maintain itself . . . its unity and identity, without a moment of the sacred, without religion, rituals, and something we can only call *belief*?" He answers, "I do not think so."[35] He adds that he has "come to this conclusion with no particular joy." Nevertheless, Critchley doubts that the sacrifices necessary to create a just society will be borne unless many people believe in and feel "the overwhelming, infinite demand" of love, "the sort of demand that Christ made in the Sermon on the Mount when he said, 'Love your enemies, bless them that curse you, do good to them that hate you, and pray for them which despitefully use you, and persecute you'" (Matt. 5:44).[36] The command to love everyone sacrificially, even your enemies, is not ultimately practical. It can't be attained in this life. It is not the kind of demand that self-interested rationality could produce. Critchley says to feel this "infinite ethical demand" requires faith in a transcendent dimension to the universe. He doubts that any significant-size movement toward justice in a society can happen unless many people have this faith and experience this demand.[37]

A Nonoppressive Absolute

We have seen the difficulties that the secular view of things has, not only accounting for moral value and human rights, but also motivating people to honor them and live by them consistently. The problems are severe enough that many secularist authors and thinkers see religion as a necessity in any move toward more just societies. But doesn't Christianity have its own problems with justice? In particular, isn't Christianity itself a "totalizing metanarrative"? Doesn't it purport to hold the true, universal values, and hasn't that truth been used to marginalize and demonize all difference and dissent as heresy?

The answer, of course, is "Yes, but not so fast." What our survey has shown us is that the denial of universal moral truth, characterized by both modernity and postmodernism, has not necessarily led to peace and freedom but to new forms of domination and marginalization. Without any belief in objective moral facts, there is no way to build a program of justice. And yet it is also true that many religions, with their absolute claims, have abused and oppressed people. What is the way forward?

Richard Bauckham of the University of St Andrews writes: "We need a story that once again affirms universal values while resisting their co-option by the forces of domination."[38] In short, we need a "nontotalizing metanarrative," a nonoppressive absolute. As we have seen, we can't work for justice without some acknowledgment of universal moral values. The modern and postmodern dissolution of moral norms has not brought the liberation and peace we have sought. So we need universal values, but we also need something that undermines the natural, powerful human inclination to dominate others.

Bauckham believes what we need lies within the pages of the Bible. He doesn't deny that "the Christian story has been . . . at least equally compromised by oppressive distortions." Nevertheless, he argues that it is possible to do a "retrieval of aspects of the biblical story that resist . . . [such] ideological distortions."[39] What are those aspects of the Christian faith that can provide a ground for doing justice yet at the same time prevent us from becoming oppressors ourselves?

First, metanarratives try to explain all reality, which can lead to the hubris that sees all opponents and dissidents as antirational or dangerously deluded. But the biblical story, while giving us many fundamental insights about human nature and purpose, nevertheless leaves much "intractable to comprehension." Psalms such as Psalm 88 give us prayers by suffering believers that sometimes end in darkness without clear resolution or answers. Job's friends smugly think they have the ways of God so figured out that they know sufferers are always being punished for some sin. This simplistic view leads them to divide the world into the good people and the bad people and to explain away "the real intractability of the evils of history." Their dogmatism leads them to condemn and dismiss people who don't agree with them. However, at the end of the book of Job, they are condemned by God. God alone has the full perspective on things. We see only in part.

So the biblical story is not the kind of neat, "comprehensive explanation of reality" that leads believers to the proud position that they have all the answers.[40]

Second, metanarratives offer the prospect of solving all the world's problems. And indeed, unlike postmodernism, the Christian story gives hope for the righting of wrongs and the redemption of all things through God's saving action in Jesus Christ. But unlike modernity, Christianity does not teach that this is a redemption human beings can bring about. This future redemption is "not in terms of [human] reason or human mastery, but in terms of the freedom and purpose of God."[41] Modern narratives—the stories of literature and stage and screen—are mainly about "human achievement," how people "can surmount disaster and achieve their freely chosen goals." This fits into the modern metanarrative that we create our own meanings and morals and, with reason and science, can solve the world's problems. Thus the temptation to domination. The biblical stories, by contrast, do not lead us to think in this way. Characters face forces both good and evil beyond their control. They win through faith and the help of supernatural grace. "Their world is more mysterious than comprehensible, and they do not expect to master it."[42]

For a Christian, then, redemption cannot be a utopian hope in inevitable progress or in human ingenuity, but only in God, and in God's time.

A Story of Reversal

Finally, metanarratives through their claims of truth can lead to domination, but the biblical plotline reveals "a story of God's repeated choice of the dominated and the wretched, the powerless and the marginal."[43]

The Bible begins with the book of Genesis, written when primogeniture—the passing of all the family's wealth and estate to the eldest son—was the iron law in virtually all societies. Yet the entirety of Genesis is subversive of this cultural norm.[44] God constantly chooses and works through the second sons, the ones without social power. He chooses Abel rather than Cain, Isaac rather than Ishmael, Jacob rather than Esau, Joseph rather than Reuben. And when he works with women, he does not choose women with the cultural power of beauty and sexuality. He does his saving work through old, infertile Sarah, not young Hagar, through unloved and unattractive Leah, not lovely Rachel. God repeatedly refuses to allow his gracious activity to run along the expected lines of worldly influence and privilege. He puts in the center the person whom the world would put on the periphery. Biblical scholar Walter Brueggemann comments on the place in Genesis 25 where God prophesies through an oracle that he will be working with the younger of two sons, Jacob rather than Esau. He explains that the lesson of Genesis is that "the oracle is against all conventional wisdom."

> *The Israelites must have wondered about this patriarch who was always in trouble. . . . This God does not align himself only with the obviously valued ones, the first-born. This oracle speaks about an inversion. It affirms that we are not fated to the way the world is presently organized.*
>
> *That is the premise of the ministry of Jesus: the poor, the mourning, the meek, the hungry . . . are the heirs to the kingdom (Matt. 5:3–7).*[45]

As the Bible's story line proceeds, we see God standing beside Israel in slavery against the oppression of the greatest empire in the world. Proceed to the story of Judges—the deliverers and leaders who one after the other led Israel whenever it fell under the domination of more powerful nations. But readers have pointed out how often the man God raises up—Jephthah, Gideon, Samson—is someone from a smaller tribe, a low-status family, or even the class of social outcasts. David the king is the youngest and smallest of Jesse's sons (1 Samuel 16). Then in the New Testament, when Jesus Christ encounters a respected male and a socially marginal woman (John 3 and 4) or a religious leader and a tax collector (Luke 18) or a religious teacher and a fallen woman (Luke 7), it is always the moral, racial, sexual outsider and socially marginalized person who connects to Jesus most readily.

Along with this narrative of the reversal of the weak and the strong, the poor and the rich, there is a wide and deep river of ethical teaching and appeal to all believers to live justly and be agents of social justice in the world. The Old Testament prophets insist that a lack of care for the poor and needy is a sign of a lack of genuine faith in God (Isaiah 1:17; 58:6–7). The New Testament likewise teaches that a practical love for the poor is a mark of a heart changed by grace (James 2:14–17; 1 John 3: 17–18). God "raises the poor from the dust and lifts the needy from the ash heap; he seats them with princes. . . . He settles the childless woman in her home as a happy mother of children" (Psalm 113:7–9), but "the proud he knoweth afar off" (Psalm 138:6, cf. James 4:6).[46]

The reason for this persistent story line in the Bible is not simply because the writers like underdogs. It is because the ultimate example of God's working in the world was Jesus Christ, the only founder of a major religion who died in disgrace, not surrounded by all of his loving disciples but abandoned by everybody whom he cared about, including his Father. He was the victim of a miscarriage of justice and he died oppressed and helpless. Jesus Christ's salvation comes to us through his poverty, rejection, and weakness. And Christians are not saved by summoning up their strength and accomplishing great deeds but by admitting their weakness and need for a savior.

Most metanarratives say: "Here's how to win through. Pull yourself together, master yourself. Master the situation. Be strong. You can do it." But Jesus says, essentially, "You can't do it. You must rely on me." "Except ye be converted, and become as little children, ye cannot enter the kingdom of heaven" (Matthew 18:3, King James Version). A salvation earned by good works and moral effort would favor the more able, competent, accomplished, and privileged. But salvation by sheer grace favors the failed, the outsiders, the weak, because it goes only to those who know salvation *must* be by sheer grace. In token of this, Jesus comes not as a wealthy and powerful person but as a poor man, the child of an unwed mother.

Thus the Bible does not show us story after story of "heroes of the faith" who go from strength to strength. Instead we get a series of narratives containing figures who are usually not the people the world would expect to be spiritual paragons and leaders. The Bible is not primarily a series of stories with a moral, though there are plenty of practical lessons. Rather, it is a record of God's intervening grace in the lives of people who don't seek it, who don't deserve it, who continually resist it, and who don't appreciate it after they have been saved by it.

If all this surprises you, it may mean that you have bought into a completely mistaken idea, namely that Christianity is about how those who live moral and good lives and consequently are taken to heaven. Rather, one of the main themes of the biblical story and stories is that even some of the ablest human beings who have ever lived, such as Abraham and David, could not rise above the brutality of their own cultures nor the self-centeredness of their own hearts. But by clinging to the wondrous promise that God's grace is given to moral failures, they triumphed.

A Story That Breaks the Cycle

The biblical story shows us a God who loves the downtrodden, but it does more than that. In a penetrating insight, Bauckham writes that belief in the story of salvation "also breaks the cycle by which the oppressed become oppressors in their turn."[47] In the Old Testament the Israelites are constantly warned not to oppress immigrants and racial outsiders "because you were foreigners in Egypt" (Leviticus 19:33–34). The memory of their salvation from slavery not by their own power but by God's grace was to radically undermine their natural human inclination to domination. But, Bauckham writes, "the cross is the event in which the cycle [of the oppressed becoming oppressor] is definitively broken."[48]

In Proverbs 14:31 we see that God identifies with the poor. If you oppress the poor, you "show contempt for their Maker," and if you give to the needy, you "honor God." But it is only in Jesus that we see how radically and literally God identified with the poor and oppressed. He was born to a poor family; he lived among the marginalized and outcast.

His trial was a miscarriage of justice. He died violently, naked and penniless. And so the Son of God himself knew what it was like to be a victim of injustice, to stand up to a corrupt system and be killed by it. And, Christians believe, he did this to make atonement for our sins, to free us from their penalty. Christians know, then, that, in the eyes of God, we were spiritually poor and powerless—we too were aliens and slaves, but God saved us by becoming oppressed for us.

Yes, of course, believing in universal moral truths can be used to oppress others. But what if that absolute truth is a man who died for his enemies, who did not respond in violence with violence but forgave them? How could that story, if it is the center of your life, lead you to take up power and dominate others? Remarkably, then, we can conclude that a professed Christian who is not committed to a life of generosity and justice toward the poor and marginalized is, at the very least, a living contradiction of the Gospel of Christ, the Son of God, whose Father "executes justice for the oppressed, who gives food to the hungry" (Psalm 146:7). Bauckham says, "Distortion of the biblical story into an ideology of oppression has to suppress the biblical meaning of the cross." All of these characteristics of the biblical story make it "uniquely unsuited to being an instrument of oppression."[49]

The cross breaks the cycle of oppression in one more way. People who are passionate for justice often become self-righteous and cruel when they confront persons whom they perceive as being oppressors. However, believers in Christ are taught to confess that they have wronged God by wronging others who are made in his image. We have not loved and honored our neighbors as we wished to be treated. In other words, every Christian who understands the Gospel admits that he or she has been an oppressor. When we lie, we deprive people of the truth they have a right to. When we break our promises, we deprive people of goods they have a right to. And if we are not poor and we close our hearts to those who are, we deprive them of sustenance they have a right to. Christians know they have the hearts of oppressors, yet have been saved by grace nonetheless. Therefore, even when they confront an oppressor, they may do it with steely and courageous determination, but the gospel teaches to do so also without self-righteousness or bullying. They cannot hate haters, or justify oppressing people they think are oppressors.

The Gospel of Jesus Christ provides a nonoppressive absolute truth, one that provides a norm outside us as a way to escape the ineffectiveness of relativism and of selfish individualism, yet one that cannot truly be used to oppress others. Terry Eagleton believes that "if religious faith were to be released from the burden of furnishing social orders with a set of rationales for their existence, it might be free to rediscover its true purpose as a critique of all such politics." He believes that "what it adds to common morality is not some supernatural support, but the grossly inconvenient news that our forms of life must undergo radical dissolution if they are to be reborn as just and compassionate communities. The sign of that dissolution is solidarity with the poor and powerless. It is here that a new configuration of faith, culture, and politics might be born."[50]

PART THREE

Christianity Makes Sense

Eleven

Is It Reasonable to Believe in God?

I began this volume assuming that my readers favored a more secular point of view than a religious one. If that is your position, you might think that religion is in long-term decline because fewer and fewer people will see or feel the need for it. You also might think that religion is purely a matter of faith rather than reason, that secularity is the more rational and scientific view of things, and that the burden of proof is on believers to prove God exists. In the first two chapters I took aim at these views and argued that they range from being major oversimplifications to grave mistakes.

Comparing Views of the World

We saw that it is not true that religion is declining or that it must decline inevitably within a modern society. I argued that all varieties of secularism are sets of beliefs, not simply the absence of faith. Indeed, to say "You must prove God to me" is to choose and believe in a form of rationality that most philosophers today consider naive. Neither religion nor secularity can be demonstrably proven—they are systems of thinking and believing that need to be compared and contrasted to one another in order to determine which makes the most sense. That is, which makes the most sense of our experience, of things we know and need to explain? Which one makes the most sense of our social experience and addresses the problems we face in living together? And which of these is the most logically consistent? In short, we need to ask which of these views of reality makes the most sense emotionally, culturally, and rationally.

I could not in this book compare all the major contemporary traditions or worldviews—for example, we barely discussed Hinduism, Buddhism, or Islam. But we did do an examined comparison of Christianity and Western secularism. We did this by looking at six givens to human life, things we cannot live without. They were meaning, satisfaction, freedom, identity, hope, and justice. In each case there are competing narratives—there is both a secular and a Christian way to understand and address the needs. I argued that in each case the secular narratives, while often partially right, are not self-evident and are attended by a host of difficulties. I then outlined Christianity's penetrating analysis and explanation of our life experience in each area. Finally, in each chapter, I looked at Christianity's unsurpassed offers—a meaning that suffering cannot remove, a satisfaction not based on circumstances, a freedom that does not hurt but rather enhances love, an identity that does not crush you or exclude others, a moral compass that does not turn you into an oppressor, and a hope that can face anything, even death.

During all these chapters I have been making the case that Christianity makes the most emotional and cultural sense. Now we are in a position to survey the rational case for belief in God and Christianity. The crucial word here is "survey." There are many other books that provide excellent, detailed, substantial evidence and arguments for the Christian faith. The volume you are reading was written to bring secular readers to a place where they might find it even sensible and desirable to explore the extensive foundations for the truth of the Christianity.

So in this chapter I will give a thirty-thousand-foot view of the case that it is rationally warranted to believe that God exists. It will outline the basic case and serve as an introduction to other books and reading that will give fuller reasoning than I can provide here.

Why Believe in God?

Traditionally it has been expected that believers should provide nonbelievers with proof of the existence of God. After all, we would not believe in beings like the yeti (the abominable snowman) or the Loch Ness monster unless there were proof of their existence. So the burden of proof, it is thought, is on the believer in God. However, these creatures are beings in the world while the Bible—and also other religions—do not understand God as a being within the material universe. They understand God rather as Being itself, the ground and condition for all other things to exist. All things that have being depend on God moment by moment for it. Without God nothing would exist at all. Those who do not believe in God, by contrast, think that material objects exist "on their own."[1]

Philosopher C. Stephen Evans writes that therefore determining the existence of God is not like determining the existence of any being inside the material world: "To believe in God is to believe the universe has a certain character; to disbelieve in God is to believe the universe . . . has a very different character."[2] So believers in God have argued that God's existence cannot be proven empirically, as if he were a physical object.

Instead, many religious philosophers have argued that God's existence can be inferred logically. Many scientific theories, especially those in physics, are established this way.[3] Theory X is more reasonable than theory Y if it explains the data (what we see) better than theory Y. This, of course, is not final proof of the kind that can be concluded in a laboratory. But most of our theories about waves and particles, about light and molecules, are established like this. In a similar way, the arguments for God contend that belief in God makes more rational sense of the world than nonbelief because it accounts for the data—what we see and know about the world.

The arguments for God's existence are many, but I will present only six here. We could call them the arguments for God from existence, from fine-tuning, from moral realism, from consciousness, from reason, and from beauty.

Cosmic Wonder

One way to argue for the existence of God is to infer his existence from existence itself.

Nothing cannot produce something. Everything must come from

something that already has being. This means that there must be some unique being that exists without a cause, that did not spring out of nothing, that is its own cause and the source of everything else. That one being who is Being itself is God. Again, because all natural beings have a cause, there must be some supernatural entity that exists without a cause, from which all has come.

There are two responses to this argument. One is to say there was no first cause, only an "infinite regress" of causes. But science knows of no chain of events without a beginning, so how could such a chain have gotten started? The other common response is to say, "If everything must have a cause, what caused God?" and then to argue that matter has just always existed.

But both these rejoinders, while trying to deny the need for God, ironically still require belief in the supernatural. If there is no God, then either original matter sprang from nothing, or original matter has always existed without a cause, or there is an infinite regress of causes without a beginning. Each of these answers takes us out of the realm of science and the universe we know. They are nothing short of miracles, for science knows nothing of beings or physical processes that spring out of nothing or that have no beginning. Ironically, then, there is an agreement that modern science is completely insufficient to explain the existence of the world. Whatever brought it about must have been something extranatural or supernatural. So even those who think they are denying this argument for a supernatural divinity are still supporting it. This material world cannot be all there is to the universe.[4]

Is this a conclusive proof of God? No, because it doesn't prove that the personal, holy, almighty God of the Bible exists. But it is a strong case that there is something beyond the natural world that brought it into existence and which even now upholds its existence.

Perhaps your eyes glaze over a bit at the logical syllogisms of the past few paragraphs. The very existence of the cosmos, however, might provide evidence to your senses more directly. As we have seen, Albert Camus believed there was no God and that the universe had no meaning or explanation. Nevertheless, Camus felt that it was absurd that it is so, that it *ought* to make sense and have a purpose. Some thinkers have pointed out Camus's inconsistency. But it may be that Camus was simply perceiving the universe to be too mysterious and wondrous to simply exist on its own. For many, the astonishing universe is evidence pointing beyond itself to Something. Many people also find this cosmic wonder to be a compelling sign of God's reality.[5]

Perceived Design

Another argument for God has to do with the apparent fine-tuning and design of the world. Recently many Christian thinkers have pointed to the constants of physics. The speed of light, the gravitational constant, the strength of the strong and weak nuclear forces—must all have almost exactly the values that they do have in order for organic life to exist. You can think of these as a set of dials, all of which must be set just where they are set. In terms of probability, the chances that all of the dials would be tuned to life-permitting settings all at once are about 10^{-100}. Of all the possible arrangements of settings, there was only one in billions of trillions that could have produced life on the planet.

The implications of this can be drawn out with an illustration. Imagine that a man is going before a firing squad. Ten crack marksmen fire at the doomed prisoner, who is only ten feet away. Every one of them misses. Could that have happened by accident? Yes, it is possible that every one of the ten sneezed or coughed or was drunk that morning and so on and all of them missed. But it would be more reasonable to conclude that it was some conspiracy, something intended and designed by someone.

So, believers in God argue, as long as you don't beg the question and assume that God could not possibly exist, then the fine-tuning of physics makes much more sense in a universe in which there is a creator and designer. It is improbable that all the physical constants just happened to be perfectly tuned for life on their own. It would be more reasonable to conclude it was something intended and designed.[6]

Is this a conclusive proof? No, because its argument is only that it is more likely that there is a God than that there is not. Yet the argument does have real force. Many atheists feel required to engage it, most often by proposing the "multiverse thesis," namely that there are an infinite number of different universes, so it is inevitable that some or one would be tuned for life. But MIT professor Alan P. Lightman, in *Harper's Magazine*, writes of "science's crisis of faith." He says that the fine-tuning argument is strong enough that scientists put forth the multiverse thesis even though there is neither a shred of evidence for it nor any way to test it.[7] In other words, either you have to take a great step of faith to believe there is a God who designed the universe or you must take a great step of faith to believe there is not. That's a testimony to the strength of the argument.

As we saw just above, the perceived order and design of the world can work directly on people's intuitions apart from a detailed series of logical propositions. The distinguished physician Lewis Thomas wrote: "I cannot make peace with the randomness doctrine: I cannot abide the notion of purposelessness and blind chance in nature. And yet I do not know what to put in its place for the quieting of my mind." C. Stephen Evans says that Thomas is a man who felt "the pull of the sign" of perceived design.[8] Evans also points out that the great philosopher Immanuel Kant, while concluding that the design argument did not constitute a rigorous proof for God, nonetheless spoke often and movingly about "the splendid order, beauty, and providence shown everywhere in nature," which, he believed, led naturally to "faith in a wise and great author of the world."[9]

Moral Realism

A third traditional case for God has been called the moral argument.[10] Some have called this the strongest of them all.[11] Since I have given ample space to this way of reasoning in chapter 9, I will only summarize it here. Most people think that not only moral feelings but also moral obligation exists. God is not necessary to explain the fact of moral feelings. But we also believe that some things are wrong for people to do, regardless of their feelings. We say to others, "You are obligated *not* to do that deed, even if you personally feel it is all right to do." What could possibly be the basis of such obligation? If there is no God, moral obligation appears to be an illusion caused by either our evolutionary biology or our culture. Most people won't grant the illusory nature of all moral values, however, and will insist that some things are absolutely wrong to do. Moral obligation, then, makes more sense in a universe created by a personal God to whom we intuitively feel responsible than it does in an impersonal universe with no God.

Another variation on the moral argument is the question of human rights. Why believe that every human being has an equal right to life and liberty? One secular answer is that we legally create rights because we have come to see that society works best that way. But if we create rights, then they can be removed by majority vote. Most Western secularists would respond that rights cannot be removed, that they are "there" whether or not an oppressive government recognizes them in law. But if we don't create them, where do they come from? If someone responds that they are not created but are somehow natural and inherent, the answer is that nature is not like that, it is "red in tooth and claw." We evolved through the strong overcoming the weak, so there is nothing natural about the idea of human rights. So again, why would rights exist? Historians tell us that the idea of rights grew out of societies that believed in the God of the Bible. That is not a proof of the existence of God. Nevertheless, human rights make more sense in a universe created by God. Without God, it is difficult to explain why or how they exist.

The moral argument also does not prove the existence of a personal God. Yet it points powerfully toward something beyond this world. A consistent materialist, who believes in nothing beyond natural, scientifically verifiable causes, struggles mightily to account for the moral obligation and human rights in which she cannot but believe. As Thomas Nagel writes:

> *I remained convinced that pain is really bad, and not just something we hate, and that pleasure is really good, and not just something we like. . . . I suspect the same is true for most people. . . .*

On the Darwinian account, this must be regarded as an illusion—
perhaps an illusion of objectivity that is itself the product of natural
selection because of its contribution to reproductive fitness.[12]

Nagel concludes that despite "the scientific credentials of Darwinism," it is "not enough to dislodge the immediate conviction that objectivity is not an illusion with respect to basic judgments of values."[13]

And here we see the force of the moral argument. If you cannot accept that objective, moral absolutes and obligation are illusions, then you, like Nagel, will have to concede that there must be *something* beyond this physical, material world that accounts for them, even if you cannot be sure what it is.

Consciousness

There are three other arguments for the existence of God that have often been presented. One has to do with human consciousness. Nagel believes that human "consciousness is the most conspicuous obstacle to a comprehensive naturalism that relies only on the resources of physical science" to explain reality.[14] Why?

In Nagel's famous article "What Is It Like to Be a Bat?" he says that a being has conscious mental states if there is something it is like to *be* that being, *for* that being.[15] David Bentley Hart provides a list of the features of consciousness that are remarkable and difficult to account for using purely biological explanations. He begins with the "qualia" that Nagel describes, namely, that all human experience has a subjective quality to it. I am not only aware of the red rose but also aware of my awareness of it, of what the rose is like to me (but is not, for example, to my wife). Another mark of consciousness involves the ability to draw abstractions and inferences about particular objects and events. These abstractions can go to many levels of complexity far beyond just the physical similarities that our physical senses may perceive between objects. Philosophers of mind also note that we can relate our past and present to each other and envision a future that is not simply like the past. And we are capable of perceiving deep mathematical structures in the world and doing complex mathematical operations as well.[16]

How do we explain all these aspects of idea making and self-consciousness? Secular thinkers must try to account for all these mental states first as the product of only neural events within our brains and second as something that developed only because, in human evolution, it enhanced the reproductive fitness of our ancestors. However, it is very hard to explain how the ability to do complex mathematics and abstract philosophy was a capacity that helped our ancestors survive.[17] Steven Pinker, a convinced materialist, has been forced by these arguments to agree. He is not sure why these capacities developed.[18] He opines that perhaps the ability to reflect on one's self and most of the other features of consciousness are excessive, unnecessary, chance products of other capabilities that we actually did find useful in earlier periods of our evolution.

But even if one accepts this somewhat tortured explanation, no one can account scientifically for the link between brain events and thoughts. Though we know that chemical processes in the brain are involved in thoughts, that does not prove that they are fully created by them. Nor has anyone shown *how* electrochemical events could produce what we call thoughts. So consciousness can't be explained simply as a means to reproductive fitness, nor can anyone explain how neurochemistry produces subjective experience. Many scientists insist, however, that it is only a matter of time before we understand it all.

However, to insist that there *must* be an evolutionary and scientific explanation is to assume that there *can't* be any nonmaterial or transcendent reality. As we have seen, that is a philosophical assumption, not a scientific hypothesis. As it stands now, human consciousness points to something beyond the natural world.

There is an additional problem with the effort to account for all consciousness with neurochemistry. Just as it is impossible for most people to accept that moral obligation is an illusion caused by our genes, so it is difficult for most people to believe that our ideas, hopes, and loves are nothing but chemical reactions. Francis Crick, a leading molecular biologist and neuroscientist, famously wrote: "You, your joys and your sorrows, your memories and ambitions, your sense of personal identity and free will, are in fact no more than the behavior of a vast assembly of nerve cells and their associated molecules."[19] If there is no God or spiritual dimension, that is pretty much the logical conclusion.

So—is what one senses about our feelings of love really and merely our genes' way to get us to pass on our genetic code? Is the air of significance surrounding it every bit as much of an illusion as is the sense of moral obligation? Strict, consistent materialists like Pinker and Jerry Coyne say yes. But most people, including atheists like Nagel, will not grant that our ideals, loves, and profoundest insights can be reduced to electrochemical processes. David Skeel writes that there is "something deeply unsatisfying about the claim that idea-making has no real meaning," that it is essentially an unnecessary by-product of more important mental abilities.[20]

If you, the reader, also believe that your self-consciousness, free choice, love, and ability to reflect on reality are central to what it means to be human, and if you believe that your sense of the significance of love is not an illusion produced by your genes, then you should be very reluctant to accept that this material reality is all there is. Consciousness and idea making make far more sense in a universe created by an idea-making, conscious God.[21]

Reason and Beauty

Over the last two generations there has developed an argument for the existence of God now called "the argument from reason." Its main proponent has been the philosopher Alvin Plantinga.[22]

The case begins by examining the assumption that our reasoning abilities are the product of natural selection. As philosopher Patricia Churchland has said, "Boiled down to essentials . . . the principal chore of a nervous system is to get the body parts where they should be in order that the organism may survive. . . . Truth, whatever that is, definitely takes the hindmost."[23] Her point is that our brains have evolved only to enable us to survive, and many creatures do this very well without any reasoning capacity at all. So our brain's ability to reason evolved not to provide true beliefs about reality but only to tell us what we needed to "feed, flee, fight, and reproduce."

Of course, we may feel and believe that our rational capacities work to tell us truth about reality, but we must remember that, according to evolutionary naturalism, our genes also lead us to feel that there are objective, moral obligations and that love and idea making are highly significant. In fact, evolutionary psychologists argue that the persistence of religious belief in human beings—faith in God and a supernatural—is also something that developed in us because it helped our ancestors survive. Most people in the human race perceive the existence of God but, according to materialistic naturalism, that perception is an illusion given to us by our genes to help us reproduce.

This, then, leads us to a question. If we can't trust our moral and religious sensibilities to tell us truth—if evolution has given us those illusions simply to help us adapt to our environment—then why should we trust our reasoning capacities to tell us truth? It is not really fair to apply the knife of evolutionary skepticism to our morality and religion and not use it on our reason.

But this, of course, would be devastating to the whole materialist view of things, which is based on the conviction that we can understand reality through our reason. Nagel writes, "Evolutionary naturalism provides an account of our capacities that undermines their reliability and in doing so undermines itself."[24] If we can't trust the minds that gave us the theory of naturalism, then naturalism undermines itself.

Finally, perhaps the least logically rigorous but most personally attractive argument for God is the argument from beauty, which we touched upon briefly in chapter 1. All of us experience some forms of art and some ideas as profoundly, movingly beautiful. "Beauty has a physical effect on us that ideas alone ordinarily do not, an admixture of longing and a sense that beauty is not as enduring as it should be." David Skeel says that this indelible sense that beauty is real, and that it reflects the universe as it *ought* to be but in large part is not, is "the paradox of beauty."[25]

As I have noted above, a common scientific explanation of the human desire for beauty is that our ancestors came to recognize certain landscapes as beautiful because it alerted them to the prospect of food.[26] But this does not explain how, for example, we came to find certain landscapes, such as an uninhabitable desert, beautiful. Other thinkers, such as Denis Dutton in *The Art Instinct*, argue that our sense of beauty had its origins in the need to display ourselves in order to attract mates or to recognize health and fertility in others. But "being stirred or excited by broad shoulders, shapely hips . . . and so forth is not the same thing as being moved or fascinated by a particular alignment of hues, or a haunting refrain, or a happy poetic image." None of these things appear to have anything remotely to do with reproductive fitness.[27]

On the contrary, as David Bentley Hart writes, when we find something intensely beautiful, it is seldom because of its utility. In fact, to find something useful is to see it as a means to an end, but to find something beautiful is different. It is marked by "utter gratuity." It is deeply satisfying immediately, in itself, not for anything it does for us. "The beautiful presents itself to us as an entirely unwarranted, unnecessary, and yet marvelously fitting gift."[28] Whatever the beautiful is, Hart writes, it cannot be identified with or reduced to "symmetry or consonance or ordonnance or brightness," because we may find any of these things "anodyne or vacuous." Beauty is something "mysterious, prodigal, often unanticipated, even capricious." We may find ourselves ambushed by some "strange and indefinable glory" in a barren field or storm-wracked forest.[29]

In the end, the argument from beauty works much like those concerning moral facts and consciousness. Evolutionary naturalism does not appear to have plausible explanations for why and how our aesthetic sense works. It also tells us that the air of significance around beauty is an illusion, and most people would not accept this reductive account of the experiences that have given such meaning to our lives.

Christianity explains the "beauty paradox" as our recognition that the world around us is good but it has been corrupted. The ugliness isn't inherent, and in fact it doesn't belong to it original design.[30] Rather, the glory we see in the world reflects the beauty of its creator as the moon reflects the light of the sun (Psalm 19:1–6).

Luc Ferry does a good job of summarizing the moral, consciousness, reason, and beauty arguments against the secular, naturalistic view of things. He writes that his experiences of "truth, beauty, justice, and love . . . whatever the materialists say, remain fundamentally transcendent." By that he means, "I cannot invent mathematical truths, nor the beauty of a work of art, nor the imperatives of the moral life. . . . [They] impose themselves on me as if they come from elsewhere." He adds, "I am not at all persuaded by the argument that I merely *choose* ethical values."[31] These things are signs that impress themselves on our minds and hearts and point us toward God.

Why Not Reconsider Your Premise?

All these arguments and signs that we have been reviewing are not so strong as to force belief, but they do make it completely rational to believe. In fact, these arguments are that it is *more* rational and takes less of a leap of faith to believe in God than to not believe. If your premise that there is no God leads most naturally to conclusions you know are not true—that moral obligation, beauty and meaning, the significance of love, our consciousness of being a self are illusions—then why not change the premise?

Ultimately, nonbelief in God is an act of faith, because there is no way to prove that the world and all that is within it and its deep mathematical orderliness and matter itself all simply exist on their own as brute facts with no source outside of themselves. If the theory that God exists leads us to expect what we find, whereas the belief that there is no God does not, why not move ahead, at least tentatively, by adopting the theory that God is there?

Twelve

Is It Reasonable to Believe in Christianity?

The Jesus Argument

Many people point out that the arguments for God not only do not prove God's existence but also give us only an "unmoved mover" or some other abstract being, not the holy, loving, all-powerful God of the Bible. But the purpose of the so-called theistic arguments is not to give us a specific description of God. The main work they do is to help us "see the inadequacies of [secular] naturalism" and bring us to see that there is probably something transcendent outside of nature.[1] These "cases for God" have been around for centuries, but in today's world our goals for their use should be targeted but modest. They primarily provide a means for "shaking up the dogmatic confidence . . . that naturalism and materialism are the default rational views of the universe."[2]

Christians believe that the main way we know specifics about God is not through our philosophical reasoning but through his self-revelation, not first through our thinking but through his speaking to us. And of course, Christians believe he has done that decisively in Jesus. If he is what is claimed, and if he rose from the dead, then we have, as it were, a strong case not just that God exists but that he is the God of the Old and New Testament Scriptures. So Jesus himself is the main argument for why we should believe Christianity.

The man Christians call Jesus Christ is the single most influential person who ever lived. As we have seen throughout this volume, Western civilization was shaped in large part by the Bible and particularly by

228

Christian theology. Even today's secularism shows the marks of the humanistic values that grew out of Christian understandings.

And Jesus's influence does not lie mainly in the past. Today a greater percentage of the world's population than ever before is Christian, and Christianity adds to its ranks over fifty thousand persons a day, or just under nineteen million new people a year.[3] Even in its beginnings, the movement of Jesus followers spread out in all directions outward from its Middle Eastern origins, not only to Europe but also to North Africa, to Turkey and Armenia, to Persia and India. "Christianity was a world religion long before it was a European one."[4] And today again, as we saw in chapter 7, Christianity is the religion that is most equally distributed across the continents of the world. So "no other [faith] . . . has so extensively crossed the cultural divisions of humanity and found a place in so many diverse cultural contexts."[5]

Even when Jesus has been used to legitimate oppression, as in the nineteenth-century American South, the African slaves themselves found the inspiration and power in Jesus to resist their domination. Even though during the early-modern period Christianity was tied too closely to European and American colonialism and empire, today most of the most vital and largest Christian populations are now nonwhite, non-Western. No matter how many efforts have been made to capture and deploy Jesus for imperialistic ends, he has always escaped them.[6]

It is difficult to argue with the well-known, somewhat overwrought saying that "all the armies that ever marched, all the parliaments that ever sat, all the kings that ever reigned," have not had the impact on the world of "this one solitary life."[7] Why has Jesus had the effect that he has had? The answer can come only from looking at his life, his words, and his actions.

The Sources for Jesus

Before we look at Jesus, however, we must assess our main source of information about him. How can we know what he said and did? Aren't the biblical sources of information about Jesus filled with legends to one degree or another? Can we trust them?

Though there is virtual unanimity among historical scholars that Jesus himself was a historical figure,[8] there is debate about the historical reliability of the four New Testament documents that give us most of our information about Jesus—the four Gospels: Matthew, Mark, Luke, and John. However, scholarly books in recent years have made a strong case for the trustworthiness of the Gospel accounts of Jesus's life.[9]

The consensus is that the Gospel of Mark was written about thirty years after Jesus's death, in approximately AD 65, while Matthew and Luke were written perhaps a decade or so later and the Gospel of John a decade or so after that. Also, "all scholars agree that Gospel traditions must originally have been formulated by disciples of Jesus and others who encountered him, witnessed the events, and remembered his teaching."[10] The real question is this: How were the accounts about his life preserved during those decades, and how did they reach the authors of the Gospels who wrote them down?

For almost a century biblical scholarship was dominated by a view called "form criticism." The form critics believed that the Gospels are folk literature, the product of oral tradition. Oral tradition was believed to be formed by communities that felt free to modify, embellish, and shape the stories to fit their own needs and to answer their own questions. It was believed that these communities did not care if the accounts were historically true at all. This was the form critics' answer to the question of how information about Jesus's life reached the Gospel writers. This view, of course, means that the Gospels cannot be trusted to tell us who the real Jesus was or what he did. Therefore, what many historians tried to do was to "get behind" the legendary accretions of the Bible to discern the true, original, historical Jesus. To say the least, the results of this "quest for the historical Jesus" have been extraordinarily disappointing, because scholars famously tend to produce a Jesus who reflects many of their own beliefs. "The fact that such diverse results have come out of the 'quest' . . . conducted on form-critical premises does not inspire confidence in the historical methods being used."[11]

But in the last twenty years the very premises of the form critics have come under attack, and they should no longer be taken for granted. We can begin with their view of oral tradition. While it is true that, for example, European fairy tales were freely altered by many anonymous handlers, anthropologists have now studied oral traditions across many cultures and discovered that this was not always the practice. When a community was remembering some shared historical origin account, the stories often had to be passed down without change.[12]

Most crucially, because the Gospel accounts were written down not after centuries of transmission (as in the case of European fairy tales) but within the lifetimes of people who had been eyewitnesses to the events, they are better characterized as oral *history* or historical testimony rather than as oral tradition.[13] The form critics assumed that even within the lifetimes of the eyewitnesses the churches felt free to take hold of the stories of Jesus's life and change them. They also assumed that the Gospel authors would not have consulted any of the firsthand witnesses when writing their texts, even though many of them were alive and were important, honored members of many of the churches.[14] Richard Bauckham, in *Jesus and the Eyewitnesses*, argues that these assumptions are highly unlikely, because good historians in the ancient world ordinarily interviewed eyewitnesses and documented it by naming them in their work. This is exactly what the Gospel writer Luke claims at the beginning of his work to have done. He says that he is recounting the events "just as they were handed down to us by those who from the first were eyewitnesses" (Luke 1:2).[15] Bauckham and others show how often the names of eyewitnesses—Simon of Cyrene, his sons Rufus and Alexander, Cleopas, Malchus, and others—are embedded in the Gospels, according to the accepted historiographical custom of the day.[16]

So one reason that the form critics are wrong is that the Gospels were written too early to be legend-encrusted folklore. They are rather eyewitness histories. The second reason that the form critics are wrong is that the Gospels do not show signs of having been shaped to fit the needs and sensibilities of the cultures and communities of the time.

Paul Eddy and Gregory Boyd, in their formidable volume *The Jesus*

Legend, point to a number of the features of the Gospel accounts—"the claims of Jesus's identity . . . [as] that of Yahweh-God and that he should receive worship, the notion of a crucified messiah, the concept of an individual resurrection, the dullness of the disciples, the unsavory crowd Jesus attracted." Eddy and Boyd call these all highly "embarrassing aspects" of the Jesus story for Christians. Every one of them went painfully against the grain of both Greek and Hebrew worldviews and subjected Christians to ridicule at best and abuse at worst.[17] Christians had every incentive to play down or eliminate all these issues from the Gospels, but instead they are prominent in the texts. This makes it highly unlikely that the stories are legendary, shaped for the Christian community's needs. Eddy and Boyd add, following Bauckham, that "the fact that this story originated and was accepted while Jesus's mother, brothers, and original disciples (to say nothing of Jesus's opponents) were still alive renders the legendary explanation all the more implausible." Their conclusion: "It is hard to understand how this story came about in this environment, in such a short span of time, unless it is substantially rooted in history."[18]

The Character of Jesus

When we read the Gospels about Jesus, then, what do we see?

One striking feature of the accounts is how they give us no description of Jesus's appearance. It is inconceivable that a modern journalistic account of any person would fail to tell us something of the kind of figure he cut or even of what he wore. We live in an age intensely concerned with image and nearly obsessed with looks. But here all the emphasis is, we might say, not on the quality of his skin but on the content of his character. And that character was remarkable.

Particularly impressive to readers over the centuries has been what one writer has called "an admirable conjunction of diverse excellencies in

Jesus Christ."[19] That is, in him we see qualities and virtues we would ordinarily consider incompatible in the same person. We would never think they could be combined but, because they are, they are strikingly beautiful. Jesus combines high majesty with the greatest humility, he joins the strongest commitment to justice with astonishing mercy and grace, and he reveals a transcendent self-sufficiency and yet entire trust in and reliance upon his heavenly Father. We are surprised to see tenderness without any weakness, boldness without harshness, humility without any uncertainty, indeed, accompanied by a towering confidence. Readers can discover for themselves his unbending convictions but complete approachability, his insistence on truth but always bathed in love, his power without insensitivity, integrity without rigidity, passion without prejudice.

One of the most counterintuitive combinations in Jesus's life, that of truth and love, is seen everywhere in the pages of the Gospels. Then as now, people rejected and shamed those who held beliefs or practices that they thought wrong and immoral. But Jesus astonished everyone by being willing to eat with tax collectors, collaborators with the occupying Roman imperial forces. This outraged those we might call the "Left," those zealous against oppression and injustice. But he also welcomed and ate with prostitutes (Matthew 21:31–32), which offended those promoting conservative, traditional morality on the "Right." Jesus deliberately and tenderly touched lepers (Luke 5:13), people who were considered physically and ceremonially contaminated but who were desperate for human contact. Yet he also ate repeatedly with Pharisees (Luke 7: 36–50; 11:37–44; 14:1–4), showing that he was not bigoted toward the bigoted. He forgave the enemies who were crucifying him (Luke 23:34) and the friends who were letting him down in the hour of his greatest need (Matthew 26:40–43).

Nevertheless, though welcoming and befriending all, Jesus was surprisingly insistent on bearing witness to the truth. Zacchaeus, the despised tax collector, was stunned by Jesus's love and embrace of him, yet, when hearing his call to repent, he stopped his government-backed extortion racket (Luke 19:1–9). When Jesus encounters women who were considered sexually immoral by the society, he engaged them with a respect and graciousness that startled onlookers (Luke 7:39; John 4:9, 27). Yet he gently points out to the Samaritan woman the wreckage of her many failed relationships with men and calls her to find the soul satisfaction she has sought in his eternal life (John 4:13–18). In the famous account of the woman caught in adultery, Jesus says to her, in one breath, "Neither do I condemn you," and in the next, "Go now and leave your life of sin" (John 8:11).[20] Here we see the counterintuitive but brilliant conjunction of both truth and love, both a passion for justice and a commitment to mercy. He is full of grace *and* truth (John 1:14).

New Testament scholar Craig Blomberg explains that the religiously respectable of Jesus's day refused to associate or eat with people considered sinners, such as tax collectors and prostitutes, for fear of becoming morally contaminated by them. Their friendship and love was given only conditionally, to those who had made themselves clean and pure. But Jesus turned the dominant social pattern on its head. He freely ate with the moral and social outcasts. He welcomed and befriended the impure and called them to follow him (Mark 2:13–17). He did not fear that they would contaminate him; rather, he expected that his wholesome love would infect and change them, and again and again this is what happened.[21]

The Wisdom and Freedom of Jesus

We speak of people as having a particular "temperament." Each of us has certain personality default modes. Some of us are introverted and some extroverted. Some of us are more outspoken and others soft-spoken. Some are quicker to lead out while others seek a consensus. Some are more rational and some more intuitive. This leaves us vulnerable, because we tend to respond with our temperaments whether or not the situation warrants it. So in a situation that requires us to speak out, we soft-spoken types miss our opportunity.

Jesus, however, appears in the Gospels to be the most versatile and wise person ever. There is never a false step or wrong note. We never see him being strong where he should be tender or tender where he should be strong. He is blunt and confrontational with a respectable religious leader (John 3), and in the very next chapter he is patient and gentle with a woman who is a social outcast (John 4). He approaches two sisters, Mary and Martha, both struggling with the same grief at their brother's death, both even saying the very same thing to him—"Lord, if you had been here, my brother would not have died" (John 11:21,32). Yet he responds to Martha with truth ("I am the resurrection and the life," John 11:25) but to Mary simply with tears and no words at all. He requires one woman whom he heals to testify to it publicly (Mark 5:30–34), but he takes a deaf-mute away from the eyes of the crowd and heals him in complete privacy (Mark 7:31–36). We see in him perfect flexibility and consummate wisdom in his relationships. He never treats people other than in the way they need, and he always knows perfectly what that is.

Readers have also been struck by the freedom of Jesus. He was free of prejudice. He continually showed his freedom from the rigidly stratified racial and gender barriers of the day, associating and eating with all sorts of people, high and low. He didn't avoid the rich and powerful, yet he showed no need for their approval at all. Although strongly committed to the truth of the Hebrew Scripture, he exhibited great freedom in reinterpreting the meaning of many of its laws and precepts. He simply disregarded many of the rabbinical rules of conduct that had come to overlay the way the Bible was read in that day. He was free too, it seems, from fear. He was constantly saying to people, "Fear not." Don't be afraid of the storm (John 6:16–24). Don't be afraid of death. If I have your hand, it is just sleep (Mark 5:35–43). And at the end of his life, when we see him bound and on trial, he seems most free of all, confidently telling one of his judges that he has no power to do anything that isn't part of the divine plan (John 19:11). "Think of Jesus at his trial," says one biblical commentator. "Was he the prisoner, or were his accusers? . . . He was calling the shots, not they. In this age that values freedom almost more than anything else, Jesus confronts us as the most liberated man who ever lived."[22]

People who have read and pondered Jesus's words, deeds, and life have groped for good ways to describe and explain what they see. And many begin to realize that the remarkable claims of Jesus about himself may be the only way forward. One writer puts it like this:

> *Imagine a man in whom the overwhelming, all-at-once perspective of the God of everything is not a momentary glimpse from which he rebounds, reeling, but a continual presence which in him is somehow adapted to the scale of the human mind, so that for him, uniquely, the shining is not other but self. . . . He's the creator in the midst of the thing made.*[23]

The Claims of Jesus

This brings us to the most startling of all the strange and beautiful juxtapositions of Jesus's life—the magnitude of his claims beside the humility, compassion, and tenderness of his character. What is surprising is not only that his claims were so self-centered but also that his character and his actions were so completely un-self-centered. We never see him pompous or offended or standing on his own dignity. He is approachable to the weakest and most broken. He is never moody or irascible. There is an unsurpassed moral and spiritual beauty about the character and the teaching of Jesus. Huston Smith, in *The World's Religions*, says that only Buddha and Jesus so impressed their contemporaries that they were asked not just "Who are you?" but also "*What* are you? What order of being do you belong to? What species do you represent?"[24] Smith makes the case that these two figures had characters that transcended ordinary human life to the degree that this question was necessary.

But the difficulty for observers comes at this point, for Buddha asserted with great clarity and emphasis that he was not a god or even some angelic, divine being.[25] But Jesus took an approach that could not be more different. He repeatedly and continually claimed to be *the* God, the creator of the universe.

This creates a great conundrum for anyone trying to understand this most influential figure in world history. Jesus is one of the very few persons in history who founded a great world religion or who, like Plato or Aristotle, has set the course of human thought and life for centuries. Jesus is in that tiny, select group. On the other hand, there have been a number of human persons over the years who have implicitly or explicitly claimed to be divine beings from other worlds. Many of them were demagogues; many more of them were leaders of small, self-contained sects of true believers. What is unique about Jesus is that he is the only member of the first set of persons who is also a member of the second.

The first group had a great impact on millions of people largely because of their brilliant teaching but also because of their admirable lives and characters, which, of course, included humility. Buddha emphatically said he was not a god, and Muhammad, of course, would never, ever have claimed to be Allah, nor did Confucius identify himself with heaven. The second group consists of those who claimed to be God but never were able to convince anyone but a small number. Why? Because it is virtually impossible to live such an extraordinary life that most people would be forced to conclude you were not merely a human being. In the whole history of the world, there is only one person who not only claimed to be God himself but also got enormous numbers of people to believe it. Only Jesus combines claims of divinity with the most beautiful life of humanity.

How do we account for this? There are only five ways to do so.

The first is to simply say that we don't care and feel no need to try to work it all out. This is more an attitude than a reason, and there's no arguing with an emotion. But imagine if you got a letter from some bank saying that some wealthy person—and here a name is given that you have never heard—had left you money. Even if you were of a skeptical nature and you had no evidence that this could be true, it would be unwise not to make inquiries. If a man has come into history claiming to have the gift of eternal life and the key to the meaning of things, and if he has not passed into obscurity like other claimants but has convinced many people that he is right, it seems unwise not to make inquiries.

The second, most common way to account for Jesus's life and claims is to insist that Jesus was a great teacher of wisdom and that this is the main way he should be regarded. This has the virtue of appreciating the extraordinary impact he had on those around him, but it keeps us from attributing to him a place above other human teachers and religious founders. The trouble with that, of course, is the power of Jesus's divine claims about himself.

There were all his indirect but deliberate claims. Jesus assumed authority to forgive all sins (Mark 2:7–10). Since we can forgive only sins that are against us, Jesus's premise is that all sins are against him, and therefore that he is God, whose laws are broken and whose love is offended in every violation. Jesus also claimed that he alone could give eternal life (John 6:39–40), though God alone has the right to give or take life. More than that, Jesus claimed to have a power that could actually eliminate death, and he claimed not just to have or bring a power to raise the dead but to be *the* Power that can destroy death (John 11:25–26). Jesus claimed to have the truth as no one else ever has. All prophets said, "Thus saith the Lord," but Jesus taught with "But *I* say unto you" out of his own authority (Mark 1:22; Luke 4:32). And more than that, he claimed not just to have or bring truth but to be *the* Truth itself, the source and locus of all truth (John 14:6).

Jesus assumed the authority to judge the world (Mark 14:62). Since God alone has both the infinite knowledge and the right (as creator and owner) to evaluate every person, Jesus's premise is that he has both divine attributes. More than that, Jesus claimed that we will be judged in the end primarily on our attitude toward him (Matthew 10:32–33; John 3:18). Jesus assumed the right to receive worship (John 5:23, 9:38, 20:28–29; Luke 5:8), which neither great persons nor even angels would accept (Revelation 22:8–9; Acts 14:11–15). Even his offhand statements and actions continually assume that he has divine status. He comes to the temple and says all the rules about observing the Sabbath are off now because the inventor of the Sabbath is now here (Mark 2:23-28). He puts his own knowledge on a par with God the Father's (Matthew 11:27). He claimed to be perfectly sinless (John 8:46). He says that the greatest person in the history of the world was John the Baptist but that the weakest follower of Christ is greater than he (Matthew 11:11). This list could be stretched out indefinitely.

But then there are his direct claims, which are just as staggering. To know him is to know God (John 8:19), to see him was to see God (John 12:45), to receive him is to receive God (Mark 9:37). Only through him can anyone know or come to God (Matthew 11:27; John 14:6). Even when Jesus called himself "*the* Son of God" he was claiming equality with the Father, because in ancient times an only son inherited all the father's wealth and position and was thus equal with him. The listeners knew that every time Jesus called him self "*the* Son," he was naming himself as fully God (John 5:18). Finally, Jesus actually takes upon himself the divine name "I am" (John 8:58, Exodus 3:14, 6:3), claiming to be "Yahweh," who appeared to Moses in the burning bush.[26]

So, as has often been said more eloquently than I can say it here, Jesus might have been a deranged demagogue or a charlatan, or perhaps the Son of God, but he couldn't simply have been a great teacher. His claims do not leave that option open to us. A merely good human being would not say such things. His statements about himself, "if not true, are those of a megalomaniac, compared with whom Hitler was the most sane and humble of men."[27]

The Conundrum of Jesus

The third way people account for the conundrum of Jesus's claims and character is to argue that he never really claimed to be divine, that these statements of deity were put into his mouth. According to some, Jesus was a man who lived an ordinary human life and died an ordinary death. He never made any declarations that he was God. It was only over the years, incrementally, that his followers gave him increasing devotion and finally elevated him to the status of a divine being. But in New Testament historical scholarship, this view was once much more dominant than it is now.

This view assumes the form critics' understanding of the transmission of the Gospels as oral folklore tradition, not as eyewitness history. But we have seen earlier in this chapter that this view of the Gospel records is hard to support. Therefore we can't dismiss the New Testament statements about the divinity of Christ as being later interpolations into the historical account.

In addition, the proposal that Jesus's followers invented his divinity is problematic. Buddha, through strenuous, emphatic protestation, could convince his followers that he was not a god. And yet his disciples had views of God that allowed the possibility of a kind of God-man. But first-century Jews had a theology and a culture that in every regard was completely resistant to the idea of God becoming human. That means that if Jesus had also, like Buddha, denied that he was God, why would he have failed to convince where the other founders succeeded, and with the least likely people on earth to divinize their teacher? The letters of Paul (written only fifteen to twenty-five years after Jesus's death) and the even earlier hymns and creeds he quotes (like Philippians 2:5–11) show that the earliest Christians—who were mainly Jewish persons—worshipped Jesus immediately after his death. The only fair explanation is that Jesus was the source of the claims—that his continual and powerful assertions of deity eventually broke through their walls of resistance.

Professor Martin Hengel of the University of Tübingen has argued that Paul's letters, written only twenty years after Jesus's death and based on his public ministry in the eastern Mediterranean less than ten years after Jesus's death, "make outstandingly elevated claims about Jesus, including his preexistence, his divine nature, and his mediation of creation and salvation."[28] Hengel and others also point out that Christians were worshipping Jesus within the lifetimes of hundreds of eyewitnesses who had heard Jesus's own words. Had he, like Buddha, eschewed any talk of divinity or worship, there would have been, at the very least, some evidence of Christian communities that insisted he was just a man while others were "evolving" toward a higher view. But there is no evidence of this. All Christians, as far as we can tell, immediately began to worship him as the resurrected Son of God. Martin Hengel, Larry Hurtado of Edinburgh University, and Richard Bauckham of the University of St Andrews have provided ample evidence from historical research that the earliest followers of Jesus were worshipping him as God.[29]

So it is impossible to slip out of the conundrum of Jesus by saying that he never really claimed to be God.

The fourth possible way to account for things is to say, perhaps sadly, that anyone who makes the megalomaniacal-sounding statements that Jesus did would *have* to be either mentally ill (if he believed them) or a fraud (if he did not). But there are reasons why very few people over the years have found this a convincing explanation.

To begin with, let's return to the fact that first-century Jews were so radically nondisposed to believe that any human being could be divine. Eastern religions were "pantheistic" and understood God to be the spiritual force in everything. So for someone in Eastern lands to say, "I am part of God" or "I am one with God," is not terribly unusual. On the other hand, many Western religions, such as those of the Greeks and Romans, were "polytheistic" and believed in various gods who could take on human guises. But when the Jews spoke of God, they meant the beginningless creator who was infinitely exalted above everything else. It had been burned into their minds and hearts that we must not worship any created, earthly thing. It permeates the Ten Commandments. So when Jesus claimed to have the same name as Yahweh, the "I am" (John 8:58), he was making the most stupendous claim that anyone has ever made, and it is not surprising that those who heard him say it tried immediately to kill him.[30]

The question is, however, why was it that Jesus was able to get the Jewish people around him to believe he was God? How could he have overcome the unthinkability of that? Why did he succeed as the only person who ever claimed deity and also founded a major—indeed, *the* largest—movement and religious faith? The first answer is that his life must have been exquisitely beautiful. The greatness we get a glimpse of in the Gospels must have smitten those around him. It is extraordinarily difficult to claim to be perfect and divine and then to get the people who actually live with you to believe it. But Jesus did it. What a life he must have lived. It is exceedingly hard to read the Gospel accounts, to see the counterintuitive brilliance of Jesus, and then to conclude that the basis for all these stories was someone who was either a "lunatic or a liar." We have seen that the historical evidence is that these narratives could not simply have been made up—they were written too early for that, and they have the form of eyewitness testimony. But even apart from that, the reader gets the sustained sense when considering Jesus that this character could not be the product of fiction, could not simply have been made up.

The Resurrection of Jesus

The other reason, however, that the unthinkable became thinkable—that Jesus was worshipped by Jews as God—is the Resurrection.

The historical evidence for the Resurrection of Jesus is formidable and has been laid out recently with massive scholarly support by N. T. Wright in *The Resurrection of the Son of God* and by many others as well.[31] These scholars argue that as long as you do not begin with an imposed philosophical bias against the possibility of miracles, the Resurrection has as much attestation as any other ancient historical event. There are three basic lines of evidence that converge.

The first is the fact of the empty tomb. Many point out that without an empty tomb, Christianity could never have begun, because it proclaimed a resurrected Lord from the earliest days. If the body could have been recovered and displayed, it certainly would have. It is also of note that there is no record of early Christians making Jesus's tomb a place of devotion and pilgrimage, which was normal for religious observance of the time. If his body had been there, this would almost certainly have been the practice. The tomb would have been inconsequential only if it was empty. So historians see the empty tomb as a given. The question is what happened to the body.

The second line of evidence is the testimony of and about the eyewitnesses. Paul is able to say in a public document about twenty years after the event that there were hundreds of eyewitnesses who saw Christ raised from the dead. Most are still alive, he says, and indicates that their testimony is available to anyone who seeks it out (1 Corinthians 15:3–7). It is interesting that Paul says that many of the sightings were by large groups. This rules out the theory that individual followers had near hallucinatory experiences of their Lord out of wish fulfillment. As we have said, the Jews were not disposed to believe in a divine man or in a single resurrection in the middle of history. But in addition, hallucinations can't happen to hundreds of people at once.

And as virtually all historians point out, every Gospel says that the first eyewitnesses of the risen Christ were women. This was at a time when the evidence of women was not admissible in court because of their low social status. If the Gospel writers had felt free to alter their narratives at all, they would have had no motivation to put women in the account. We know that early pagan critics of Christianity latched onto this and dismissed their testimony as being that of "hysterical females."[32] Therefore, there was no reason that the women would have been reported as the first witnesses unless they were. We can conclude, then, that many people really did see Jesus, alive again after his crucifixion.

The third line of evidence has to do with the impact of the Resurrection on Jesus's followers. Despite the fact that they were poor, few, and marginal, they developed a confidence and fearlessness that enabled them to spread the Gospel gladly, even at the cost of their own lives. Some have thought that the disciples stole the body, but people do not die for a hoax. N. T. Wright and Richard Bauckham point out that there were several other messianic pretenders, such as Bar Kokhba, who also died in their attempt to establish themselves. In each case their movements withered immediately on the argument that their death proved that they could not have been the Messiah. "Had Jesus' story ended with his death on the cross, he too would have been remembered only as a failed would-be Messiah."[33] Bauckham concludes that, therefore, something extraordinary must have happened to the disciples to change history's normal course. We must come up with a historically plausible alternative explanation for why thousands of Jews would overnight come to believe that a human being was the risen Son of God and then go out and die for their faith.

As the Japanese novelist Shusaku Endo says, if we don't believe in the Resurrection, we will be "forced to believe that what did hit the disciples was some other amazing event different in kind yet of equal force in its electrifying intensity."[34] If we try to explain the changed lives of the early Christians, we may find ourselves making even greater leaps of faith than if we believed in the Resurrection itself.

"I Am the Way"

So at the heart of the evidence for Christianity is a great conundrum. Here is a man who claimed to be God yet who lived a life so great that he became the only person to convince a sizable part of humanity that he was. How do we account for that? I've argued that we can't be indifferent to such a claim. We can't resolve the issue by saying he was only a great teacher, because his declarations don't allow that. We can't respond that he never made such claims because of the historical evidence. We can't be content with the explanation that he was deranged or a fraud because of the evident wisdom, greatness, and impact of his life on his followers and because of the case for the Resurrection.

This leaves us with the final possible explanation, namely, that he is who he said he is. As hard as it is to believe that he is God come to earth, it may be just as difficult not to. Is it really impossible for God to become human? Why, if God is really all-powerful, could he not have done it? And why, if God is really all-loving, would he not have done it?

This chapter certainly does not make the full case for believing the

Christian faith. A good number of very powerful objections to the Christian faith have been posed over the years, and they require thoughtful, extensive, and well-worked-out responses. Perhaps the strongest is the argument against the loving, all-powerful God of the Bible based on the presence of evil and suffering in the world. Another has to do with both the record within the Bible of God's commanding holy war, as well as the record of religion and Christianity promoting violence in subsequent world history. Another objection is to the biblical teachings on judgment and hell. Other objections arise around the Bible, including its relationship to science. I have written a book, *The Reason for God*, that gives answers to these objections, but there are many other volumes that should be consulted. While these books may not be ultimately convincing to all readers, I believe they will help us conclude what we have been seeking to establish in these last two chapters, that is, that it is quite rational to believe in God and Christianity. There are lots of good reasons to do so.[35]

When Jesus spoke to the woman at the well in Samaria, she spoke about the "Messiah" (John 4:25). The Samaritans had a belief in a *Taheb*, a prophet or teacher who would appear and show them the ultimate Truth.[36] Jesus said to her, "I, the one speaking to you—I am he" (John 4:26). Yet by the end of the chapter the woman and the other Samaritans are confessing him as "Savior of the world" (John 4:42). They had been hoping for a teacher, not a savior, and one just for their nation, not for the world. Jesus built on their aspirations and hopes yet radically challenged them as well.

This is always the case. Jesus comes to every individual and every culture and offers to fulfill their deepest desires and best aspirations. But in the same stroke he also fundamentally challenges their beliefs and practices; he tells them they have been going about seeking the fulfillment of those desires in profoundly wrong ways. He offers them all they want—meaning, satisfaction, freedom, identity, hope, and justice—but calls them to repent and seek their all in him. This is his basic message, and it makes sense of the magnitude of his language. As one summarized it:

Others said, "This is the truth about the universe. This is the way you ought to go." He says, "I am the way, and the truth, and the life." He said, "No man can reach absolute reality except through me. Try to retain your own life, and you will be inevitably ruined. Give yourself away, and you will be saved. . . . Finally, do not be afraid. I have overcome the whole universe."[87]

Epilogue

Only in God

Langdon Gilkey grew up in the most enlightened, educated environment possible. Born in 1919, he went to elementary school at the University of Chicago Laboratory School, a progressive educational institution founded by John Dewey. Gilkey's father was on the faculty of the University of Chicago, as were the parents of half of the school's students. In 1939 he graduated from Harvard magna cum laude with a degree in philosophy. The next year he went to teach English at a university in China. When the Japanese overran the region where he was teaching, he was put under house arrest with other Westerners and finally sent to an internment compound in Shandong Province. Gilkey survived his experience and wrote about it years later in the book *Shantung Compound*.[1]

Fragile Existence

A wall with electrified barbed wire surrounded the compound, along with guard towers filled with machine gun–armed soldiers.[2] It was about the size of a large city block, about two and a half acres, yet contained two thousand people. His personal living space consisted of a bed with eighteen inches on either side and three feet at its foot in which to keep all his possessions. "In that little world, 9 feet by 54 inches, each single person had to keep intact all his possessions and at the same time somehow to maintain his own personal being."[3] Food was extremely scarce and sanitation was poor. There were only twenty or so toilets—none of them flush—for two thousand persons, and so the lines were perpetual.[4] The ordinary symbols of status—money, family pedigree, and education— did nothing to change one's status or living space or influence in the compound. No one could accrue or protect any privacy. Most of all, the prisoners' very lives were always in doubt under the constant "harangues" from their captors and the guns trained on them.

Like most bright, educated young adults, Gilkey had a "view of life," a set of beliefs about human meaning, nature, and purpose. He began his time in the compound with "the confident humanism so characteristic of liberal academic circles."[5] He described that as consisting of two basic parts. First, he believed in the "rationality and goodness" of human beings, who had the ingenuity to solve basic human problems.[6] Second, he saw religion as "merely a matter of personal taste, of temperament, essential only if someone wants it" and useless to achieving the broad concerns of the human race. He believed "secularity, with its techniques, its courage, and its idealism is quite able to create a full human life without religion."[7] "'Why,' I asked myself, 'add religious frills to the ethical commitments . . . to the moral absolutes of peace in the world and justice in society?'" These moral commitments, he thought, did not need religious "frills" for support. In fact, religious belief distracted people from what was really important.[8]

Gilkey's first couple of months in the compound seemed to confirm his "secular humanism." When two thousand strangers suddenly found themselves thrown together, they began to organize themselves, discovering what every person was trained to do vocationally and putting everyone to work. The challenges of food preparation, sanitation, health care all were met with ingenuity. The actors and musicians created a stage and put on arts events. Also, people learned new skills. "Those who had never seen a mason's trowel built clever brick stoves in their rooms . . . that not only heated the room, but baked a modest cake." All of this confirmed his belief that "the capacity of [human beings] to develop the technical aspects of civilization—know-how—is limitless. I knew I would never again despair of man's ability to progress in both knowledge and practical techniques."[9] He felt that human ingenuity in dealing with the problems of human life was "unlimited," whereas the metaphysical issues that religion and philosophy "pretended to deal with" were "irrelevant."[10]

Human Nature

But the rest of Gilkey's account reveals how thoroughly his "secularity" was dismantled by his unusually up-close two-year confrontation with fundamental human nature. People began to steal coal and food, and no amount of public shaming could stop it. Fights broke out over space and distribution of goods, and those with marginally more of these things fiercely defended them rather than sharing. Crisis after crisis occurred "that involved not a breakdown in techniques, but a breakdown in character." The trouble with his "humanism" was "not its confidence in science and technology . . . [but] its naïve and unrealistic faith in the rationality and goodness of the men who wielded these instruments."[11] What he discovered was that all human beings were intensely self-interested and selfish but found the most ingenious ways to cloak those motives in moral and rational language. He called this "the essential intractability of the human animal," and it not only was a problem for the people from the lower or less educated classes but characterized the missionaries and priests in their midst as well.[12]

He realized that this created a great crisis for their "microcivilization." "These moral breakdowns were so serious that they threatened the very existence of our community." In particular, very few people seemed regularly capable of self-sacrifice, but that was what was required. "I began to see that without moral health, a community is as helpless and lost as it is without material supplies."[13]

One of the most instructive incidents came early in his time as the elected head of the Housing Committee. Eleven single men living in a small room discovered that there were nine single men living in an identical-sized space. They went to Gilkey asking that one of them be allowed to move into the other residential room, so that there would be ten living in each one. Gilkey was pleased. "Here at last was a perfectly clear-cut case. Surely the injustice in this situation was, if it ever was in life, clear and distinct. . . . Anyone who could . . . count and measure could see the inequity involved." He assumed that "the average man, when faced with a clear case of injustice . . . will at least agree to rectify that injustice even if he himself suffers from the rectification." And surely, he reasoned further, we are all in a common difficulty here, like persons on a raft at sea. So he assumed that the nine residents of block 49 would agree with him to accept a new resident, if not enthusiastically.

On the contrary, they did not. "Sure we're sorry for those chaps over there," said one, "but what has that got to do with us? We're plenty crowded here as it is, and their worries are their tough luck." Gilkey passionately argued against what he called "the sheer irrationality of nine men in one room and eleven in the other when both were the same size." It seemed only rational to share fairly, and, he argued, to do so was ultimately in their self-interest, because this way they could count on fair treatment if they were in a position to need it. Gilkey, of course, was speaking and later writing before John Rawls's influential books that argued almost in the identical way. There was no need to appeal to anything but rationality and self-interest to establish a peaceful and just order.

The men of block 49 heard Gilkey's excellent logic, and one replied, "That may be, friend. But let me tell you a thing or two. Fair or not fair, if you put one of them in here, we are merely heaving him out again. And if you come back here about this, we are heaving you out too."[14] Several others tried to take a more moderate tone, but they were just as adamant against the move. They tried to engage Gilkey's argument, finding ways to explain why they were not being impractical, unreasonable, or unjust.

As Gilkey went home, defeated, a thought struck him. "I almost laughed aloud when a queer thought struck me: Why *should* a man wish to be reasonable or moral if he thereby lost precious space?" What obliged a person to be rational? If you argue that to be rational is simply to be in your best interests, well, you are appealing to no higher value than selfishness. So why *shouldn't* the person act selfishly? Rationality and logic, then, were insufficient to bring human beings to agreement and to move them to action that promoted the social good. Something else was needed.

True Virtue

Gilkey came home that night confused, shaken, and losing faith in humanity's "basic goodness." "Self-interest seemed almost omnipotent next to the weak claims of logic and fair play." As the months went by, he constantly faced this same self-centered "intractability," namely, that "the fundamental bent of the total self in all of us was inward, toward our own welfare. And so immersed [are] we in it that we hardly are able to see this in ourselves, much less extricate ourselves from our dilemma."[15] People never could admit to themselves or others what they were doing. They always found "afterward . . . rational and moral reasons for what they had already determined to do."[16] The most moral and religious people, like everyone else, "found it incredibly difficult, not to say impossible, to will the good; that is, to be objective . . . generous and fair. . . . Some power within seemed to drive us to promote our own interests against those of our neighbors. . . . Though quite free to will whatever we wanted to do in a given situation, we were not free to love others, because the will did not really want to."[17]

The Shandong compound had stripped away the masks of politeness. "The thin polish of easy morality" had worn off. In more comfortable settings, people can feign the virtues of justice, compassion, and integrity. But in the compound, to be truly "fair and rational . . . just and generous . . . required the sacrifice of some precious good," and that did not come naturally to anyone. Shandong showed that true virtue is extremely costly and goes deeply against the grain of human nature. Gilkey had been taught in Chicago and at Harvard by teachers who believed that when the chips were down, and humans were revealed as they "really are," they would be good to one another. He now saw that "nothing could be so totally in error."[18] If the social order was to improve or even to survive, people had to be capable of virtue. But in their natural state they were not. In the compound Gilkey found true virtue to be "rare indeed."[19]

Gilkey discovered a number of ideas for which we have been contending in his book. He saw that Western secularity was not just the absence of belief but a new set of beliefs. Those beliefs included the goodness and rationality of human beings and especially the sufficiency of unaided human reason to guide us toward the goals of peace and justice. This worldview, these beliefs, could not stand up to the reality of human nature and human life under less-than-ideal circumstances.

He saw that rationality alone could not give people a basis for moral obligation. Why *should* people make sacrifices for others, especially if they could not see how it benefited them? Not only that, Gilkey saw an intractable inclination to selfishness and cruelty in the human heart that simple appeals to moral ideals could neither dislodge nor even enable people to see in themselves. This led Gilkey to a radical reversal in thinking.

> *It was a rare person indeed in our camp whose mind could rise beyond that involvement of the self in crucial issues to view them dispassionately. Rational behavior in communal action is primarily a moral and not an intellectual achievement, possible only to a person morally capable of self-sacrifice. In a real sense, I came to believe, moral selflessness is a prerequisite for the life of reason—not its consequence, as so many philosophers contend.*[20]

In short, if we are going to live rationally and use our minds well, we need new hearts. We need something that draws us out of our desperate search for self-fulfillment, affirmation, and value and makes us capable of loving other beings, not for our sake but for theirs. Gilkey came to believe that only faith in God could do all this.

> *[Human beings] need God because their precarious and contingent lives can find final significance only in His almighty and eternal purposes, and because their fragmentary selves must*

find their ultimate center only in His transcendent love. If the meaning of men's lives is centered solely in their own achievements, these too are vulnerable to the twists and turns of history, and their lives will always teeter on the abyss of pointlessness and inertia. And if men's ultimate loyalty is centered in themselves, then the effect of their lives on others around them will be destructive of that community on which we all depend. Only in God is there an ultimate loyalty that does not breed injustice and cruelty, and a meaning from which nothing on heaven and earth can separate us.[21]

My wife, Kathy, and I originally discovered *Shantung Compound* because we understood that it contained an account of Eric Liddell (called by the pseudonym "Eric Ridley" in the book), the former Olympic star and missionary to China whose story is told in the movie *Chariots of Fire*. Liddell was a prisoner in the compound and died during his internment. Gilkey candidly describes how the other missionaries and clergy in the camp were fully as selfish and ungenerous as others, and in many cases more so, because they often accompanied their behavior with sanctimony. But Liddell was different. Gilkey makes a startling statement about him: "It is rare indeed when a person has the good fortune to meet a saint, but he came as close to it as anyone I have ever known."[22] Liddell was especially concerned to minister to the teenagers of the camp. He cooked for them and supervised recreation for them and poured himself out for them. More than anyone else there he was overflowing with humor, love of life, sacrificial kindness for others, and inward peace. When he died suddenly of a brain tumor, the entire camp was stunned.

Liddell was a committed Presbyterian missionary who believed in Christ and that his salvation was accomplished by God's sheer and free grace. Gilkey wisely points out that "religion" all by itself does not necessarily produce the changed heart capable of moral selflessness. Often religion can make our self-centeredness worse, especially if it leads us to pride in our moral accomplishments. In Liddell we had a picture of what a human being could be if he was both humbled yet profoundly affirmed and filled with the knowledge of God's unconditional love through un-deserved grace. Gilkey, quoting Reinhold Niebuhr, says:

> *Religion is not the place where the problem of man's egotism is automatically solved. Rather, it is there that the ultimate battle between human pride and God's grace takes place. Insofar as human pride may win the battle, religion can and does become one of the instruments of human sin. But insofar as there the self does meet God and so can surrender to something beyond its own self-interest, religion may provide the one possibility for a much needed and very rare release from our common self-concern.*[23]

ACKNOWLEDGMENTS

I am privileged to have three young colleagues in ministry who live in New York City and who, in recent years, have been important conversation partners and consultants to me. Craig Ellis, Mai Hariu-Powell, and Michael Keller never tire of seeking ways to help our urban friends and neighbors better understand the offers and claims of (what appears to so many New Yorkers to be) the strange religious faith of Christianity. Thanks to all of them, and to Rose Shabet, for giving me feedback on the manuscript of this book and the ideas within it.

I want to thank those who gave me great places and spaces to work on this book, including Ray and Gill Lane of The Fisherbeck Hotel in Ambleside, Cumbria, UK, and Janice Worth in Florida. As always, I am grateful to David McCormick and Brian Tart, without whose editorial and literary wisdom I could not have brought this or the other books to readers. And most of all, thanks to Kathy, whose iron sharpens mine (Proverbs 27:17.)

NOTES

Preface: The Faith of the Secular

1. Samuel G. Freedman, "Evangelists Adapt to a New Era, Preaching the Gospel to Skeptics," *New York Times*, March 16, 2016. The article is a good account of what goes on in these kinds of discussions sponsored by our church. I would add that the approach described here for talking about faith is not new. It is the only way I have ever talked to others about faith in my forty years of ministry, and I have many colleagues who have done the same.

2. "Evangelists Adapt to a New Era, Preaching the Gospel to Skeptics," Reddit.com, March 4, 2016, www.reddit.com/r/skeptic/comments/48zdpe/evangelists _adapt_to_a_new_era_preaching_the/.

3. These three ways to use the term "secular" are based on Charles Taylor's analysis in his book *A Secular Age* (Cambridge, MA: Harvard University Press, 2007), pp. 1–22. First he gives the two most common definitions of secularity. The first is that *a secular society is one in which the government and main social institutions are not tied to one religion.* In a religious society all institutions including the government are based on and promote a particular set of religious beliefs. In a secular society the institutions and political structures are disconnected from any one religion (except in historical but not substantial ways, as in Britain and Scandinavian countries). Political life and power are shared equally between believers and nonbelievers. The second is that *a secular society is one in which many or most people do not believe in God or in a nonmaterial, transcendent realm.* In this definition to be secular is to be personally nonreligious, to not believe in a supernatural dimension to life and the universe. While some secular people may be explicit atheists or agnostics, others might continue to attend a religious service and extrapolate moral truths for living from religion. But ultimately they find all the resources they need—for meaning in life and personal fulfillment, for morality and working for justice—in purely human, this-world resources. Taylor calls this a "self-sufficing or exclusive humanism. . . . A secular age is one in which the eclipse of all goals beyond human flourishing becomes conceivable" (p. 19). Even people who retain connections to religious institutions are nonetheless secular if they perceive the fulfilled life in completely self-actualizing, this-worldly terms and reject the idea of self-denial and obedience to God in order to reach eternal life. The culture warns people that self-denial out of service to others or to higher ideals can be emotionally unhealthy and a way to collaborate with oppressive forces. While granting that the word "secular" usually has one of these first two meanings, Taylor offers a third. He considers *a secular society one in which the conditions for belief have changed* (pp. 2–3). In religious societies faith is simply assumed. Religion is not something you choose. That

would be considered a dangerous, outrageously self-centered attitude. In a secular culture, however, religion is seen as something that you must choose, and indeed the pluralism of secular societies does ultimately mean that your religion is something you can choose or lay aside. Therefore, you must have some justification for your beliefs, whether those grounds are rational or more intuitive and practical. In a secular culture belief is no longer automatic or axiomatic. In this sense, says Taylor, we are all (in Western society) persons of a secular age and society.

4. In *A Secular Age* Charles Taylor talks about what he calls a "social imaginary," which is "a way of constructing meaning and significance" (p. 26). It is something like what we would call a worldview—a set of deep background beliefs that shape everything. But Taylor avoids the word "worldview" and instead uses this term in order to get across some important aspects of how we live our lives that the term "worldview" simply does not capture. He wants to get at "something much broader and deeper than . . . intellectual schemes" (p. 171). He says a social imaginary includes not only propositions of how we are to live but also "deeper normative notions and images which underlie these expectations" (p. 171). What does that mean?

   First, a social imaginary is largely unconscious—some of it is identifiable as specific, expressed beliefs, but much or perhaps most of it, like an iceberg, is under the surface. Much of what shapes our view of the world are called by Michel Foucault "unthoughts" (p. 427) or "background"—the "largely unstructured and inarticulate understanding of our whole situation" (p. 173). These deepest "normative notions" are not usually consciously held propositions. They are more like "unchallenged common sense" about what is real, possible, and imaginable. Because they are considered self-evident, they are not based on any thought-out justifications, and the holders often become very defensive if such justifications are asked for. We don't feel they need them. It is just the way things are. It is literally unthinkable or unimaginable to us that they not be the true. To disagree with them is not to be merely mistaken, but ridiculous and "beyond the pale."

   Second, a social imaginary is much more than an intellectual framework. It is "carried" not in theoretical terms but in "images, stories . . . etc." It is formed largely through experiences (which we instinctively interpret in narrative form) and stories we are told. It forms, then, not merely (or perhaps not even mainly) the mind but also the imagination (pp. 171–72). It determines what we can imagine as possible and shapes what captures the imagination as good, desirable, beautiful.

   Third, a social imaginary is "social" in two complementary ways. It is an "implicit grasp of social space"—it has to do with how we live with others (p. 173). That grasp of social space contains both the factual and the normative—"how things usually go . . . interwoven with an idea of how they ought to go" (p. 172). But in addition, a social imaginary is social because it is a "*common* understanding," a "widely shared sense of legitimacy," which makes possible common practices (p. 172). One of the reasons it is so obvious and needs no theoretical justification is that "everybody I know feels the same way." So a social imaginary is formed communally—we come to find most plausible the beliefs of the people we associate with the most, and especially of the people and communities of which we want to be an accepted member.

Taylor notes, however, that social imaginaries, while not themselves theoretical frameworks, often begin as such. The way social imaginaries change is that at first a small minority of people *do* theorize and think them up and out. They come up with new ideas and they argue for them and they produce art to shape the imagination with the ideas. But "what starts off as theories held by a few people may come to infiltrate the social imaginary—first of elites perhaps, and then of the whole society" (p. 172). Eventually the new idea, argued for theoretically, comes to be "the taken-for-granted shape of things, too obvious to mention" (p. 176). In sum: The social imaginary is the "felt context" for life, the way we "make sense of any given act" (p. 174), something that people pick up from others in their social groupings, often without ever really adopting the conscious beliefs that created it.

Chapter One: Isn't Religion Going Away?

1. Sarah Pulliam Bailey, "The World Is Expected to Become More Religious—Not Less," *Washington Post*, April 24, 2015.

2. Ibid., https://www.washingtonpost.com/news/acts-of-faith/wp/2015/04/24/the-world-is-expected-to-become-more-religious-not-less/. See the comments by "KoltirasRip Tallus."

3. Maureen Cleave, "The John Lennon I Knew," *Telegraph*, October 5, 2005, www.telegraph.co.uk/culture/music/rockandjazzmusic/3646983/The-John-Lennon-I-knew.html.

4. This is the well-argued thesis of Stephen LeDrew in *The Evolution of Atheism: The Politics of a Modern Movement* (Oxford: Oxford University Press, 2015).

5. See Alasdair MacIntyre, *Whose Justice? Which Rationality?* (Notre Dame, IN: University of Notre Dame Press, 1988) and *After Virtue*, 3rd ed. (Notre Dame, IN: University of Notre Dame Press, 2007); Charles Taylor, *A Secular Age* (Cambridge, MA: Harvard University Press, 2007); Alvin Plantinga, *Warranted Christian Belief* (Oxford: Oxford University Press, 2000) and *Where the Conflict Really Lies: Science, Religion, and Naturalism* (Oxford: Oxford University Press, 2011). Not only are believers in God producing high-level scholarship, but a surprising number of leading secular thinkers in recent years have argued that science and reason alone cannot answer all the big human questions. They include Jürgen Habermas, Thomas Nagel, Ronald Dworkin, Terry Eagleton, and Simon Critchley. In various ways they make the case that a completely naturalistic view of the world—a world in which everything has a scientific, material cause—cannot explain the reality of moral values or support human rights and a program of justice. See Jürgen Habermas, et al., *An Awareness of What Is Missing: Faith and Reason in a Post-Secular Age* (Cambridge: Polity Press, 2010); Thomas Nagel, *Mind and Cosmos: Why the Materialist Neo-Darwinian Conception of Nature Is Almost Certainly False* (Oxford: Oxford University Press, 2012); Ronald Dworkin, *Religion Without God* (Cambridge, MA: Harvard University Press, 2013); Simon Critchley, *The Faith of the Faithless: Experiments in Political Theology* (London: Verso, 2012); Terry Eagleton, *Reason, Faith, and Revolution: Reflections on the God Debate* (New Haven, CT: Yale University Press, 2009)

and *Culture and the Death of God* (New Haven, CT: Yale University Press, 2015). We will be returning to consider each of these thinker's contributions later in this volume.

6. The literature on this subject is vast. The first scholarship to catch the attention of many was Philip Jenkins, *The Next Christendom: The Coming Global Christianity* (Oxford: Oxford University Press, 2002; 3rd ed., 2011). A recent review of the literature can be found in Rodney Stark, *The Triumph of Faith: Why the World Is More Religious Than Ever* (Wilmington, DE: Intercollegiate Studies Institute, 2015). See also David Barrett, George T. Kurian, and Todd M. Johnson, *World Christian Encyclopedia*, 2nd ed. (Oxford: Oxford University Press, 2001); Scott W. Sunquist, *The Unexpected Christian Century: The Reversal and Transformation of Global Christianity, 1900–2000* (Grand Rapids, MI: Baker Academic, 2015); Peter Berger, Grace Davie, and Effie Fokas, *Religious America, Secular Europe?* (Burlington, VT: Ashgate, 2008).

7. For these numbers and others in these paragraphs, see the Pew study "The Future of World Religions: Population Growth Projections 2010–2050," which can be found online at www.pewforum.org/2015/04/02/religious-projections -2010-2050/. Keep in mind that other reputable research companies have said that Pew's projections are, if anything, actually too conservative because they underestimate church growth in China. See this response to the Pew Study by the Center for the Study of Global Christianity at Boston University and Gordon-Conwell Seminary: www.gordonconwell .edu/ockenga/research/documents/CSGCPewResponse.pdf.

8. Zhuo Xinping is a member of the Standing Committee of the National People's Congress, China, and the director of the Institute of World Religions, Chinese Academy of Social Sciences. He writes, "Only by accepting this [Christian] understanding of transcendence as our criterion can we understand the real meaning of such concepts as freedom, human rights, tolerance, equality, justice, democracy, the rule of law, universality, and environmental protection." Zhuo Xinping, "The Significance of Christianity for the Modernization of Chinese Society," *Crux* 33 (March 1997): 31. Also quoted in Niall Ferguson, *Civilization: The West and the Rest* (New York: Penguin Books, repr. ed., 2012) p. 287. See Ferguson, pp. 256–94, for an overview of the remarkable growth of Christianity in China as well as its broad, positive, cultural impact. See also Zhuo Xinping, "Christianity and China's Modernization," a paper that can be found at www.kas.de/wf/doc/ kas_6824-1522-1-30.pdf?051011091504. "Since . . . 1978 . . . more and more Chinese people have envisaged that Christian values have a manifold potential influence in the development of Chinese civilization and modernization. Today, the Christian concept of sin helps Chinese self-understanding from a new perspective. The concept of salvation and transcendence inspires the Chinese people moving toward democracy." Jinghao Zhou, *China's Peaceful Rise in a Global Context: A Domestic Aspect of China's Road Map to Democratization* (Lanham, MD: Lexington, 2012), p. 169. As an example of the kind of favorable analysis Chinese scholars are giving Christianity, see Zhuo Xinping, *Christianity*, trans. Zhen and Caroline

Mason (Leiden, Germany: Brill, 2013), p. xxv: "The conundrum that Christianity holds to original sin, yet protects and enhances the dignity of human beings, whereas much Confucian thought promotes the original goodness of human nature, yet in practice has undermined human rights." It is important to keep in mind that scholars such as Zhuo do not expect or want China to be thoroughly Christianized or Westernized, and yet he and others see the growth of Christianity in China as a good thing in that they believe that Christianity provides a better basis than Western secularism for human rights, equality, and rule of law.

9. For years Habermas argued that by working together human beings could determine how to conduct our lives without any of the deliverances of religion. "The [former] authority of the holy," he once wrote, "is . . . replaced by the authority of a [rationally] achieved consensus." (Quoted by Stanley Fish in "Does Reason Know What It Is Missing?" *New York Times*, April 12, 2010). A brief account of Habermas's "evolution" on the subject of reason and religion is given in the essay "Habermas and Religion" by Michael Reder and Josef Schmidt, in Habermas, et al., *An Awareness of What Is Missing*, pp. 1–14. See also Jürgen Habermas, *Between Naturalism and Religion* (Cambridge: Polity, 2008).

10. Habermas, et al., *An Awareness of What Is Missing*, pp. 18–21. Another thinker who has more recently made this same point is historian Karen Armstrong in a November 23, 2014, interview in *Salon* magazine. She was asked if religion isn't a "strain of irrationality" in our society and if we should "purge this irrationality wherever we see it." Armstrong responds that though communism was "said to be a more rational way to organize a society" it was based on a myth of the healing state, and though the French revolutionaries were "imbued with the spirit of the Enlightenment" and were strongly antireligious and antichurch and even talked about "the goddess of reason," they publicly beheaded seventeen thousand people. Armstrong argues that no one is perfectly rational because science and rationality cannot speak to right and wrong, significance and meaninglessness. They cannot ultimately guide behavior beyond telling us what is the most efficient and practical way to reach particular goals. They cannot tell us if those goals are good or right. Human beings, therefore, need "the stories . . . we tell ourselves, that enable us to inject some kind of ultimate significance, however hard we try to be rational." She concludes that because rationality alone cannot give meaning, and because it is often the only public discourse allowed, "there's been a very strong void in modern culture, despite our magnificent achievements." She perceives a "nihilism," ennui, and aimlessness that are behind a great deal of crime and unrest in our culture. "A lack of meaning is a dangerous thing in a society." See Michael Schulson, "Karen Armstrong on Bill Maher and Sam Harris," *Salon*, November 23, 2014, www.salon.com/2014/11/23/karen _armstrong_sam_harris_anti_islam_talk_fills_me_with_despair/.

11. Someone may retort that social science can measure happiness and it can tell us how to live life in order to maximize happiness. But that leads to the question—Why believe that human beings should live for happiness? Science cannot answer that question. It requires a moral or philosophical argument.

See Miroslav Volf, *Flourishing: Why We Need Religion in a Globalized World* (New Haven, CT: Yale University Press, 2015), for an extended argument that globalization and secular states need religion to provide what only religion can—a vision of human good and flourishing that puts limits on science and the market.

12. Habermas, *An Awareness of What Is Missing*, p. 81.

13. Thomas C. Leonard, *Illiberal Reformers: Race, Eugenics, and American Economics in the Progressive Era* (Princeton, NJ: Princeton University Press, 2016).

14. Ibid., p. 111.

15. Frank M. Spinath and Wendy Johnson, "Behavior Genetics," in *The Wiley-Blackwell Handbook of Individual Differences*, ed. Tomas Chammoro-Premuzic, et al. (Oxford: Wiley-Blackwell, 2011), pp. 295–96.

16. Leonard, *Illiberal Reformers*, p. 190.

17. The full quote: "Universalistic egalitarianism, from which sprang the ideals of freedom and a collective life in solidarity, the autonomous conduct of life and emancipation, the individual morality of conscience, human rights and democracy, is the direct legacy of the Judaic ethic of justice and the Christian ethic of love. This legacy, substantially unchanged, has been the object of continual critical appropriation and reinterpretation. To this day, there is no alternative to it. And in light of the current challenges of a postnational constellation, we continue to draw on the substance of this heritage. Everything else is just idle postmodern talk." Jürgen Habermas, *Time of Transitions* (Cambridge: Polity, 2006), pp. 150–51. This essay also appears in Jürgen Habermas, *Religion and Rationality: Essays on Reason God, and Modernity* (Cambridge: Polity, 2002), p. 149. In short, even the modern state's commitment to equal rights, Habermas argues, was inherited from the Bible. Some would say that in this line of reasoning Habermas was following the lead of his teacher in the famous Frankfurt School, Max Horkheimer. Horkheimer similarly argued that secular reasoning alone cannot honor human dignity nor satisfy our deepest yearnings. He traces out how modern secular reason moved us away from belief in any absolute, mind-independent, and universal truths by which we could determine if a human action was right or wrong. *See* Max Horkheimer and Theodor W. Adorno, *Dialectic of Enlightenment: Philosophical Fragments*, ed. Gunzelin Schmid Noerr, trans. Edmund Jephcott (Stanford, CA: Stanford University Press, 2002) and Stephen Eric Bronner, in *Critical Theory: A Very Short Introduction* (Oxford: Oxford University Press, 2011). Horkheimer and Adorno argued that secular thought, which denied nonmaterial realities, became "instrumental." That is, an action was reasonable and right as long as it efficiently served the advancement and preservation of the people doing the reasoning. That "good" was now free to be defined by the majority as anything it deemed in its best interests. It could be argued that starving the poor or removing a particular ethnic minority from the national gene pool was "the greatest good

for the greatest number," and secular reason could not dispute such a conclusion. Science could judge only efficiency and cost-benefit, which could lead to treating people as objects and cogs in an economic machine. Horkheimer and Adorno were writing in the wake of World War II and had seen how both the Left of communism and the Right of fascism had used this understanding of scientific reason to justify violence. See Max Horkheimer, *Eclipse of Reason* (Oxford: Oxford University Press, 1947). This led to their critique of all modern economic-political orders—from socialism to free-market capitalism. They all in their own way "transform the qualitative into the quantitative." They seek to reduce personal, spiritual, moral, and human goods to commodities that can be managed and defined through metrics. They all offer material prosperity as the ultimate good, but it can never fulfill the desire for "eternity, beauty, transcendence, salvation, and God," or what Horkheimer called "the longing for the totally other" (quoted in Bronner, *Critical Theory*, p. 92). See also Max Horkheimer, "The Ego and Freedom Movements," in *Between Philosophy and Social Sciences*, trans. G. F. Hunter, M. S. Kramer, and John Torpey (Cambridge, MA: MIT Press, repr. ed., 1995).

18. Peter Watson also cites Thomas Nagel and Ronald Dworkin, as well as Habermas, as "three philosophers on either side of the Atlantic and each at the very peak of his profession" who are all likewise saying that materialistic atheism simply cannot account for the things we know are true, things like moral value, human consciousness, and free will. All three maintain that they are nonbelievers in a personal God but acknowledge that "we cannot escape the search for transcendence." Peter Watson, *The Age of Nothing: How We Have Sought to Live Since the Death of God* (London: Weidenfeld & Nicolson, 2014), p. 5. Watson is referring to Habermas's works already cited and to Nagel, *Mind and Cosmos*, and Dworkin, *Religion Without God*.

19. This was a speech written by William Jennings Bryan, who prosecuted Scopes. This is quoted in a review of Leonard's book by Malcolm Harris, "The Dark History of Liberal Reform," *New Republic*, January 21, 2016, https://newre public.com/article/128144/dark-history-liberal-reform. For more of the speech see www.pbs.org/wgbh/amex/monkeytrial/filmmore/ps_bryan.html.

20. Paul Kalanithi, *When Breath Becomes Air* (New York: Random House, 2016).

21. Ibid., p. 168.

22. Ibid., p. 169.

23. Ibid., p. 169–70.

24. Ibid., pp. 168 and 171. Once Kalanithi became open to the existence of God, he began to look at the religions and discovered Christianity's teaching on grace and redemption more compelling than other religions, which stressed earning God's blessing through moral accomplishment. Chapters 3–9 in this book will cover much of this territory.

25. Rebecca Pippert, *Hope Has Its Reasons: The Search to Satisfy Our Deepest Longings* (Downers Grove, IL: InterVarsity, 2001), p. 117.

26. Ibid., p. 119.

27. James Wood, "Is That All There Is? Secularism and Its Discontents," *New Yorker*, August 14, 2011.

28. Ibid.

29. Walter Isaacson, *Steve Jobs* (New York: Simon & Schuster, 2011), p. 571. Quoted in James K. A. Smith, *How (Not) to Be Secular: Reading Charles Taylor* (Grand Rapids, MI: Wm. B. Eerdmans, 2014), p. 13.

30. Lisa Chase, "Losing My Husband—and Finding Him Again Through a Medium," *Elle*, October 5, 2014.

31. Andrew Delbanco, *The Real American Dream: A Meditation on Hope* (Cambridge, MA: Harvard University Press, 1999), p. 3.

32. Julian Barnes, *Nothing to Be Frightened Of* (London: Jonathan Cape, 2008), p. 54.

33. Steven Pinker, *How the Mind Works* (New York: Norton, 1997), p. 524 and 537. Quoted in David Skeel, *True Paradox: How Christianity Makes Sense of Our Complex World* (Downers Grove, IL: InterVarsity, 2014), p. 67.

34. Taylor, *A Secular Age*, p. 607.

35. C. S. Lewis, "On Living in an Atomic Age," in *Present Concerns* (New York: Harcourt, 1986), p. 76.

36. Leonard Bernstein, *The Joy of Music* (New York: Simon & Schuster, 2004), p. 105.

37. Taylor's discussion of "fullness" can be found in *A Secular Age* on pp. 1–22 and in the chapter "Cross Pressures," pp. 594–617.

38. Ibid., p. 6.

39. Frank Bruni, "Between Godliness and Godlessness," *New York Times*, August 30, 2014.

40. Hubert Dreyfus and Sean Dorrance Kelly, *All Things Shining: Reading the Western Classics to Find Meaning in a Secular Age* (New York: Simon & Schuster, 2011), p. 201. Cornelius Plantinga also writes about this experience in "Longing and Hope," the first chapter in his book *Engaging God's World: A Christian Vision of Faith, Learning, and Living* (Grand Rapids, MI: Wm. B. Eerdmans, 2002), pp. 1–16.

41. Roger Scruton, *The Soul of the World* (Princeton, NJ: Princeton University Press, 2014). A philosopher, Scruton uses the discipline of phenomenology to "make space" for religious belief.

42. Quoted in Stuart Babbage, "Lord Kenneth Clark's Encounter with the 'Motions of Grace,'" *Christianity Today*, June 8, 1979, p. 28.

43. Václav Havel, *Letters to Olga* (New York: Knopf, 1988), pp. 331–32. Quoted in Taylor, *A Secular Age*, p. 728–29.

44. Havel's prison "conversion" did not result in a profession of faith in Christianity or even in belief in the traditional God of the monotheistic religions. But he developed a view of divine "Being" that lies behind all religions and cultures. See M. C. Putna, "The Spirituality of Vaclav Havel in Its Czech and American Contexts," *East European Politics and Societies* 24, no. 3 (August 2010): 353–78, available at http://eep.sagepub.com/content/24/3/353.full.pdf+html.

45. Kristin Dombek, "Letter from Williamsburg," *Paris Review* 205 (Summer 2013), www.theparisreview.org/letters-essays/6236/letter-from-williamsburg-kristin-dombek. Note: The online version of this essay reads, "I have been an atheist now for more than fifteen years," while the print version reads, "It has been fifteen years since I stopped believing." I used the quote from the former version, though I don't know which phrase was the revision.

46. Barbara Ehrenreich, *Living with a Wild God: A Nonbeliever's Search for the Truth About Everything* (New York, Twelve Books, 2014), p. 1.

47. Ibid., pp. 37–44 and 77.

48. Ibid., p. 115.

49. Ibid., p. 116.

50. Ibid., p. 203.

51. Ibid., p. 127.

52. Ibid., p. 197.

53. Ibid., p. 226–27.

54. Augustine, *Confessions*, book VII, chapter 23. This translation is by Maria Boulding in Saint Augustine of Hippo, *The Confessions: With an Introduction and Contemporary Criticism*, ed. David Vincent Meconi (San Francisco: Ignatius, 2012), p. 186.

55. Henry Chadwick, *Augustine: A Very Short Introduction* (Oxford: Oxford University Press, 1986), p. 23.

56. Cf. C. S. Lewis: "An 'impersonal God'—well and good. A subjective God of beauty, truth and goodness, inside our own heads—better still. A formless life-force surging through us, a vast power which we can tap—best of all. But God himself, alive, pulling at the other end of the cord, perhaps approaching at an infinite speed, the hunter, King, husband—that is quite another matter." C. S. Lewis, *Miracles* (New York: Touchstone, 1996), p. 125.

57. See the review of Ehrenreich's book by Francis Spufford, "Spiritual Literature for Atheists," *First Things*, no. 257 (November 2015). "*Wild* justice—justice unmediated and unfiltered—is different than the thing we painstakingly try to make in courtrooms." Spufford also writes that *wild* love, a love that searingly insists on our good and will not let us harm ourselves—"is fearfully unlike the adulterated product we are used to. . . . To call the presence you meet *'amoral'* [as Ehrenreich does] is at least to acknowledge its difference" (pp. 47–48).

58. Rudolf Otto, *The Idea of the Holy* (London: Oxford University Press, 1931), p. 28.

59. Ehrenreich, *Living with a Wild God*, pp. 203 and 215.

60. Taylor, *A Secular Age*, p. 8.

61. Mark Lilla, "The Hidden Lesson of Montaigne," *New York Review of Books* 58, no. 5 (March 24, 2011), cited in James K. A. Smith, *How (Not) to Be Secular: Reading Charles Taylor* (Grand Rapids, MI: Wm. B. Eerdmans, 2014), p. 1.

62. Matt Ridley, "Why Muslims Are Turning Away from Islam," *Times* (London), November 23, 2015.

63. Peter Berger, Grace Davie, and Effie Fokas, *Religious America: Secular Europe? A Theme and Variation* (Farnham, UK: Ashgate, 2008), p. 10.

64. Not only has China become more Christian as it modernizes, but it is understood by Chinese scholars that the growth of Christianity is leading greater modernization and democracy. See the work of Zhuo Xinping and others cited above in note 8.

65. See sociologist José Casanova's landmark work *Public Religions in the Modern World* (Chicago: University of Chicago Press, 1994). He compares Spain, Poland, Brazil, and the United States and finds very different trajectories (both up and down) for religion and churches under modernization. The trajectory depends in great part upon how churches respond to modern culture. In general, churches that are either too hostile (withdrawing or attacking) or too friendly (adapting and assimilating) decline. The path also depends on whether, in the past, religious affiliation has been more traditional and statist or more local and voluntaristic. The more a religion is tied to a national identity through a past monopoly (e.g., state churches), the more religion declines. The more religion is based on free and voluntary associations, the stronger it remains in modern culture. In short, it is not religion itself that declines under modernity but inherited religion. Chosen religion that is based on conversion can thrive.

    See also Mark Noll, *From Every Tribe and Nation: A Historian's Discovery of the Global Christian Story* (Grand Rapids, MI: Baker Academic, 2014), pp. 72–75.

66. Eric Kaufmann, *Shall the Religious Inherit the Earth? Demography and Politics in the Twenty-First Century* (London: Profile Books, 2010), pp. 1–45.

67. Ibid., p. 253.

68. See Caspar Melville, "Battle of the Babies," *New Humanist*, March 22, 2010, http://newhumanist.org.uk/2267/battle-of-the-babies. This is a review of *Shall the Religious Inherit the Earth?* as well as an interview with the author.

69. In fact, those who never go to worship have fewer children than those who go infrequently, and they in turn have fewer offspring than those who go weekly. See the work of German scholar Michael Blume, who has shown that there is a global-level positive correlation between the frequency of worship and the number of offspring. Jesse Bering, "God's Little Rabbits: Religious People Out-Reproduce Secular Ones by a Landslide," *Scientific American*, December 22, 2010: "Those who 'never' attend religious services bear, on average, 1.67 children per lifetime [below the 2.0 replacement level]; 'once per month,' and the average goes up to 2.01 children; 'more than once a week,' 2.5 children."

70. Ibid.

71. See Jeffrey Sachs, *The End of Poverty: Economic Possibilities for Our Time* (New York: Penguin, 2015) pp. xli–xlii.

72. Kaufmann, *Shall the Religious Inherit the Earth?*, p. 45. Kaufmann also writes: "We have a long way to go before all regions of the planet complete their demographic transitions. . . . By the time the transition runs its course in the twenty-second century, the secular nations of the planet will account for a much smaller share of the world's population than they do today. And this assumes that the West [itself] will remain as secular as it is now: which is unlikely. . . . The 'browning' of the West is injecting a fresh infusion of religious blood into secular society. . . ." p. 254.

73. Ibid., p. 255.

74. See David Brooks, "Creed or Chaos," *New York Times*, April 21, 2011.

75. Berger, Davie, and Fokas, *Religious America, Secular Europe?* pp. 40–41.

76. Ibid., pp. 41–42. See also pp. 33–34.

77. The Pew Center study found that evangelical and Pentecostal churches, those that require decision and conversion, had actually grown by two million people over the previous seven years while both mainline Protestant and Catholic affiliation declined sharply. See Sarah Pulliam Bailey, "Christianity Faces Sharp Decline as Americans Are Becoming Even Less Affiliated with Religion," *Washington Post*, May 12, 2015.

78. Noll, *From Every Tribe and Nation*, p. 130.

79. "Christianity in Its Global Context, 1970–2020: Society, Religion, and Mission," Center for the Study of Global Christianity, Gordon Conwell Theological Seminary, June, 2013, http://www.gordonconwell.edu/ockenga/ research/documents/ChristianityinitsGlobalContext.pdf, p. 36.

80. Ibid., p. 22.

81. Noll, *From Every Tribe and Nation*, p. 130.

82. Kaufmann, *Shall the Religious Inherit the Earth?*, p. 269.

83. Melville, "Battle of the Babies."

84. Rabbi Jonathan Sacks, *Not in God's Name: Confronting Religious Violence* (New York: Schocken Books, 2015), p. 18.

85. Saint Augustine of Hippo, *The Confessions: With an Introduction and Contemporary Criticism*, ed. David Vincent Meconi (San Francisco: Ignatius, 2012), p. 3.

Chapter Two: Isn't Religion Based on Faith and Secularism on Evidence?

1. S. A. Joyce, "One Night I Prayed to Know the Truth. The Next Morning I Discovered I Was an Atheist," no date, quoted in "Into the Clean Air: Extended Testimonies," Patheos.com, www.patheos.com/blogs/daylightatheism/essays/ into-the-clear-air-extended-testimonies/.

2. I am aware that this is not the only narrative for a deconversion story. Some are driven more directly by terrible experiences of unjust evil and suffering. Others are triggered by the hypocrisy and even abusiveness of the religious communities in which the narrators grew up. However, these three elements—the rational (lack of evidence), the existential (experience of evil or other intuitions that led away from faith), and the social (unattractive religious people)—are usually found together in one degree or another. The deconversion narrative I relate in the body of the text—that of the rational, thinker type—is, perhaps, more typical on the Internet.

3. "Barry Benedict," found at www.mlive.com/news/kalamazoo/index.ssf/ 2015/11/agnostics_evangelicals_growing.html.

4. Ibid.

5. Talal Asad, *Formations of the Secular: Christianity, Islam, Modernity,* (Stanford, CA: Stanford University Press, 2003). "The defense of liberal principles in the modern world cannot . . . be effectively carried out by making abstract arguments. . . . The image [a secularist] employs to present and defend liberalism is . . . 'making a garden in a jungle that is continually encroaching' and a 'world that is a dark place, which needs redemption by the light'" (p. 59). This image is cited in Stephen LeDrew, *The Evolution of Atheism: The Politics of a Modern Movement* (Oxford: Oxford University Press, 2015), for use as the title of his chapter 3, "A Light in a Dark Jungle," pp. 55–91.

6. Charles Taylor, *A Secular Age* (Cambridge, MA: Harvard University Press, 2007), pp. 26–29.

7. Barbara Ehrenreich, *Living with a Wild God*, pp. 37 and 61.

8. William Kingdon Clifford, "The Ethics of Belief," *Contemporary Review* 29 (December 1876–May 1877): 289, www.uta.edu/philosophy/faculty/burgess -jackson/Clifford.pdf.

9. Atheist philosopher Bertrand Russell assumed it when asked what he would do if he died and found himself before God. He answered that he would defend himself by saying, "Sir, why did you not give me better evidence?" Leo Rosten, "Bertrand Russell and God: A Memoir," *Saturday Review,* February 23, 1974, pp. 25–26.

10. See Peter van Inwagen, "Quam Dilecta," in *God and the Philosophers: The Reconciliation of Faith and Reason*, ed. Thomas Morris (Oxford: Oxford University Press, 1994), pp. 44–47.

11. There are some secularists, such as the "New Atheists" Richard Dawkins and Sam Harris, who continue to try to apply Clifford-style exclusive rationality to all knowledge. But they are now rare. Van Inwagen's point is that, while most secularists have abandoned exclusive rationality as a way of knowledge in general, most of them continue to apply it to religious belief. This is at least inconsistent, if not disingenuous.

12. Doubting that P is true "implies the acceptance of some not strictly indubitable framework within which *P* can be said to be . . . provable or not-provable." Michael Polanyi, *Personal Knowledge: Toward a Post-Critical Philosophy* (New York: Harper Torchbooks, 1964), p. 274.

13. Michael P. Lynch, *In Praise of Reason: Why Rationality Matters to Democracy* (Cambridge, MA: MIT Press, 2012), p. 4. Lynch makes a good, pragmatic case that we should use reason in our public discourse rather than simply yelling ideological slogans at one another. Nevertheless, it is striking that Lynch, a professor of philosophy at the University of Connecticut, says, "I will not defend reason with a capital R, nor the illusion that reason is value-free—nor that there are unfounded foundations, nor that there is a bare, unbiased 'given' in experience" (p. 5).

14. See Charles Taylor, "Overcoming Epistemology," in *Philosophical Arguments* (Cambridge, MA: Harvard University Press, 1995), pp. 1–19. James K. A. Smith makes a Christian case for the kind of knowing explained by Merleau-Ponty, Pierre Bourdieu, and other Continental thinkers in the first half of *Imagining the Kingdom* (Grand Rapids, MI: Wm. B. Eerdmans, 2013).

15. This is taken from Ludwig Wittgenstein, *On Certainty*, ed. G. E. M. Anscombe and G. H. Von Wright, trans. Denis Paul and G. E. M. Anscombe (New York: Harper & Row, 1969), sections 83–110, pp. 12c–15.

16. C. Stephen Evans, *Why Christian Faith Still Makes Sense: A Response to Contemporary Challenges* (Grand Rapids, MI: Baker Academic, 2015), p. 23.

17. Ibid.

18. Lesslie Newbigin, *The Gospel in a Pluralist Society* (Grand Rapids, MI: Wm. B. Eerdmans, 1991), p. 20. For a summary of Polanyi's thought and its application to matters of religious faith and doubt, see the first sixty-five pages of Newbigin's book.

19. If someone was to counter that the "uniformity of nature"—that "if X is the cause of Y, then Y will necessarily exist whenever X exists"—has been proven, eighteenth-century philosopher David Hume would deny it. He famously and powerfully argued we cannot prove that just because one thing follows another in a laboratory, it will ever do so again. Our belief that causally the future will be like the past is a premise of faith, it cannot be empirically demonstrated. Hume says, therefore, that inferences of cause-effect relationships aren't "'determin'd by reason,' [so] there must be 'some principle of equal weight and authority' that leads us to make them. Hume maintains that this principle is *custom* or *habit*. . . . It is therefore custom, not reason, which 'determines the mind . . . to suppose the future conformable to the past' (Abstract 16). . . . Hume concludes that custom alone 'makes us expect for the future, a similar train of events with those which have appeared in the past' (EHU 5.1.6/44)." William Edward Morris and Charlotte R. Brown, "David Hume," in *The Stanford Encyclopedia of Philosophy* (Spring 2016 ed.), ed. Edward N. Zalta, http://plato.stanford.edu/entries/hume/. See also the essay "Probable Reasoning Has No Rational Basis." "Our belief is in the uniformity of nature. By this means, our experience is able to yield us a rich bounty of causal information, which in turn permits us to connect up the reality with which our senses acquaint us (impressions) to the greater reality that lies beyond the purview of the senses, yet, in truth, exists only in our imaginations in the form of vivid ideas. However, although the uniformity principle is the foundation of all empirical reason as such, it is not itself founded on reason, demonstrative or probable." This essay is part of a course offered by Wayne Waxman at New York University, "The History of Modern Philosophy" found at www.nyu.edu/gsas/dept/philo/courses/modern05/ Hume_on_empirical_reasoning.pdf.

20. Polanyi, *Personal Knowledge*, p. 88. Much of the material in this part of the chapter is based on Polanyi's chapters "The Critique of Doubt" and "Commitment," pp. 269–324.

21. "Paradigm" is the term made famous by Thomas Kuhn in Thomas S. Kuhn, *The Structure of Scientific Revolutions*, 4th ed. (Chicago: University of Chicago Press, 2012). "Tradition" is the term used in Alasdair MacIntyre, *After Virtue*, 3rd ed. (Notre Dame, IN: University of Notre Dame Press, 2007). Robert Bellah defines a "tradition" like this: "A tradition is a pattern of understandings and evaluations that a community has worked out over time. Tradition is an inherent dimension of all human action. There is no way of getting outside of tradition altogether, though we may criticize one tradition from the point of view of another. *Tradition* is not used in contrast to *reason*. [In fact] tradition is often an ongoing reasoned argument about the good of the community or institution whose identity it defines." Robert Bellah, et al., *Habits of the Heart: Individualism and Commitment in*

American Life, with a New Preface (Oakland, CA: University of California Press, 2007), p. 336.

22. Martin Heidegger's student Hans-Georg Gadamer, in his influential book *Truth and Method*, developed this idea of our *Vorurteil* (literally, in German, "prejudice"). We are all unavoidably situated in cultures and communities and times. There is no "view from nowhere"—we begin with a perspective and we analyze a text by comparing its world with our world. See Robert J. Dostal, "Introduction," in *The Cambridge Companion to Gadamer*, ed. Robert J. Dostal (Cambridge, UK: Cambridge University Press, 2002), p. 6. Also see Fred Dallmayr, *Integral Pluralism: Beyond Culture Wars* (Lexington, KY: University of Kentucky Press, 2010), pp. 103–22. Many believe that Thomas Kuhn applied Heidegger's and Gadamer's hermeneutics to scientific inquiry.

23. James Wood, *The Broken Estate: Essays on Literature and Belief* (New York: Picador, 2010). "Life-under-God seems a pointlessness posing as a purpose (the purpose, presumably being to love God and to be loved in return); life-without-God seems to me also a pointlessness posing as a purpose (jobs, family, sex, and so on—all the usual distractions). The advantage, if it can be described as one, of living in the latter state, without God, is that the false purpose has at least been invented by man, and one can strip it away to reveal the *actual* pointlessness" (p. 261). Ehrenreich writes that the monotheistic God "can be blamed for natural disasters and birth defects." *Living with a Wild God*, p. 226.

24. Taylor, *A Secular Age*, p. 232.

25. Polanyi, *Personal Knowledge*, p. 272.

26. "Into the Clean Air," Pathos.com. no date, www.patheos.com/blogs/daylight atheism/essays/into-the-clear-air/#sthash.LosBmEcu.dpuf.

27. Polanyi, *Personal Knowledge*, p. 265.

28. See A. I. Jack et al., (2016) Why Do You Believe in God? Relationships Between Religious Belief, Analytic Thinking, Mentalizing and Moral Concern," *PLoS ONE* 11, no. 3 (2006): e0149989.

29. Michael Polanyi, *Personal Knowledge*, p. 266. Polanyi claimed that Augustine had initiated postcritical philosophy because he taught that ultimately all knowledge is a gift of God's grace. Reason works only on the basis of antecedent faith. *Nisi credideritis, non intelligetis*—unless you believe you will not understand. See also p. 268.

30. The assertion that secularity is not an absence of faith and metaphysical beliefs but a different set of such beliefs is still highly contested in popular forums, but in scholarly circles the case for this is being made with increasing power and sophistication. To acquaint yourself with that scholarship, a good place to start is Stephen LeDrew, *The Evolution of Atheism: The Politics of a Modern Movement* (Oxford: Oxford University Press, 2015). LeDrew, himself an atheist, is highly critical of the New Atheists, who in his view will not

admit that their position is not merely one of pure scientific rationality but is rather an ideology, which he defines as "a stable structure of beliefs and attitudes that determine how knowledge is constructed and interpreted to legitimate a form of authority" (p. 56). LeDrew agrees with the contention in this chapter that the New Atheists' epistemology—its claim that reason does not require faith in order to function—is naive. However, though he does not seem to share the New Atheists' "naked rationality," he does share with them their "humanistic morality." LeDrew correspondingly holds there are "Two Atheisms: Scientific and Humanistic" (p. 32). The other scholarship that LeDrew summarizes and draws upon includes the following: Asad, *Formations of the Secular*; Terry Eagleton, *Reason, Faith and Revolution: Reflections on the God Debate* (New Haven, CT: Yale University Press, 2009) and *Culture and the Death of God* (New Haven, CT: Yale University Press, 2014); Max Horkheimer and Theodor W. Adorno, *Dialectic of Enlightenment: Philosophical Fragments*, ed. Gunzelin Schmid Noerr, trans. Edmund Jephcott (Stanford, CA: Stanford University Press, 2002); Craig Calhoun et al., *Rethinking Secularism* (Oxford: Oxford University Press, 2011); Philip Gorski et al., *The Post-Secular in Question: Religion in Contemporary Society* (New York: New York University Press, 2012); Eduardo Mendieta and Jonathan VanAntwerpen, eds., *The Power of Religion in the Public Square* (New York: Columbia University Press, 2011). LeDrew also draws upon Taylor and Habermas. See Taylor, *A Secular Age*, and Jürgen Habermas et al., *An Awareness of What is Missing: Faith and Reason in a Post-Secular Age* (Cambridge: Polity Press, 2010); Jürgen Habermas, *Between Naturalism and Religion* (Cambridge: Polity, 2008) and *Religion and Rationality: Essays on Reason God, and Modernity* (Cambridge: Polity, 2002). It should be noted that LeDrew is especially concerned with analyzing the "New Atheists," a strain of what he calls "scientific atheism" that is particularly ideological and that refuses to admit that it is. Nevertheless, LeDrew's efforts to show the historical genealogy of secularist beliefs applies to all its forms.

31. "Now the traditional unbelieving attack on religion since the Enlightenment contains . . . the 'moral' facet of the 'death of God' critique. . . . The unbeliever . . . knows that human beings are on their own [without God]. But this doesn't cause him just to cave in. On the contrary, he determines to affirm human worth, and the human good, and to work for it, without the false illusion or consolation. . . . Moreover, he has no reason to exclude anyone as heretic; so his philanthropy is universal. . . . So goes one story." Taylor, *A Secular Age*, pp. 561–62.

32. Charles Mathewes and Joshua Yates, "The 'Drive to Reform' and Its Discontents," in Carlos D. Colorado and Justin D. Klassen, *Aspiring to Fullness in a Secular Age: Essays on Religion and Theology in the Work of Charles Taylor* (Notre Dame, IN: University of Notre Dame Press, 2014), p. 153.

33. "Casey K.," commenting on Tony Schwartz, "The Enduring Hunt for Personal Value," *New York Times*, May 1, 2015, www.nytimes.com/2015/05/02/busi ness/dealbook/the-enduring-hunt-for-personal-value.html?_r=0.

34. Quoted in Taylor, *A Secular Age*, p. 596.

35. Jacques Derrida, "On Forgiveness: A Roundtable Discussion with Jacques Derrida," moderated by Richard Kearny, in *Questioning God* (Bloomington: Indiana University Press, 2001), p. 70.

36. These thinkers include Larry Siedentop (Oxford), Philip S. Gorski (Yale), Eric T. Nelson (Harvard), and Charles Taylor, among many others. Some of their particular works will be cited in these notes.

37. Again: "The ideals of freedom and a collective life in solidarity, the autonomous conduct of life and emancipation, the individual morality of conscience, human rights and democracy, is the direct legacy of the Judaic ethic of justice and the Christian ethic of love. . . . To this day, there is no alternative to it. . . . We continue to draw on the substance of this heritage. Everything else is just idle postmodern talk." Habermas, *Religion and Rationality*, p. 149.

38. Luc Ferry, "The Victory of Christianity over Greek Philosophy," in *A Brief History of Thought: A Philosophical Guide to Living*, trans. Theo Cuffe (New York: Harper Perennial, 2011), pp. 55–91.

39. Ibid., p. 58.

40. Ibid., pp. 72–73.

41. Horkheimer noted that the very concept that each soul, regardless of race or class, could be "the dwelling place of God, came into being only with Christianity, and all antiquity has an element of emptiness and aloofness by contrast." He adds that the Gospel accounts of "simple fishermen and carpenters" being anointed by God to become great leaders and teachers, healers and preachers, in contrast "seem to make Greek masterpieces mute and soulless . . . and the leading figures of antiquity roughhewn and barbaric." Ibid. For a full-blown exposition of the biblical, Jewish/Christian roots of Western liberalism, human rights, and individualism, see Larry Siedentop, *Inventing the Individual: The Origins of Western Liberalism* (New York: Allen Lane, 2014). This is not to denigrate Greek philosophy's contribution to both Western individualism and democracy. Among the aristocracy the importance of the individual was asserted. See, for example, Christian Meier, *A Culture of Freedom: Ancient Greece and the Origins of Europe* (Oxford: Oxford University Press, 2009). But as has been pointed out, the radical idea of equality across the human race is an idea that came from the Bible.

42. See Brian Tierney, *The Idea of Natural Rights: Studies on Natural Rights, Natural Law and Church Law 1150–1625* (Atlanta, GA: Scholars Press for Emory University, 1997). Tierney makes the case that it was within Christian jurisprudence of the twelfth and thirteenth centuries that human-rights thinking began, rooted particularly in the Christian doctrine that all human beings are created in the image of God and therefore have inherent dignity. See also Brian Tierney, "The Idea of Natural Rights: Origins and Persistence," *Northwestern Journal of International Human Rights* 2 (Spring 2004); Richard Tuck, *Natural Rights Theories: Their Origin and Development* (Cambridge, UK: Cambridge University Press, 1979); Michael

J. Perry, *Toward a Theory of Human Rights: Religion, Law, Courts* (Cambridge, UK: Cambridge University Press, 2006), p. 18; Martin Luther King Jr., "The American Dream," preached at Ebenezer Baptist Church, Atlanta, Georgia, July 4, 1965. It can be accessed at http://kingencyclopedia .stanford.edu/encyclopedia/documentsentry/doc_the_american_dream/.

43. Peter Brown, *The Body and Society: Men, Women, and Sexual Renunciation in Early Christianity* (New York: Columbia University Press, 1988), p. 34.

44. "All mankind stood before the majesty of God as other and inferior to Him. Body and soul faced him together. He had created both and would judge both. Every believer confronted God not as a soul committed, for a time, to the necessary if thankless task of bringing order to an alien body, but rather as the possessor of a 'heart.'" Ibid., p. 35.

45. Ibid.

46. See Taylor, *A Secular Age*, pp. 274–76. This is a necessarily high-level discussion of a complex field.

47. Henry Chadwick, *Augustine of Hippo: A Life* (Oxford, UK: Oxford University Press, 2009), p. 93. Chadwick argues that classical Greek and Latin thinkers saw the virtues—courage, honesty, prudence, wisdom, and loyalty—as largely the product of suppressing unruly emotions. "Rationality was the supreme thing." But St. Augustine taught that "our emotions are disordered, but the feelings are not themselves the cause of the disorder." They need to be not repressed but redirected away from other things toward God.

48. Augustine's *Confessions* established the importance of understanding one's self and "pioneered a highly positive evaluation of human feelings" in which the intellect does not "have the last word." Henry Chadwick, *Augustine: A Very Short Introduction* (Oxford, UK: Oxford University Press, 2001), p. 4. See also Sandra Dixon et al., *Augustine and Psychology: Tradition and Innovation* (Lanham, MD: Lexington Books, 2012). Again, we must be careful not to overdraw the distinctions between Christianity and Greek philosophy. The Greeks' conception of emotion was not completely negative, as Peter Brown points out. See also David Konstan, *Pity Transformed* (New York: Bristol Classical, 2001) and *The Emotions of the Ancient Greeks: Studies in Aristotle and Classical Literature* (Toronto: University of Toronto Press, 2007).

49. See Diogenes Allen, "The Christian Roots of Modern Science and Christianity's Bad Image," in *Christian Belief in a Postmodern World: The Full Wealth of Conviction* (Louisville, KY: John Knox, 1989), pp. 23–35; and Rodney Stark, *How the West Won: The Neglected Story of the Triumph of Modernity* (Wilmington, DE: Intercollegiate Studies Institute, 2014). Indeed, as Luc Ferry points out, the Christian doctrine of the Resurrection, and of the eventual perfection of the material world, is "unique among all the major religions." It gives us the most elevated and positive view of the material world possible. We will live permanently, endlessly, not merely in a nonphysical paradise but in a renewed world with resurrected bodies. This means that ordinary experiences of seeing and hearing, of embracing and

eating, of physical enjoyment and pleasure, are so important that God will extend these gifts and goods to us forever. This also means that we will be ourselves in the eternal future. See Ferry, *Brief History of Thought*, pp. 88–91.

50. Ferry, *Brief History of Thought*, pp. 85–86.

51. Ibid., pp. 60–61.

52. Ibid., p. 60.

53. Ibid.

54. Taylor, *A Secular Age*, p. 279.

55. "The modern slide to Deism, and later atheism, integrated a great deal of the original package of changes effected by the Fathers. . . . Modern Deism integrated the first five in my list: the body, history, the place of individuals, contingency [Taylor's term for the significance of our choices and actions], and the emotions. That is, it integrated these as essential dimensions of our understanding of human life but it excluded them altogether from our relationship to God." Ibid., p. 288.

56. Ferry, *Brief History of Thought*, p. 152.

57. Friedrich Nietzsche, *Twilight of the Idols and the Anti-Christ*, trans. R. J. Hollingdale (New York: Penguin Classics, 1990), p. 40. Also cited in a different translation in Ferry, *Brief History of Thought*, p. 153.

58. Eagleton, *Culture and the Death of God*, pp. 156–57.

59. "When one gives up Christian belief one thereby deprives oneself of the *right* to Christian morality. For the latter is absolutely *not* self-evident: one must make this point clear again and again in spite of English shallowpates. Christianity is a system, a consistently thought out and *complete* view of things. If one breaks out of it a fundamental idea, the belief in God, one thereby breaks the whole thing to pieces: one has nothing of any consequence left in one's hands." Nietzsche, *Twilight of the Idols*, pp. 80–81.

60. "Christianity [and its values of egalitarian benevolence and compassion] . . . possesses truth only if God is truth—it stands or falls on belief in God. If the English really do believe they will know, of their own accord, 'intuitively,' what is good and evil; if they consequently think they no longer have need of Christianity as a guarantee of morality; that is merely the consequence of the ascendency of Christian evaluation and an expression of the strength and depth of this ascendency: so that the origin of English morality has been forgotten, so that the highly conditional nature of its right to exist is no longer felt. For the Englishman morality is not yet a problem." Ibid., p. 81.

61. "He dismisses conventional virtue in *Twilight of the Idols* as little more than social mimicry, and in *Beyond Good and Evil* scoffs at the concept of the common good. Not only is he unconcerned to retain religious belief for social

utilitarian reasons, but he regards such a project as self-contradictory. How can selfless values serve self-interested social ends?" Eagleton, *Culture and the Death of God*, p. 163.

62. Ronald Dworkin, *Religion Without God* (Cambridge, MA: Harvard University Press, 2013), p. 2.

63. Ibid., p. 6.

64. "What Nietzsche recognizes is that you can get rid of God only if you also do away with innate meaning. . . . As long as there appears to be some immanent sense to things, one can always inquire after the source from which it springs. Abolishing given meanings involves destroying the idea of depth, which in turn means rooting out beings like God who take shelter there." Eagleton, *Culture and the Death of God*, p. 155.

65. Ibid., p. 163. This quote is Eagleton's words, summarizing Nietzsche's views.

66. Ibid., p. 161. This quote is Eagleton's words, summarizing Nietzshe's views.

67. John Gray writes that Nietzsche did not escape his own net. "His early work contained a profound interrogation of liberal rationalism, a modern view of things that contains no tragedies, only unfortunate mistakes and inspirational learning experiences. Against this banal creed, Nietzsche wanted to revive the tragic world-view of the ancient Greeks. But that world-view makes sense only if much that is important in life is fated. As understood in Greek religion and drama, tragedy requires a conflict of values that cannot be revoked by any act of will; in the mythology that Nietzsche concocted in his later writings, however, the godlike Superman, creating and destroying values as he pleases, can dissolve and nullify any tragic conflict. . . . Aiming to save the sense of tragedy, Nietzsche ended up producing another anti-tragic faith: a hyperbolic version of humanism." John Gray, "The Ghost at the Atheist Feast," *New Statesman*, March 13, 2014.

68. Eagleton, *Culture and the Death of God*, p. 161. For further critique of Nietzsche and the school of "Deconstruction" that he founded, see Ferry, *Brief History of Thought*, pp. 193–204.

69. Many have claimed that this—the lack of secular grounding for humanistic values—is the greatest problem that the contemporary secularity faces. So we will revisit it in chapters 9 and 10.

70. See Peter Watson, *The Age of Nothing: How We Have Sought to Live Since the Death of God* (London: Weidenfeld & Nicolson, 2014). In his review of Watson's book John Gray summarizes Watson's material. "First published in 1882, Nietzsche's dictum 'God is dead' described a situation in which science (notably Darwinism) had revealed 'a world with no inherent order or meaning.' With theism no longer credible, meaning would have to be made in future by human beings—but what kind of meaning, and by which human beings? In a vividly engaging conspectus of the formative ideas of the past century, *The Age of Nothing* shows how Nietzsche's diagnosis evoked

responses in many areas of cultural life, including some surprising parts of the political spectrum. While it is widely known that Nietzsche's ideas were used as a rationale for imperialism, and later fascism and Nazism, Watson recounts how Nietzsche had a great impact on Bolshevik thinking, too. The first Soviet director of education, Anatoly Lunacharsky (who was also in charge of state censorship of the arts and bore the delicious title of Commissar of Enlightenment), saw himself as promoting a communist version of the Superman. 'In labour, in technology,' he wrote, in a passage cited by Watson, '[the new man] found himself to be a god and dictated his will to the world.' Trotsky thought much the same, opining that socialism would create 'a higher social-biologic type.' Lenin always resisted the importation of Nietzsche's ideas into Bolshevism. But the Soviet leader kept a copy of Nietzsche's *Birth of Tragedy* in his personal library and one of *Zarathustra* in his Kremlin office, and there is more than a hint of the cult of the will in Lenin's decree ordering the building of 'God-defying towers' throughout the new Soviet state." Gray, "Ghost at the Atheist Feast."

71. David Sessions, "What Really Happens When People Lose Their Religion?" *Patrol*, April 30, 2013, www.patrolmag.com/2013/04/30/david-sessions/what -really-happens-when-people-lose-their-faith/. Sessions's account is remarkably insightful and honest, both personally and intellectually. It is a profitable read for believers, nonbelievers, and those in between. He writes: "It has a certain noble appeal: we're good Westerners who can no longer believe in God, but are still heirs of a great civilization who can press on, being as reasonable and dispassionate as possible, for the sake of humanity. It explains why we used to believe the myths and shrouds our disenchantment in courage and moral duty; it's no surprise a great number of homeless ex-believers end up there. The point is not to insult liberal humanism; after all, there are far worse things. The point is to remind us that it is a construal in a culture where it tends to assert itself as natural and uncontroversial, to all sorts of cultural and political detriment that I can't get into here. I hope, if possible, people who have had the privilege of going between, of actually feeling the persuasive power of different kinds of construals that co-exist in our culture, can elevate the conversation above the crude Doug Wilson vs. Christopher Hitchens–type spectacle that is so clickable. I think reading Taylor is an excellent tonic; even a few chapters of *A Secular Age* will do those hovering between belief and unbelief far more good than the collected works of 'Ditchkins.' Ending up in a 'cross-pressured' no-man's land—torn between immanence and transcendence—may feel inconclusive, but it's creatively productive, and is certainly better than exchanging one half-baked ideology for another. One needn't remain religious to admit potential harm in the lack of self-awareness in certain secular construals of the world, and to be able to see religious belief, with a kind humility and respect, as a construal that can be equally as plausible as our own. And one that is to be studied carefully, especially by philosophy and politics, for its crucial insights about human be-ing. For those who inhabit a religious construal, and are perhaps working to deepen, enrich, and preserve it, there are also important lessons to be found in Taylor (who is, after all, on your side). I'll address one to evangelical Protestantism, since I know it best: the unqualified disaster of apologetics that have focused on rational-empirical argumentation as a means of persuasion, intensifying the already-problematic tendency of Protestantism to be in one's

head than in the practices of one's body. The thrust of 'resurgent' evangelical activity in my lifetime has been mostly to embrace and even radicalize the most harmful features of the modern obsession with rational control. If you can begin to pull your religion out of that abyss, there's no telling what a powerful countercurrent it might become."

72. By styling itself as an absence of faith, secularity is doing something that cultural theorists have called "mystification": taking a contestable viewpoint or belief and denigrating any views that challenge it, marginalizing all rival forms of thought, and denying the social reality that the belief is not universally held. This gives the opinion the appearance of being a universal, self-evident, inevitable fact that may not be questioned. See Terry Eagleton, *Ideology: An Introduction* (New York: Verso, 1991), pp. 5–6. Critical theorists and their heirs have pointed out that there is a strong tendency to domination in modern Western culture, so that in the name of personal freedom and social emancipation new forms of oppression, marginalization, forced conformity, and dehumanization are continually generated. See Max Horkheimer and Theodor Adorno's classic *Dialectic of Enlightenment*. Western cultural elites of both the Left and the Right are generally oblivious to this perennial danger.

73. I have argued that secularism is a set of new beliefs, but I could go on to add that, like any religion, secularism has "denominations." The first, using Stephen LeDrew's terminology, would be *secular scientism*, one manifestation of which has been dubbed the "New Atheists." LeDrew critiques this group as believing not in science but in "scientism," which is marked by the naive belief (which I have critiqued above) in scientific rationality as the only form of true knowledge. He argues that their agenda is to establish the hegemony of scientists and scientific thought as the supreme authorities and arbiters of truth in society. LeDrew says that this position is one of exclusive ideological commitments rather than, as its adherents style it, just one of "openness to reason." LeDrew, *Evolution of Atheism*, pp. 32 and 55–91. A second "denomination" could be called *secular humanism*, the viewpoint of many modern liberals. This group of secularists, like LeDrew himself, are willing to grant that scientific reason is not the only arbiter of knowledge. Their concern is not to see the triumph of science but to work for freedom, equality, and the common good of society. See LeDrew, pp. 44–48. A good example of this denomination, cited by LeDrew, is Greg Epstein, the humanist chaplain at Harvard, who defines secular humanism as "a cohesive world movement based on the creation of good lives and communities, without God." Greg M. Epstein, *Good Without God: What a Billion Nonreligious People Do Believe* (New York: Harper, 2010), p. xiv. A third "denomination" of secularism consists of *secular antihumanists*. This is a small but still influential school of thought, including thinkers such as Foucault, Derrida, and Bataille, who follow Nietzsche very closely. This group critiques modern liberalism as well as religion and in this sense follows the path of Nietzsche and the Critical Theory of the Frankfurt School. See Charles Taylor, "The Immanent Counter-Enlightenment," in *Canadian Political Philosophy: Contemporary Reflections, ed.* Ronald Beiner and Wayne Norman (Oxford: Oxford University Press, 2001), pp. 386–400. In an intriguing passage Taylor rightly

points out that the fragmentation of our culture today comes because modern culture is *not* the scene of a simple "liberal/secular"–versus–"religious/conservative" conflict. Rather, it is the scene of a four-cornered battle. The parties are what he names: (1) "Those who acknowledge some good beyond life" (p. 397), who believe in the *transcendent,* "a point of life that is beyond life" (p. 387). He believes this includes not only people of all religions but also even less religiously committed thinkers who hold that there is a reality beyond the material, natural world. (2) "Secular humanists," those who do not believe in a transcendent, supernatural reality yet continue to hold the values of universal benevolence, of the imperative to work for the freedom and safety of all, of the elimination of suffering. (3) The "neo-Nietzscheans," who question and critique any moral values or claims as exercises of power and who "valorize" death and sometimes violence (p. 397). (4) Then he adds a fourth party by acknowledging that those who believe in transcendence are divided between those who think the whole move toward secularism was a terrible mistake and needs to be wholly undone and those who see good coming out of the move toward secularism, good that would not have come into the world unless the power of religious institutions hadn't been broken in some measure. Taylor puts himself in that category and adds as an aside, "We might even be tempted to say that modern unbelief is providential, but that might be too provocative a way of putting it." (Taylor, *A Secular Age,* p. 637.) Taylor puts into his category of "secular humanist" both groups that LeDrew calls scientific and humanistic secular. If we take into account the very real differences that LeDrew points out, the cultural "battlefield" becomes even more complex than Taylor's description would have it.

74. Blaise *Pascal, Pensées,* trans. A. J. Krailsheimer (London: Penguin Books, 1966), p. 147. In another part of the *Pensées,* Blaise Pascal lays down two principles to guide us as we consider evidence and arguments for God. "If [God] had wished to overcome the obstinacy of the most hardened, he could have done so by revealing himself to them so plainly that they could not doubt the truth of his essence, as he will appear on the last day. . . . It was, therefore, not right that he should appear in a manner manifestly divine and absolutely capable of convincing all men, but neither was it right that his coming should be so hidden that he could not be recognized by those who sincerely sought him. . . . There is enough light for those who desire only to see, and enough darkness for those of a contrary disposition." Ibid., pp. 79–80. Philosopher C. Stephen Evans gives names to both principles. The first he calls the "Wide Accessibility Principle," the idea that, if a loving God exists, he would likely not want to restrict the knowledge of his existence to intellectuals capable of assessing complicated arguments, any more than to one gender or to one continent or country. The second he calls the "Easy Resistibility Principle," the concept that, if a just God exists, he would not want to force his knowledge on people. Rather, this "God wants the relationship humans are to enjoy with him to be one in which they love and serve him freely and joyfully." C. Stephen Evans, *Natural Signs and Knowledge of God: A New Look at Theistic Arguments* (Oxford: Oxford University Press, 2010), p. 15. What Evans and Pascal say here fits in better with a Roman Catholic or Arminian understanding of free will and human

agency than with a Lutheran or Reformed view, but Pascal can get some grounding in texts like Mark 4:11–12, where Jesus tells his disciples his teaching was designed to be understandable to some but hard to understand for those with closed eyes and ears.

75. I will reserve until the last two chapters a fuller outline of the rational case for faith, which I laid out in more detail in *The Reason for God*. How can we weigh the offers and claims of Christianity and see if they make more sense emotionally, culturally, and rationally than other views of life? Here's what to keep in mind as you read. Most modern people imagine that the way to test out a comprehensive viewpoint or "worldview" is simply to look at the "proofs" for it. So, it is thought, either the classic proofs of God work or they don't. If they don't, we can be atheist or agnostic; if they do, we move on to look at the different religions. But as we have seen, no comprehensive viewpoint or "worldview" can prove its case so that no reasonable person can doubt it. Alasdair MacIntyre points out that Aristotle, Thomas Aquinas, and David Hume each had an approach to how reason worked that was significantly different from the others'. Alasdair MacIntyre, *Whose Justice? Which Rationality?* (Notre Dame, IN: University of Notre Dame Press, 1988). This was because each approach to reason was deeply embedded in a matrix of beliefs about justice, human purpose, the nature of the material world, and how we know things. There are, then, no "standards of truth and rational justification" that are independent and can be used to judge all viewpoints, because any standards you come up with will come from and already assume one of these worldviews and therefore the wrongness of all the others. Alasdair MacIntyre, *After Virtue*, 3rd ed. (Notre Dame IN: University of Notre Dame Press, 2007), p. xii. Do we then have any way to proceed and test out different viewpoints? Yes, we do. MacIntyre points to a path forward for persons inhabiting one worldview (what he calls a "tradition") to assess another one. First they must "come to understand what it is to think in the terms prescribed by that particular rival tradition." Ibid., p. xiii. They must do everything they can to sympathetically put themselves in the shoes of the other. They should engage only the strongest, not the weakest presentations of the other viewpoint. Second, in both their own worldview and the one they are assessing, they should identify "unresolved issues and unsolved problems—unresolved and unsolved *by the standards of that tradition."* Ibid., p. xiii. MacIntyre goes on to say that every "tradition" has such issues and problems. Notice that these are tensions felt by the believers not because of criticisms coming from outside but because of problems caused by holding the beliefs themselves. One kind of problem is inconsistency, so that some beliefs of the worldview contradict others. Another kind of problem is unlivability, so that some beliefs are impossible for the bearer to actually practice. This means the beliefs don't fit one another internally or the real world externally. The sign that this is happening, according to MacIntyre, is when adherents of one worldview are found smuggling in ideas and values from other worldviews in order to deal with their own tradition's contradictions and inconsistencies. It is when one worldview "lacks the resources to address those issues and solve those problems . . . so long as it remains faithful to its own standards and presuppositions" and when it becomes clear that "the means of overcoming this predicament" can come only from "that [other] rival tradition" that "it is possible for one such tradition to defeat another in respect of the adequacy of

its claims to truth." Ibid. If, while claiming to have one set of beliefs, you must constantly borrow from another set of beliefs in order to live your life, then you are bearing witness that the other worldview makes more emotional, cultural, and rational sense than yours does. This is what I will attempt to show in the rest of this book, namely, that secularity in particular does this unacknowledged borrowing in a heavy way, and that Christianity makes more overall sense than its rival(s).

Chapter Three: A Meaning That Suffering Can't Take from You

1. Thomas Nagel, *What Does It All Mean? A Very Short Introduction to Philosophy* (Oxford: Oxford University Press, 1987), p. 101.

2. Ibid.

3. Rodney Stark, *The Triumph of Faith,* p. 211. See the charts 213–222.

4. Cited and summarized by Terry Eagleton, *The Meaning of Life: A Very Short Introduction* (Oxford: Oxford University Press, 2003), p. 12.

5. Atul Gawande, *Being Mortal: Medicine and What Matters in the End* (New York: Metropolitan Books, 2014), p. 112.

6. Ibid., p. 113.

7. Ibid., p. 125.

8. Anton Chekhov, *Three Plays: The Sea-Gull, Three Sisters, and The Cherry Orchard,* trans. Constance Garnett (New York: Modern Library, 2001), p. 89.

9. Franz Kafka, *The Trial* (New York: Tribeca Books, 2015), p. 32.

10. Jean-Paul Sartre, *Being and Nothingness,* trans. Hazel E. Barnes (New York: Philosophical Library, 1956), p. 615.

11. Albert Camus, *The Myth of Sisyphus and Other Essays,* trans. Justin O'Brien (New York: Random House, Vintage Books, 1955), p. 21.

12. "I do not want to believe that death is the gateway to another life. For me, it is a closed door. . . . If I had to speak of it, I would find the right word here between horror and silence to express the conscious certainty of death without hope." Albert Camus, "The Wind at Djemila." "And what more legitimate harmony can unite a man with life than the dual consciousness of his longing to endure and his awareness of death?. . . . [This desert landscape] took me out of myself in the deepest sense of the word. It assured me that but for my love and the wondrous cry of these stones, there was no meaning in anything. The world is beautiful [but] outside it there is no salvation." Albert Camus, "The Desert." Both quotes are from Harold Bloom, ed., *Albert Camus,* Bloom's BioCritiques (Philadelphia: Chelsea House, 2003), p. 59.

13. Albert Camus, *The Rebel: An Essay on Man in Revolt* (New York, Vintage, 1992), p. 261.

14. Bertrand Russell, "A Free Man's Worship," 1903, available at www.skeptic .ca/Bertrand_Russell_Collection.pdf and many other places on the Internet.

15. Eagleton, *Meaning of Life*, p. 16.

16. Nagel, *What Does It All Mean?* p. 101.

17. Eagleton, *Meaning of Life,* pp. 64 and 17.

18. Stephen Jay Gould was one of numerous "scientists, authors, and artists" who answered the question "What is the Meaning of Life? Why are we here?" in "The Meaning of Life: The Big Picture" in *Life Magazine*, December 1988.

19. Many prefer the term "late modern" to "postmodern" in order to emphasize not the discontinuities but the continuities between our current cultural climate and its roots in the Enlightenment. I have the same preference, but for the rest of this chapter I follow Terry Eagleton, who shows the great changes made within the last generation in how the "meaning of life" question is regarded.

20. Quote from *Fargo*, season 2, episode 5, See *Fargo (2014) Episode Scripts*, http://www.springfieldspringfield.co.uk/view_episode_scripts.php?tv-show= fargo-2014&episode=s02e05.

21. Quote from *Fargo*, season 2, episode 8, See *Fargo (2014) Episode Scripts*, http://www.springfieldspringfield.co.uk/view_episode_scripts.php?tv-show= fargo-2014&episode=s02e08.

22. Quotes in this paragraph and the last are from *Fargo*, season 2, episode 10. See *Fargo (2014) Episode Scripts*, http://www.springfieldspringfield.co.uk/ view_episode_scripts.php?tv-show=fargo-2014&episode=s02e10.

23. Eagleton, *Meaning of Life*, p. 58.

24. Jerry A. Coyne, "Ross Douthat Is on Another Erroneous Rampage Against Secularism," *New Republic*, December 26, 2013, https://newrepublic.com/ article/116047/ross-douthat-wrong-about-secularism-and-ethics.

25. Daniel Florian, "Does Atheism Make Life Meaningless?" Patheos.com, August 5, 2009, www.patheos.com/blogs/unreasonablefaith/2009/08/ does-atheism -make-life-meaningless/.

26. Eagleton, *Meaning of Life*, p. 17.

27. Ibid., p. 67.

28. Ibid., pp. 69–70.

29. Thomas Nagel, "The Absurd," in *The Meaning of Life*, ed. E. D. Klemke and Steven Cahn (Oxford: Oxford University Press, 2008), pp. 146–47.

30. Many have criticized Shakespeare's definition of meaninglessness in *Macbeth*, act 5, scene 5: "Out, out brief candle! Life's but a walking shadow, a poor player, that struts and frets his hour upon the stage, and then is heard no more." The question is posed—why does the brevity of life make life meaningless? Just because a drama lasts only an hour and then ends does not mean that the drama was meaningless. But the drama, though ended, is not meaningless because the spectators continue. There are still people who exist who remember the drama with profit. What Nagel and others are arguing is that it is not merely our own deaths but the inevitable death of everyone and everything that makes life meaningless.

31. Nagel, *What Does It All Mean?* p. 96.

32. "I guess (strict sense) that you think man a more important manifestation than I do. . . . Of course from the human point of view he is important [to himself]; he would hardly live if he didn't think so. Also I hasten to admit that I don't dare pronounce any fact unimportant that the Cosmos has produced. I only mean that when one thinks coldly I see no reason for attributing to man a significance different in kind from that which belongs to a baboon or a grain of sand. But the time approaches when I must go down stairs and play solitaire I fear." Richard Posner, ed., *The Essential Holmes: Selections from the Letters, Speeches, Judicial Opinions, and Other Writings of Oliver Wendell Holmes, Jr.* (Chicago: University of Chicago Press, 1997), p. 108. Also see where he writes: "My bet is that we have not the kind of cosmic importance that the parsons and philosophers teach. I doubt if a shudder would go through the spheres if the whole ant heap were kerosened. . . . Man of course has the significance of fact: that he is part of the incomprehensible, but so has a grain of sand. I think the attitude of being a little god, even if the great one has vanished, is the sin" (p. xxvi).

33. Leo Tolstoy, *A Confession* (Grand Rapids, MI: Christian Classics Ethereal Library), 1998, p. 16.

34. C. S. Lewis, "On Living in an Atomic Age," in *Present Concerns* (San Diego, CA: Harcourt Books, 2002), p. 76.

35. Eagleton, *Meaning of Life*, p. 21.

36. Royce's book is discussed in Gawande, *Being Mortal*, pp. 115–16.

37. Ibid., p. 116.

38. Ibid.

39. Charles Taylor, *The Malaise of Modernity* (Concord, ON: Anansi, 1991), p. 14.

40. Ibid., p. 18.

41. Ibid.

42. Ibid. Much more on this secular problem with moral values will be presented in chapter 7.

43. The speech is easily found in many places on the Internet. See, for example, www.americanrhetoric.com/speeches/mlkihaveadream.htm.

44. Eagleton, *Meaning of Life*, p. 22.

45. Ibid., p. 24.

46. Charles Taylor, "A Catholic Modernity?" in *Dilemmas and Connections: Selected Essays* (Cambridge, MA: Belknap, 2011), p. 173.

47. Victor Frankl, *Man's Search for Meaning* (New York: Washington Square, 1959).

48. See the dramatic account in *Man's Search for Meaning* at p. 96. A fellow inmate confided to Frankl that he had had a dream that they would be liberated by February 1945. When the month came and went, the man almost immediately ran a high fever, then became unconscious and died. Chapter 8 will further discuss the importance of hope.

49. Ibid., p. 24.

50. Ibid., p. 54.

51. Ibid., p. 90.

52. Ibid., p. 104.

53. Taylor says our secular age is marked by "the widespread inability to give any human meaning to suffering and death, other than as dangers and enemies to be avoided or combated. This inability is not just the failing of certain individuals—it is entrenched in many of our institutions and practices—for instance, the practice of medicine, which has great trouble understanding its own limits or conceiving of some natural term to human life." Taylor, "Catholic Modernity?" p. 176. See also his comments that "clinging to the primacy of life in the second (let's call this the 'metaphysical') sense is making it harder to affirm it wholeheartedly in the first (or practical) sense" (p. 177).

54. See Richard A. Shweder et al., "The 'Big Three' of Morality (Autonomy, Community, Divinity) and the 'Big Three' Explanations of Suffering," in Richard A. Shweder, *Why Do Men Barbecue? Recipes for Cultural Psychology* (Cambridge, MA, Harvard University Press, 2003); and Timothy Keller, "The Culture of Suffering" and "The Challenge to the Secular," in *Walking with God Through Pain and Suffering* (New York: Dutton, 2013), pp. 13–34 and 64–84.

55. Shweder, *Why Do Men Barbecue?*, p. 113. This is quoted and explained in my *Walking with God Through Pain and Suffering*, pp. 30–31.

56. Søren Kierkegaard, *The Sickness unto Death,* trans. Edna Hatlestad Hong, Howard Vincent Hong (Princeton, NJ: Princeton University Press, 1983).

Chapter Four: A Satisfaction That Is Not Based on Circumstances

1. Jonathan Haidt, *The Happiness Hypothesis: Putting Ancient Wisdom and Philosophy to the Test of Modern Science* (London: Arrow Books, 2006).

2. Ibid., p. 82. I have added the italics.

3. Ibid., p. 89.

4. Quoted in Haidt, *Happiness Hypothesis.*

5. From the *Dhammapada*, verse 83, in J. Mascaro's translation (1973), as quoted in Haidt, *Happiness Hypothesis*, p. 81.

6. Ibid.

7. Haidt, *Happiness Hypothesis*, p. 82.

8. "If you want to predict how happy someone is, or how long she will live . . . you should ask about her social relationships." Ibid., p. 133. See also Haidt, *Happiness Hypothesis*, chapter 6 ("Love and Attachments"), pp. 107–34.

9. De Botton thinks that every adult life is defined by two love stories—the search for love and affirmation through sex and romance and the search for those things through success. "This second love story is no less intense than the first, it is no less complicated, important, or universal, and its setbacks are no less painful." Alain de Botton, *Status Anxiety* (New York: Vintage Books, 2004), p. 5.

10. Haidt, *Happiness Hypothesis*, pp. 90–91.

11. Julian Baggini, *What's It All About?* (Oxford: Oxford University Press, 2004), p. 97.

12. Thomas Nagel, "Who Is Happy and When?," *New York Review of Books,* December 23, 2010, www.nybooks.com/articles/2010/12/23/who-happy-and -when/.

13. Terry Eagleton, *The Meaning of Life: A Very Short Introduction* (Oxford: Oxford University Press, 2003), p. 81.

14. Horace, *The First Book of the Satires of Horace*, www.authorama.com/works -of-horace-6.html.

15. Wallace Stevens, "Sunday Morning," www.poets.org/poetsorg/poem/sunday -morning.

16. For the song lyrics, see www.azlyrics.com/lyrics/peggylee/isthatallthereis .html. For a great, world-weary rendition, see www.youtube.com/watch?v=

LCRZZC-DH7M. For the historical connection to Thomas Mann, see David E. Anderson, "Is That All There Is?" *Religion and Ethics Newsweekly*, Public Broadcasting Service, July 24, 2009.

17. Cynthia Heimel, "Tongue in Chic," *Village Voice*, June 2, 1990, pp. 38–40.

18. Henrik Ibsen, *The Wild Duck*, trans. Christopher Hampton (New York: Samuel French, 2014), p. 108. This line is spoken by the character Dr. Relling in act V.

19. C. S. Lewis, "Hope," in *Mere Christianity* (New York: HarperCollins, 2001), pp. 134–38.

20. James Wood, *The Broken Estate: Essays on Literature and Belief* (New York: Picador, 2010), p. 261.

21. Haidt, *The Happiness Hypothesis*, p. 86.

22. Francis Spufford, *Unapologetic: Why, Despite Everything, Christianity Can Still Make Surprising Emotional Sense* (London: Faber & Faber, 2012), pp. 27–28.

23. Tony Schwartz, "The Enduring Hunt for Personal Value," *New York Times*, May 1, 2015, www.nytimes.com/2015/05/02/business/dealbook/the -enduring-hunt-for-personal-value.html?_r=0.

24. See Charles Taylor, "A Catholic Modernity?" in *Dilemmas and Connections: Selected Essays* (Cambridge, MA: Belknap, 2011), pp. 181–87.

25. Quoted in Luc Ferry, *A Brief History of Thought: A Philosophical Guide to Living*, trans. Theo Cuffe (New York: Harper Perennial, 2011), p. 48.

26. Haidt, *Happiness Hypothesis,* pp. 83–84. Modern psychology often tries to explain various human traits as adaptations of natural selection. It is helpful to keep in mind that these theories of what evolutionary function various human features may have served originally are untestable hypotheses.

27. Henry Chadwick, *Augustine: A Very Short Introduction* (Oxford: Oxford University Press, 1986), p. 11.

28. Ibid.

29. *Enchiridion*, chapters 31, 117. See Augustine, *The Augustine Catechism: The Enchiridion on Faith, Hope, and Love*, trans. Bruce Harbert (Hyde Park, NY: New City, 1999), p. 130.

30. Augustine called virtues "the various movements of love" and described the four cardinal virtues in terms of love: "I hold that virtue is nothing other than perfect love of God. Now, when it is said that virtue has a fourfold division, as I understand it, this is said according to the various movements of love. . . . We may, therefore, define these virtues as follows: temperance is love

preserving itself entire and incorrupt for God; courage is love readily bearing all things for the sake of God; justice is love serving only God, and therefore ruling well everything else that is subject to the human person; prudence is love discerning well between what helps it toward God and what hinders it. Augustine, *Of the Morals of the Catholic Church*, chapter XV, section 25, available at www.newad vent.org/fathers/1401.htm.

31. Augustine, *Confessions*, Oxford World Classics, trans. Henry Chadwick (Oxford: Oxford University Press, 1991), p. 278 (book XIII, chapter 9).

32. Saint Augustine, *On Christian Teaching*, trans. R. P. H. Green (Oxford: Oxford University Press, 1997), p. 21.

33. Augustine, *Confessions*, trans. R. S. Pine-Coffin (London: Penguin UK, 1961), pp. 228–29 (book X, chapter 22).

34. Augustine, *The City of God*, trans. Henry Bettenson (London, Penguin Books, 1972), p. 637 (book XV, chapter 23).

35. Augustine, *Confessions*, trans. Chadwick, p. 3 (book I, chapter 1).

36. Augustine, *Commentary on the Psalms*, Psalm 35:9. This is a modernization of the translation in Phillip Schaff, *Nicene and Post-Nicene Fathers*, series 1, vol. 8, available at www.ccel.org/ccel/schaff/npnf108.ii.XXXV.html.

37. C. S. Lewis, "Hope," pp. 136–37. In a personal letter Lewis puts this argument even more succinctly: "If you are really the product of a materialistic universe, how is it that you don't feel at home here? Do fish complain of the sea for being wet?" See "A Letter to Sheldon Vanauken, December 23, 1950," in *The Collected Letters of C. S. Lewis*, vol. 3, ed. Walter Hooper (New York: HarperCollins, 2007), p. 75.

38. Lewis's famous chapter "Hope" in *Mere Christianity* has been called a form of his "Argument from Desire." For a summary and analysis of that argument see Peter Kreeft and Ronald K. Tacelli, *Handbook of Christian Apologetics: Hundreds of Answers to Crucial Questions* (Downers Grove, IL: InterVarsity, 1994), pp. 78–81.

39. This follows Ferry's discussion of Augustine and the Christian supplanting of the older, classical view of happiness. Ferry, *Brief History of Thought*, pp. 80–81.

40. We don't merely need "somebody to lean on." Serving and caring for others is more conducive to physical and mental well-being than being cared for. See Haidt, *Happiness Hypothesis*, p. 133.

41. Ferry, *A Brief History of Thought*, pp. 83–84. The quotes by Augustine are from the translation used in the Ferry chapter on these pages.

42. Luc Ferry, an atheist philosopher, adds here to his survey of Augustine's view of love: "[In the Christian view] no one can lose the individuals he loves, unless he ceases to love them in God; in other words, ceases to love what is

eternal in them, bound to God and protected by Him. This promise is, to say the least, tempting." Ibid., p. 85.

43. Miroslav Volf, *Flourishing: Why We Need Religion in a Globalized World* (New Haven, CT: Yale University Press, 2015), p. 204. The substance of this paragraph, and the use of Paul Bloom's work, is from Volf's book, pp. 203–4. Volf uses Bloom's idea to refute the critique that religion devalues ordinary pleasures and drains them of joy because it elevates the spiritual and demotes the physical. Volf agrees (as do I) that much religion can indeed be antipleasure, particularly those more legalistic religions that see salvation as being earned through deprivation. In these religions ordinary life is just a "discardable ladder for the ascent to the divine" (p. 198). Nietzsche calls this the "passive nihilism" of religion, something that "bleaches value and beauty out of ordinary life" (p. 198). Nietzsche is quite right to flag religions that have this shape and effect. But Volf argues two things: First, that secularism can also bring about "active nihilism" that literally sees no point to life and no purpose to anything. That, obviously, can also drain life of joy and satisfaction. Second, he argues compellingly that Christianity does not participate in either form of "nihilism" toward pleasure and satisfaction. Loving God more than material things enhances the joys of ordinary life because they are seen as free gifts from our Father. This is in Volf's epilogue, pp. 195–206. Also see Paul Bloom, *How Pleasure Works: The New Science of Why We Like What We Like* (New York: W. W. Norton, 2011).

44. Volf, *Flourishing*, p. 203.

45. There is much more to say about what "loving God" entails in the Christian Augustinian view than can be said here. Here are two brief, important points to make. (1) Loving God means loving him with the whole heart. In the Bible the heart is the seat of the mind, will, *and* emotions, together. The Hebrew *leb* ("heart") is the center of the entire personality. The heart's "love," then, means much more than emotional affection. What the heart most loves is what it most trusts (Proverbs 3:5) and delights itself in (Proverbs 23:26). Matthew 6:21 says, "Where your treasures is, there your heart will be also." What you treasure is what absorbs your attention and commitment the most. Whatever captures the heart's trust and love controls our thoughts, feelings, and behavior too. What the heart most loves and wants the mind finds reasonable, the emotions find valuable, and the will finds doable. (2) Loving God means loving him for himself. In Augustine's theology, to love God supremely is to love him for himself alone, and not just for what you can get from him. "For there is a joy that is not given to those who do not love you, but only to those who love you for your own sake. You yourself are their joy. Happiness is to rejoice in you and for you and because of you" (*Confessions*, book X, chapter 22). Notice that it is possible to be very religious, to do prayers and religious observances, to be very ethical—but all so that God will give you good things. It is to use God rather than to love him, which Augustine says must never be done. See Augustine, *On Christian Teaching*, trans. R. P. H. Green, p. 9. Conditional service to God—serving him as long as he is answering prayers and giving you a good life—is a sign you are using him. When you stop obeying him when things go wrong in your life, that reveals that the good things and circumstances are the real nonnegotiables, your real loves. You were

using God and loving things, rather than using things to love God. To love God for his own sake is to find him beautiful. It is to find our delight in what delights him, to find our pleasure in what pleases him, and not to serve him only as a means to get something that is more delightful or pleasurable to us than he is.

Chapter Five: Why Can't I Be Free to Live as I See Fit, as Long as I Don't Harm Anyone?

1. Robert Bellah et al., *Habits of the Heart: Individualism and Commitment in American Life* (Berkeley: University of California Press, 2008), pp. xlvii–xlviii.

2. See Keith Bradley, *Slavery and Rebellion in the Roman World, 140 B.C.–70 B.C.* (Bloomington: Indiana University Press, 1989).

3. Alan Ehrenhalt, *The Lost City: The Forgotten Virtues of Community in America* (*New York:* Basic Books, 1995), p. 2. Quoted in Charles Taylor, *A Secular Age* (Cambridge, MA: Harvard University Press, 2007), p. 475.

4. Ibid., p. 484.

5. Ibid., p. 224.

6. Ibid., pp. 165–66.

7. Ibid., p. 484.

8. Stephen Eric Bronner, *Critical Theory: A Very Short Introduction* (Oxford: Oxford University Press, 2011), p. 1. Bronner is here describing the work of the Frankfurt School at the Institute for Social Research, founded in 1923. While the scholars in the institute were humanist Marxists, the events of World War II showed them the limitations of both capitalism and state socialism. Bronner writes that their turn toward critiquing *all* systems of politics and thought and all absolute claims as potentially oppressive and destructive of freedom was highly influential in the later development of the suspicion of postmodernism and poststructuralism toward all absolute claims and all systems of authority and power.

9. Terry Eagleton, *The Illusions of Postmodernism* (Oxford: Blackwells, 1996), p. 41. See Eagleton's chapter "Ambivalences" on the paradox of freedom in late-modern or postmodern times, pp. 20–44.

10. Charles Taylor, *The Malaise of Modernity* (Concord, ON: Anansi, 1991), p. 3.

11. Eagleton, *Illusions of Postmodernism*, p. 42.

12. Taylor writes that John Locke would have said that to give the individual total freedom to choose his or her own moral values would be "not so much to seek one's happiness as to head towards perdition." Taylor, *A Secular Age*, p. 485.

13. It might be more accurate to say that there are two interdependent cultural narratives: freedom ("No one has the right to tell me how to live my life, unless I hamper the freedom of others") and the other being identity ("I ought to be true to myself and express my deepest desires and dreams, no matter what others say"). We will examine that in the next chapter.

14. Mark Lilla, "Getting Religion," *New York Times Magazine,* September 18, 2005.

15. John Michael McDonagh, screenplay for *Calvary,* 2012, available at http:// d97a3ad6c1b09e180027-5c35be6f174b10f62347680d094e609a.r46.cf2 .rackcdn.com/film_scripts/FSP3826_CALVARY_SCRIPT_BOOK_C6.pdf.

16. Atul Gawande, *Being Mortal: Medicine and What Matters in the End* (New York: Metropolitan Books, 2014), pp. 139–40.

17. McDonagh, *Calvary.*

18. John Donne, "No Man Is an Island," Meditation XVII, *Devotions upon Emergent Occasions (1624),* available at https://web.cs.dal.ca/~johnston/poetry/ island.html and elsewhere online.

19. Charles Taylor calls this the "harm principle" of John Stuart Mill. See Taylor, *A Secular Age,* p. 484.

20. Michael J. Klarman of Harvard Law School says that by itself negative freedom—freedom *from* without any definition of what our freedom is *for*—"is an empty concept," a wax nose.Some people see freedom as a freedom from government interference in their lives, which comes from shirking federal agencies and reach. Others define freedom as freedom from discrimination, which comes through increased government regulation and enforcement. Some desire "freedom from want" and poverty while others desire only freedom of opportunity in the free market. Everyone insists that they are for "freedom," but Klarman says that the term is meaningless unless you look at the value or good that the freedom is being invoked *for.* "Whether freedom is good or bad depends entirely on the particular substantive cause on behalf of which freedom is invoked." See Michael J. Klarman, "Rethinking the History of American Freedom," *William and Mary Law Review,* vol. 42 (October, 2000). This paper can also be accessed on the Web site of the Social Science Research Network, http://papers.ssrn.com/sol3/papers.cfm?abstract _id=223776.

21. Jonathan Haidt, *The Happiness Hypothesis: Putting Ancient Wisdom and Philosophy to the Test of Modern Science* (London: Arrow Books, 2006), p. 134.

22. Ibid., p. 133.

23. Ibid.

24. Bellah et al., *Habits of the Heart,* p. xlviii. See also Marc J. Dunkelman, *The Vanishing Neighbor: The Transformation of American Community,* (New York: W. W. Norton, 2014) and Yuval Levin, *The Fractured Republic:*

Renewing America's Social Contract in an Age of Individualism (New York: Basic Books, 2016). Each of these books details the ways in which the emphasis on unconstrained individual freedom has eroded human community. Dunkelman and Levin make the same analysis, though the former is politically liberal and the latter conservative.

25. In Taylor's *The Malaise of Modernity,* he also cites Tocqueville. Taylor believes that the rise of "self-determining freedom" means that democracy will break down. First, many people will not "want to participate actively in self-government," will not feel part of a community or body, but will expect the government only to give them the freedom to pursue their own lives as they see fit. Also, because people will not be able to agree on shared values, there will be polarization and a lack of consensus. So through indifference and anger democratic institutions will cease to really function. This will lead to a "soft despotism." "It will not be a tyranny of terror and oppression as in the old days. The government will be mild and paternalistic. It may even keep democratic forms, with periodic elections. But in fact, everything will be run by an 'immense tutelary power' over which people will have little control. The only defence against this . . . is a vigorous political culture in which participation is valued, at several levels of government and in voluntary associations as well. But the atomism of the self-absorbed individual militates against this. Once participation declines, once the lateral associations that were its vehicles wither away, the individual citizen is left alone in the fact of the vast bureaucratic state and feels, correctly, powerless." Taylor, *Malaise of Modernity,* pp. 9–10. For more on this, see Taylor, *Malaise of Modernity,* chapter 10, "Against Fragmentation," pp. 109–21.

26. Quoted in John Stott, *The Contemporary Christian* (InterVarsity, 1992), p. 55. The interview's English translation appeared in the *Guardian Weekly,* June 23, 1985.

27. See Ian Carter, "Positive and Negative Liberty," *The Stanford Encyclopedia of Philosophy* (Spring 2012 ed.), ed. Edward N. Zalta, http://plato.stanford.edu/archives/ spr2012/entries/liberty-positive-negative/. Carter says in this article that philosopher Isaiah Berlin taught that negative and positive liberty are not just two sides of the same coin but can be rival ways of thinking about freedom. Berlin, like Bellah, argued that an overemphasis on absolute negative freedom can lead to self-interested behavior that requires the government to pass more laws and regulations and become more totalitarian in law enforcement. So negative freedom can lead to the loss of democratic freedom.

28. Gawande, *Being Mortal,* p. 140.

29. Both the "dust dancing" and the "freedom demands closure" quotes are from Eagleton, *Illusions of Postmodernism,* p. 42.

30. There is, arguably, another major problem with modern secular freedom. If we are free because we are strictly the product of materialistic, evolutionary forces, then it could be argued that our freedom is an illusion. Everything that our brains tell us—everything that makes sense to us or seems desirable to us—is so only because that neural pattern helped our ancestors survive.

Our choices are therefore determined by our genes and biological impulses. There is no free choice. Steven Pinker of Harvard represents many scientists when he claims that our actions are triggered by chemical events in the brain before we choose them and that free will is therefore a myth. Steven Pinker, *The Blank Slate: The Modern Denial of Nature* (New York: Penguin Books, 2002). Philosopher John Gray, in *The Soul of the Marionette: A Short Inquiry into Human Freedom* (New York: Farrar, Straus and Giroux, 2015), looks beyond neuroscience and evolution to make his case that freedom of choice is an illusion and myth. He points (1) to the power of the unconscious, (2) to how society and culture work to conform and control us, and (3) to how our psychological defense mechanisms hide the truth from us. He makes a powerful case that we simply do not have the freedom of choice we think we have, and "in a kind of godless religiosity" he urges us to "accept our fallen [unfree] state." (Julian Baggini, "*The Soul of the Marionette* by John Gray; *The Challenge of Things* by A. C. Grayling—review" in *The Guardian*, March 21, 2015). The irony is that the scientists who speak of the illusion of free will are only accepting the implications of a materialistic worldview that originally was promoted, in part, to free us from any outside constraints on our choices. These assertions about free will have not penetrated the public consciousness at all. Part of the reason is that our intuition that our choices are free is extraordinarily strong. Any claims to the contrary, no matter how well reasoned and seemingly grounded in science, have no plausibility. Interestingly, even some secular thinkers argue that if free will does exist, it means that the current, dominant atheistic account of a completely naturalistic world must be false. Thomas Nagel, *Mind and Cosmos: Why the Materialist Neo-Darwinian Conception of Nature Is Almost Certainly False* (Oxford: Oxford University Press, 2012), pp. 113–15. Despite the serious implications, these debates about free will and determinism in the rarefied circles of academia have not really registered in the popular imagination or made a dent in our powerful belief in our free agency.

31. David Foster Wallace, commencement address at Kenyon College, May 21, 2005, available at http://moreintelligentlife.com/story/david-foster-wallace -in-his-own-words. See also a printed version in Dave Eggers, *The Best Nonrequired Reading 2006* (New York: Houghton Mifflin Harcourt, 2006), pp. 355–64.

32. Tony Schwartz, "The Enduring Hunt for Personal Value," *New York Times,* May 1, 2015, www.nytimes.com/2015/05/02/business/dealbook/the -enduring-hunt-for-personal-value.html?_r=0.

33. Marilynne Robinson, *The Givenness of Things: Essays* (New York: Farrar, Straus, and Giroux, 2015).

34. For a survey of the biblical view of freedom, see the chapter "Human Freedom" in G. C. Berkouwer, *Man: The Image of God* (Grand Rapids, MI: Wm. B. Eerdmans, 1962), pp. 310–48.

35. John Newton, *The Works of John Newton*, vol. 3, *Olney Hymns* (Edinburgh: Banner of Truth Trust, 1985), from "We Were Once as You Were," p. 572, and "Love Constraining to Obedience," p. 635.

Chapter Six: The Problem of the Self

1. Tony Schwartz, "The Enduring Hunt for Personal Value," *New York Times*, May 1, 2015.

2. Philosophers give most of their attention to the former issue—the persistence of the sense of being the same self over time. Psychologists give their attention more to the latter issue—the question of self-esteem or self-worth. Sociologists give their attention to the question of the relationship of the individual self to the community and its social roles. For classic early- and late-modern philosophical essays on the concept of personal identity, including those by Locke and Hume, along with Bernard Williams, see John Perry, ed.. *Personal Identity*, Topics in Philosophy, 2nd ed. (Berkeley: University of California Press, 2008). See also the older volume, Amélie Oksenberg Rorty, ed., *The Identities of Persons* (Berkeley: University of California Press, 1976). For a classic sociological perspective on identity, individualism, and American culture, see Robert Bellah et al., *Habits of the Heart: Individualism and Commitment in American Life* (Berkeley: University of California Press, 2008). For two Christian approaches, see Rick Lints, *Identity and Idolatry: The Image of God and Its Inversion* (Downers Grove, IL: IVP Academic, 2015), and Dick Keyes, *Beyond Identity: Finding Yourself in the Image and Character of God* (Milton Keynes, UK: Paternoster, 1998). Lints's book is a scholarly survey of the biblical material, and Keyes's book is an accessible, practical Christian treatment.

3. Charles Taylor, *A Secular Age* (Cambridge, MA: Harvard University Press, 2007), p. 35.

4. See chapter 3, "Finding Oneself," in Robert Bellah et al., *Habits of the Heart: Individualism and Commitment in American Life* (Berkeley: University of California Press, 2008), pp. 55–84. Taylor writes that the social order—from kings down to servants—was seen as embedded in a higher spiritual order, a chain of being, of which human social order was just a reflection. Taylor, *Secular Age*, p. 25. The Greeks (Plato in particular) believed that behind the physical universe there was a set of metaphysical essences/forms/universals of which every individual in the world was just an expression. This meant that every person occupied a place in society—peasant, artisan, noble, king, male, female—that also existed in the spiritual realm. By fulfilling your social role—knowing your place and doing your duty—you were contributing to universal harmony, you were connecting with your own essence, and you were assuming your rightful place in the cosmos. That meant that you did not relate to the rest of society as an individual but rather through your social class or grouping. No one thought of their individual interests as being in any way distinct from the good of their family or tribe or nation. Only if your community thrived could you even survive. If someone strayed from faith and proper fulfillment of their station—it was thought—it brought judgment on the whole community. The pressure toward orthodoxy and submission to one's lot, then, was enormous. The idea of individual choice did not exist, let alone the concept of creating one's own beliefs. Taylor, *Secular Age*, pp. 42–43. Because society was grounded in a spiritual order and could be maintained only with everyone submitting to those above them and to God,

it was impossible to imagine a society "not grounded in common religious beliefs." Taylor, *Secular Age*, p. 43.

5. According to Taylor, in older cultures the self was "porous." It had to align itself with spiritual and social realities—with God and moral truth and spiritual forces and family and social structures—in order to find meaning and happiness. The modern "buffered" self, however, is not vulnerable to or dependent on outside spiritual and social forces in this way. "My ultimate purposes," Taylor writes, "are those which arise within me, the crucial meanings of things are those defined in my responses to them." Taylor, *Secular Age*, p. 38. Taylor uses the example of melancholy or depression. Ancient people would feel despondent or guilty because of certain events. Taylor says that the modern person who is depressed, with a "buffered self," can "take a distance from this feeling." He may say, "Things don't really have this meaning—it just feels this way." He may decide that he will not feel guilty over this or that action or that he will get another job. This is because the modern buffered self is understood to have the power to assign and create meaning within (p. 37). "By definition for the porous self, the source of its most powerful and important emotions are outside the 'mind'" (p. 38). But today *we* decide what things mean, whether to be sad or happy, what is right and wrong. We create our own meaning. "The [buffered] self can see itself as invulnerable, as master of the meaning of things for it" (p. 38). The older porous self, for example, was subject to sin. When we sinned, it led to wrath, emptiness, guilt, and shame. But the buffered self feels it has the right to define what sin is for itself (p. 39). Taylor says that to have a porous self was "inherently living socially" (p. 42). Feeling vulnerable to outside forces of good and evil—which we did not define but had to deal with—gave everyone a sense that "we're all in this together" (p. 42). If meanings are "out there"— not self-created but with their own mind-independent reality—then we share them. Demons are demons for us all, and God is God for us all. If, instead, meanings are created within, and therefore every person worships God "as they conceive of him," then we are ultimately alone.

6. Bellah et al., *Habits of the Heart*, pp. 333–34.

7. Ibid., p. 55.

8. Ibid., chapter 3, "Finding Oneself," pp. 55–84.

9. M. H. Abrams, ed., *The Norton Anthology of English Literature, Revised*, vol. 1 (New York: W. W. Norton, 1968), p. 99.

10. Sung by the mother abbess at the close of the first act of the musical *The Sound of Music*, by Richard Rodgers and Oscar Hammerstein, 1959, lyrics available at www.metrolyrics.com/climb-every-mountain-lyrics-the -sound-of-music.html.

11. Robert Lopez and Kristen Anderson-Lopez, "Let It Go," available at www.azlyrics.com/lyrics/idinamenzel/letitgo.html.

12. Charles Taylor, *The Malaise of Modernity* (Concord, ON: Anansi, 1991), p. 26.

13. David L. Chappell, *A Stone of Hope: Prophetic Religion and the Death of Jim Crow* (Chapel Hill: University of North Carolina Press, 2005). Chappell's book stresses what most secular thinkers have not seen about the history of the civil rights movement, namely the importance of biblical "prophetic" religion. In the November 2003 issue of the *Atlantic Monthly*, in the "New & Noteworthy" column by Benjamin Schwarz, Schwarz summarizes: "Chappell's is one of the three or four most important books on the civil-rights movement, but because its conclusions will unsettle, or at least irritate, much of its natural constituency, it will surely fail to gain the attention it deserves. This unusually sophisticated and subtle study takes an unconventional and imaginative approach by examining both sides in the struggle: Chappell asks what strengthened those who fought segregation in the South and what weakened their enemies. His answer in both cases is evangelical Christianity."

14. Francis Spufford, *Unapologetic: Why, Despite Everything, Christianity Can Still Make Surprising Emotional Sense* (London: Faber & Faber, 2012), p. 28.

15. Philip Rieff, *Freud: The Mind of the Moralist* (Chicago, IL: University of Chicago Press, 1959), p. 35. The rest of this chapter's material on Freud is taken from Rieff's landmark book.

16. Ibid., p. 60.

17. Ibid., p. 375.

18. Ibid., p. 343. For Freud's pessimism and realism about human nature in contrast to the modern "culture of the therapeutic," see Rieff's classic chapter "The Emergence of Psychological Man" in *Freud: The Mind of the Moralist*, pp. 329–57. In this chapter Rieff provides a justly famous thumbnail sketch of Western cultural history. He calls premodern civilization, with its belief in normative moral orders grounded in tradition and religion, "Political Man"; he calls early-modern culture, with its normative moral order of self-interested, individual rationality, "Economic Man"; he calls late-modern (or postmodern) society, with its lack of any normative moral order outside the self, "Psychological Man." Rieff and others have pointed out that Freud sowed the seeds of this latest stage, which Rieff calls, in a later book, "the Triumph of the Therapeutic" (also the title of the book). Freud believed all guilt was "false" guilt—imposed coercively by some power in order to keep power. But he also believed false guilt was necessary for civilization. Today our culture believes the first view—that all guilt is false, imposed on us by others in a power play. But it doesn't believe Freud's second view. Our culture naively thinks that we will be happy if we throw off all guilt and social strictures and express our inmost desires even against family or cultural expectations. Rieff believes that this therapeutic stance— making no value judgments at all, leading the person to look inward and identify their deepest desires, and siding with them against any sense of binding moral absolutes—which once was deployed only in the counseling room, has now become the method by which society and all human life are being ordered.

19. Bellah et al., *Habits of the Heart*, pp. 78–79.

20. Ibid., p. 80.

21. Ibid., p. 75.

22. Gail Sheehy, *Passages: Predictable Crises of Adult Life* (New York: Bantam Books, 1976), pp. 364 and 513, quoted in Bellah et al., *Habits of the Heart*, p. 79.

23. "There is no such thing as inward generation [of identity], monologically understood. My discovering my identity doesn't mean I work it out in isolation." Taylor, *The Malaise of Modernity.*, p. 47.

24. Quoted in Philip G. Ryken, *City on a Hill: Reclaiming the Biblical Pattern for the Church in the 21st Century* (Chicago: Moody, 2003), p. 92.

25. *Star Trek: The Next Generation*, episode 1.18, "Coming of Age," 1988, written by Sandy Fries. The quote can be found at www.imdb.com/character/ch0001464/quotes.

26. Bellah et al., *Habits of the Heart*, pp. 334–35. This is his definition of a "tradition."

27. Ibid., p. 65. "The American understanding of the autonomy of the self places the burden of one's own deepest self-definitions on one's own individual choice. . . . The notion that one discovers one's deepest beliefs in, and through, tradition and community is not very congenial to Americans. Most of us imagine an autonomous self existing independently, entirely outside any tradition and community."

28. Ibid., p. 81.

29. Ibid., p. 84.

30. See Alain de Botton, *Status Anxiety* (New York: Vintage Books, 2004), pp. 45–72.

31. Ibid., pp. xiv–xv.

32. Ibid., p. 15.

33. Ibid., p. 81.

34. Taylor, *Malaise of Modernity*, pp. 48–49.

35. Quoted in Peter C. Moore, *One Lord, One Faith* (Nashville, TN: Thomas Nelson, 1994), p. 128.

36. Benjamin Nugent, "Upside of Distraction," *Opinionator* (blog), *New York Times*, February 2, 2013.

37. Ernest Becker, *The Denial of Death* (New York: Free Press, 1973), p. 160.

38. Ibid., p. 167.

39. Ibid. Becker's brilliant analysis merits being quoted at length. "Once we realize what the religious solution did, we can see how modern man edged himself into an impossible situation. He still needed to feel heroic, to know that his life mattered in the scheme of things. . . . He still had to merge himself with some higher, self-absorbing meaning, in trust and gratitude. . . . If he no longer had God, how was he to do this? One of the first ways that occurred to him, as [Otto] Rank saw, was the "romantic solution." . . . The self-glorification that he needed in his innermost nature he now looked for in the love partner. The love partner becomes the divine ideal within which to fulfill one's life. All spiritual and moral needs now become focused in one individual. Spirituality, which once referred to another dimension of things, is now brought down to this earth and given form in another human being. Salvation . . . can be sought in the 'beatification of the other.' . . . To be sure, all through history there has been some competition between human objects of love and divine ones—we think of Heloise and Abelard, Alcibiades and Socrates. . . . But the main difference is that in traditional society the human partner would not absorb into himself the whole dimension of the divine; in modern society he does. . . . Modern man fulfills his urge to self-expansion in the love object just as it was once fulfilled in God. . . . In one word, the love object is God. . . . Man reached for a 'thou' when the world-view of the great religious community overseen by God died. . . . [But] sex is a 'disappointing answer to life's riddle,' and if we pretend that it is an adequate one, we are lying both to ourselves and to our children. . . . If the partner becomes God he can just as easily become the Devil; the reason is not far to seek. For one thing, one becomes *bound* to the object in dependency. One needs it for self-justification. . . . How can a human being be a god-like 'everything' to another? No human relationship can bear the burden of godhood. . . . God's greatness and power is something that we can nourish ourselves in, without its being compromised in any way by the happenings of this world. No human partner can offer this assurance. . . . However much we may idealize and idolize him, he inevitably reflects earthly decay and imperfection. . . . If your partner is your 'All' then any shortcoming in him becomes a major threat to *you*. . . . We see that our gods have clay feet, and so we must hack away at them in order to save ourselves, to deflate the unreal over-investment that we have made in them in order to secure our own apotheosis. . . . But not everyone can do this because many of us need the lie in order to live. We may have no other God and we may prefer to deflate ourselves in order to keep the relationship, even though we glimpse the impossibility of it and the slavishness to which it reduces us. . . . After all, what is it that we want when we elevate the love partner to the position of God? We want redemption— nothing less. We want to be rid of our faults, our feeling of nothingness. We want to be justified, to know that our creation has not been in vain. . . . Needless to say, human partners cannot do this. The lover . . . cannot give absolution in his own name. The reason is that as a finite being he too is doomed, and we read that doom in his own fallibilities, in his very deterioration. Redemption can only come from outside the individual, from beyond." (pp. 160–68.)

40. Taylor, *Malaise of Modernity*, p. 43.

41. Bellah et al., *Habits of the Heart*, p. 72.

42. Taylor, *Malaise of Modernity*, p. 43.

43. See especially Bellah et al., "Preface to the 2008 edition" and "Preface to the 1996 edition," in *Habits of the Heart*, pp. vii–xlv.

44. Ibid., p. xvii. Bellah's provocative thesis is that America is the product of four "traditions." There are two forms of individualism—one hard (for the public life) and one soft (for private life). "Utilitarian individualism" analyzes everything in terms of cost-benefit. It is the way public life is conducted. Everything is weighed as to its efficiency and maximum profit. Your work, for example, can have a "social benefit" only if, in the end, it brings more income to you. "Expressive individualism" is the way the private life is conducted. It thinks of everything in terms of "feeling" and happiness. What matters is what makes you happy, fulfilling your inmost desires and dreams. To become your authentic self, you must assert these desires over and against societal expectations and social roles. Together these two forms of American individualism make individual interests more important than any social tie, any group identity, or the common good (pp. xiv–xv). Because individualism does not recognize the reality of human interdependence and tends to valorize success and to shame and punish the poor and the weak (p. xv), why has it not wreaked more havoc on our social fabric, creating a more brutal, dog-eat-dog society than we have? The answer is the counterweight of two other cultural traditions, both of which offset radical individualism with appreciation for the social dimension of human beings (p. xv). Bellah calls these the biblical and republican traditions.

   The biblical tradition teaches the dignity and worth of every individual, not because of their reason or other capacities but because of their relationship to God. This tradition obligates respect and compassion for all persons. It puts a great check on selfishness (which expressive individualism can increase) and exploitation by the strong and successful of the weak (which utilitarian individualism can increase).

   The republican tradition teaches the importance of government by both the consent and participation of the governed. The republican tradition puts great emphasis on liberty, but a liberty of self-government that is exercised through strong involvement in politics, both local and national.

   In the second chapter of *Habits of the Heart*, Bellah profiles four early Americans who each typifies one of the traditions—John Winthrop (biblical), Thomas Jefferson (republican), Benjamin Franklin (utilitarian), and Walt Whitman (expressive) (pp. 27–51). Each of the traditions defines success, freedom, and justice differently. Yet it is these conflicting "central strands" of our culture, in creative tension with one another, that have produced the American experiment. Individualism can tend to destroy community, but the counterbalancing traditions may tend to limit too much personal freedom. It is only when these traditions conduct intense debates and arguments with one another that America "remains alive" and thrives (p. 28). The crucial conclusion of Bellah's study is that the individualistic traditions are now overwhelming the counterbalancing, socializing traditions and that there are many resulting problems in our culture.

Chapter Seven: An Identity That Doesn't Crush You or Exclude Others

1. Isak Dinesen, *Out of Africa* (New York: Random House, 2002), p. 261.

2. Howard V. Hong and Edna H. Hong, trans. and eds., *Kierkegaard's Writings*, vol. 19, *The Sickness unto Death: A Christian Psychological Exposition for Upbuilding and Awakening* (Princeton, NJ: Princeton University Press, 2013), p. 35.

3. J. R. R. Tolkien, *The Lord of the Rings*, vol. 2, *The Two Towers* (Boston: Houghton Mifflin, 1994), p. 291.

4. See Anthony A. Hoekema, *Created in God's Image* (Grand Rapids, MI: Wm. B. Eerdmans, 1994); and John F. Kilner, *Dignity and Destiny: Humanity in the Image of God* (Grand Rapids, MI: Wm. B. Eerdmans, 2015).

5. The essence of this verse is expressed vividly in William Billings's early-American (seventeenth-century) hymn:
   Can a kind woman er'e forget the infant of her womb?
   And 'mongst a thousand tender thoughts her suckling have no room?
   Yet, saith the Lord, should nature change and mothers monsters prove,
   Zion still dwells upon the heart of everlasting love.
   See "Africa" *The Complete Works of William Billings*, vol. 1 (Boston: The American Musicological Association and the Colonial Society of Massachusetts, 1981), p. 88. Hear it sung on the album *A Land of Pure Delight. William Billings Anthems and Fuging Tunes*, performed by His Majestie's Clerks, conducted by Paul Hilliar, Harmonia Mundi, 1993.

6. The first question of the seventeenth-century German catechism written for the Lutheran and Reformed churches is "What is your only comfort in life and in death?" The answer is "That I am not my own, but belong—body and soul, in life and in death—to my faithful Savior, Jesus Christ. He has fully paid for all my sins with his precious blood, and has set me free from the tyranny of the devil. He also watches over me in such a way that not a hair can fall from my head without the will of my Father in heaven; in fact, all things must work together for my salvation. Because I belong to him, Christ, by his Holy Spirit, assures me of eternal life and makes me wholeheartedly willing and ready from now on to live for him." Notice that the first words of this classic expression of Christian identity contradict the modern view bluntly. I am infallibly assured and secure in the love of my Father because "I am not my own" but his. This is the translation used by the Christian Reformed Church. It can be found at www.crcna.org/welcome/beliefs/confessions/heidelberg-catechism.

7. Eric T. Olsen, "Personal Identity," in *The Stanford Encyclopedia of Philosophy* (Spring 2016 ed.), ed. Edward N. Zalta, http://plato.stanford.edu/entries/identity-personal/#UndPerQue.

8. Erving Goffman, *The Presentation of Self in Everyday Life* (New York, Doubleday Anchor Books, 1959).

9. This translation is from *The New English Bible with the Apocrypha* (Oxford and Cambridge: Oxford and Cambridge University Presses, 1961), p. 54.

10. C. S. Lewis, *Mere Christianity* (New York: HarperCollins, 2001), pp. 226–27.

11. For a survey of recent thought on this subject, see Mark Currie, *Difference* (London: Routledge, 2004).

12. Zygmunt Bauman, *Modernity and Ambivalence* (Cambridge: Polity, 1993). "In dichotomies crucial for the practice and vision of social order, the differentiating power hides [its existence] as a rule behind one of the members of the opposition. The second member is but *the other* of the first, the opposite (degraded, suppressed, exiled) side of the first and its creation. . . . The first depends on the second for its self-assertion" (p. 8).

13. Claude Lévi-Strauss, quoted in Miroslav Volf, *Exclusion and Embrace: A Theological Exploration of Identity, Otherness, and Reconciliation* (Nashville, TN: Abingdon, 1996), p. 75.

14. These four forms of exclusion are outlined by Volf in *Exclusion and Embrace*, pp. 74–78.

15. Vamik Volkan, quoted in Volf, *Exclusion and Embrace*, p. 78.

16. See Bauman's list in *Modernity and Ambivalence*, pp. 8–9.

17. Volf, *Exclusion and Embrace*, p. 20.

18. Terry Eagleton, *The Illusions of Postmodernism* (Oxford: Blackwells, 1996), pp. 25–26.

19. Ibid., p. 26.

20. Volf, *Exclusion and Embrace*, p. 21. The italics are Volf's.

21. Ibid., pp. 22–25. See also Volf's discussion of the ways that faith in the cross "breaks the cycle of violence" (pp. 291–95) and John Stott, "Self-Understanding and Self-Giving" and "Loving our Enemies," in *The Cross of Christ* (Downers Grove, IL: InterVarsity, 1986), pp. 274–310.

22. Ibid., p. 67.

23. Ibid., p. 124.

24. Ibid.

25. Stott, *Cross of Christ*, pp. 278–81.

26. Volf, *Exclusion and Embrace*, p. 71.

27. Donald B. Kraybill et al., *Amish Grace: How Forgiveness Transcended Tragedy* (San Francisco: Jossey-Bass, 2010); Mark Berman, "I Forgive You: Relatives of

Charleston Church Shooting Victims Address Dylann Roof," *Washington Post*, June 19, 2015.

28. Kraybill et al., *Amish Grace*, pp. 114 and 138.

29. These are average figures from Pew Research Center, "Global Christianity: A Report on the Size and Distribution of the World's Christian Population," December 19, 2011, www.pewforum.org/2011/12/19/global-christianity -exec/; Center for the Study of Global Christianity; for more detailed statistics on the world Christian population, see the resources at www.gordonconwell .edu/resources/csgc-resources.cfm; and Todd M. Johnson et al., *The World's Religions in Figures: An Introduction to International Religious Demography* (Oxford, UK: Wiley-Blackwell, 2013).

30. Richard Bauckham, *Bible and Mission: Christian Mission in a Postmodern World* (Grand Rapids, MI: Baker, 2003), p. 9. Bauckham's call for a "non-modern metanarrative" (pp. 83–89) is also relevant to our discussion. Bauckham's point is that without a "metanarrative" of some kind, you slide into soft relativism and individualism and this paves the way for oppression and inequality. But a "modern" metanarrative, in Bauckham's analysis, is one used to oppress others. He argues that the Gospel of Jesus Christ provides a nonoppressive absolute truth, one that provides a norm outside of ourselves as the way to escape relativism and selfish individualism, yet one that cannot be used to oppress others, because at its heart it has a man dying for his enemies to forgive them. See chapter ten for more on this theme.

31. Lamin Sanneh, *Whose Religion Is Christianity?* (Grand Rapids, MI: Wm. B. Eerdmans, 2003), p. 43.

32. It may be fair to say that Islam is more of a "hyperidentity" that removes Muslims from local cultures because of its emphasis on salvation through obedience. See Christopher Caldwell, *Reflections on the Revolution in Europe: Immigration, Islam, and the West* (New York: Anchor Books, 2009), pp. 129–31.

Chapter Eight: A Hope That Can Face Anything

1. Sabrina Tavernise, "U.S. Suicide Rate Surges to 30-Year High," *New York Times*, April 22, 2016.

2. "Bookends: Which Subjects Are Underrepresented in Contemporary Fiction?" *New York Times Book Review*, April 12, 2016.

3. See Robert Joustra and Alissa Wilkinson, *How to Survive the Apocalypse: Zombies, Cylons, Faith, and Politics* (Grand Rapids, MI: Wm. B. Eerdmans, 2016), for a review of the apocalyptic turn of contemporary popular culture.

4. E. Tenney, J. Logg, and D. Moore, "(Too) Optimistic About Optimism: The Belief That Optimism Improves Performance," *Journal of Personality and Social Psychology*,108, no. 3 (2015): 377–99.

5. In *After Virtue* Alasdair MacIntyre famously illustrates how stories are necessary if we are to assign significance to anything. He imagines standing at a bus stop, when a young man he has never met comes up to him and says, "The name of the common wild duck is *Histrionicus histrionicus histrionicus.*" How does he make sense of this incident? Even though he knows what the young man's sentence literally conveys, he cannot understand it without placing it into a narrative. One possible story is that, alas, the young man is mentally ill. That sad life story would explain it all. Another possible story is that the young man has mistaken him for someone he had a conversation with the day before. He thinks he is completing the discussion but he doesn't realize the two have never met. Another more sinister and exciting story is that the young man is a foreign spy "waiting at a prearranged rendezvous and uttering the ill-chosen code sentence which will identify him to his contact." The point is that, if there is no story, then there is no way to understand the significance of what happened. Alasdair MacIntyre, *After Virtue: A Study in Moral Theory*, 3rd ed. (Notre Dame, IN: University of Notre Dame Press, 2007), p. 210.

6. Andrew Delbanco, *The Real American Dream: A Meditation on Hope* (Cambridge: Harvard University Press, 1999), p. 1.

7. Ibid., p. 4. Delbanco is quoting Michael Oakeshott, who insists that hope depends on finding some "end to be pursued more extensive than mere instant desire."

8. See N. T. Wright, "Stories, Worldviews and Knowledge," *The New Testament and the People of God* (Minneapolis, MN: Fortress Press, 1992), pp. 38–80.

9. Ibid., pp. 1–2.

10. Robert Nisbet, *History of the Idea of Progress* (New York: Basic Books, 1980).

11. Charles Taylor, *A Secular Age* (Cambridge, MA: Harvard University Press, 2007), p. 716–17.

12. Christopher Lasch, *The True and Only Heaven: Progress and Its Critics* (New York and London: W. W. Norton, 1991), p. 530.

13. Eric Uslaner, "The Real Reason Why Millennials Don't Trust Others," *Washington Post*, March 17, 2014.

14. Adam Davidson, "Why Are Corporations Hoarding Trillions?" *New Yorker*, January 20, 2016.

15. Lasch, *True and Only Heaven*, p. 78.

16. Robert Bellah et al., *The Good Society* (New York: Random House, 1991), p. 180.

17. Ibid., p. 80.

18. Eric Kaufmann, *Shall the Religious Inherit the Earth? Demography and Politics in the Twenty-First Century* (London: Profile Books, 2010), p. 260.

19. Lasch, *The True and Only Heaven*, p. 530.

20. Ibid., p. 81 (note).

21. Ibid., p. 81.

22. Howard Thurman, *A Strange Freedom: The Best of Howard Thurman on Religious Experience and Public Life,* Walter Earl Fluker, ed. (New York: Beacon, 1991). See "The Negro Spiritual Speaks of Life and Death," pp. 55–79.

23. Ibid., p. 77.

24. Ibid., p. 71.

25. Delbanco, *Real American Dream*, p. 89.

26. Ibid., pp. 4–6.

27. Julian Barnes, *Nothing to Be Frightened Of* (London, Jonathan Cape, 2008).

28. Epicurus's position is summarized in Luc Ferry, *A Brief History of Thought: A Philosophical Guide to Living*, trans. Theo Cuffe (New York: Harper Perennial, 2011), p. 4.

29. Diana Athill, "It's Silly to Be Frightened of Being Dead," *Guardian*, September 23, 2014.

30. Diana Athill, *Alive, Alive Oh! And Other Things That Matter* (London: W. W. Norton, 2016), p. 159.

31. See www.lionking.org/scripts/Script.txt.

32. The story is told by Peter Kreeft in *Love Is Stronger than Death* (San Francisco: Ignatius, 1979), pp. 2–3.

33. Peter Kreeft, *Christianity for Modern Pagans: Pascal's Pensées Edited, Outlined, and Explained* (San Francisco: Ignatius, 1993), p. 141.

34. James Boswell, *Life of Samuel Johnson* (London: Penguin Classics, 2008), p. 665.

35. Osborn Segerberg, *The Immortality Factor* (New York: Dutton, 1974), pp. 9–13, cited in Boswell, *Life of Samuel Johnson*, p. 3.

36. Ibid.

37. From Dylan Thomas, *In Country Sleep, and Other Poems* (London: Dent, 1952). Also available at www.poets.org/poetsorg/poem/do-not-go-gentle -good-night.

38. H. P. Lovell Cocks, quoted in Stuart Barton Babbage, *The Mark of Cain: Studied in Literature and Theology* (Grand Rapids, MI: Wm. B. Eerdmans, 1966), p. 80.

39. C. G. Jung, *Memories, Dreams and Reflections* (New York: Vintage, 1965), p. 314, quoted in John W. de Gruchy, *Led into Mystery: Faith Seeking Answers in Life and Death* (London: SCM Press, 2013), pp. 178–79.

40. Quoted in Stuart Barton Babbage, *The Mark of Cain: Studied in Literature and Theology* (Grand Rapids, MI: Wm. B. Eerdmans, 1966), p. 90.

41. William Shakespeare, *Hamlet*, act III, scene 1.

42. John Dryden, *Aureng-Zebe*, IV, I, quoted in Babbage, *Mark of Cain*, p. 91.

43. Babbage, *Mark of Cain*, p. 90.

44. T. S. Eliot, *Murder in the Cathedral*, in *The Complete Plays of T. S. Eliot* (New York: Harcourt, Brace, and World, 1935), p. 43.

45. The Greek word is *embrimaomai*, a word that in extrabiblical Greek could refer to the snorting of horses and when applied to human beings always meant anger. Jesus's anger was toward the "sin and death" he saw around him. D. A. Carson, *The Gospel According to John* (Leicester, UK: Inter-Varsity, 1991), p. 416.

46. I have inserted the word "champion" for the the more frequently employed words "pioneer" or "author" to translate *archegos*. Here I follow the translation and commentary of William L. Lane, *Hebrews 1–8*, Word Biblical Commentary (Dallas: Word Books, 1991), p. 56. "The language of Hebrews 2:10, 18 displays a close affinity with the descriptions and panegyrics of some of the most popular cult figures of the Hellenistic world, the 'divine hero' who descends from heaven to earth in order to rescue humankind. Although Jesus is of divine origin, he accepts a human nature, in which he can serve humanity, experience testing, and ultimately suffer death. Through his death and resurrection he attains to his perfection, wins his exaltation to heaven, and receives a new name or title to mark his achievement in the sphere of redemption. . . . Hearers familiar with the common stock of ideas in the hellenistic world knew that the legendary hero Hercules was designated ἀρχηγός, 'champion,' and σωτήρ, 'savior.' . . . They would almost certainly interpret the term ἀρχηγός in v 10 in the light of the allusion to Jesus as the protagonist who came to the aid of the oppressed people of God in vv 14–16. . . . This representation of the achievement of Jesus was calculated to recall one of the more famous labors of Hercules, his wrestling with Death, 'the dark-robed lord of the dead.' Euripides, *Alcestis*, ll. 843, 844; see below

on vv 14–15. The designation of Jesus as ἀρχηγός in a context depicting him as protagonist suggests that the writer intended to present Jesus to his hearers in language that drew freely upon the Hercules tradition in popular Hellenism (cf. W. Manson, *The Epistle to the Hebrews*, 103–4; see Comment on 12:2). A translation of ἀρχηγός sensitive to the cultural nuances of the term in Hellenism and appropriate to the literary context of v 10 is 'champion.' Jesus is 'the champion' who secured the salvation of his people through the sufferings he endured in his identification with them, particularly through his death" (pp. 56–57).

47. Christian F. Gellert, "Jesus Lives, and So Shall I," 1757, translated by John Dunmore Lang (1826). Available at www.hymnary.org/text/jesus_lives_and_so_shall_i.

48. George Herbert, "Time" (1633), in *The English Poems of George Herbert*, ed. Helen Wilcock (Cambridge: Cambridge University Press, 2007), p. 432.

49. John Updike, *Self-Consciousness: Memoirs* (London and New York: Penguin Books, 1990), p. 204.

50. See David Skeel, "Is Heaven a Cosmic Bribe?" in David Skeel, *True Paradox: How Christianity Makes Sense of Our Complex World* (Downers Grove, IL: IVP Books, 2014), pp. 140–44.

51. C. S. Lewis, "The Weight of Glory," *Theology* 43 (November 1941): 263–74, available at www.verber.com/mark/xian/weight-of-glory.pdf. The italics are mine.

52. Updike, *Self-Consciousness*, p. 204.

53. Jonathan Edwards, "Heaven Is a World of Love," in *The Sermons of Jonathan Edwards: A Reader*, ed. Wilson H. Kimnach, Kenneth P. Minkema, Douglas Sweeney (New Haven, CT, and London: Yale University Press, 1999), pp. 242–72.

54. Ibid., p. 245.

55. Ibid., p. 248.

56. Ibid., p. 245.

57. Ibid., p. 254.

58. Ibid., p. 252.

59. Ibid., p. 253–54.

60. Ibid., pp. 252–53.

61. Ibid., p. 249.

62. Ibid., p. 252.

63. Ibid., pp. 257–58.

64. Ibid., pp. 260–61.

65. Updike, *Self-Consciousness*, pp. 216 and 239.

66. Ibid., p. 206.

67. Vinoth Ramachandra, *The Scandal of Jesus* (Downers Grove, IL: InterVarsity, 2001), p. 24.

68. Edgar Allan Poe, *The Complete Poetry of Edgar Allan Poe*, Signet Classic (New York: Penguin, 1996), pp. 92–99.

69. For an elaboration of this argument, see Miroslav Volf, *Exclusion and Embrace: A Theological Exploration of Identity, Otherness, and Reconciliation* (Nashville, TN: Abingdon, 1996), pp. 303–4.

70. J. R. R. Tolkien, "On Fairy-Stories," in *Tree and Leaf* (New York: HarperCollins, 2001), p. 13.

71. Ibid., pp. 13 and 68.

72. Ibid., pp. 15 and 66.

73. Ibid., pp. 56–69.

74. Ibid., p. 72.

75. Ibid.

76. Ibid.

77. Ibid., p. 69.

78. Ibid., p. 73.

79. Wolfhart Pannenberg, *Systematic Theology* (Grand Rapids, MI: Wm. B. Eerdmans, 1994), pp. 343–63; N. T. Wright, *The Resurrection of the Son of God* (Minneapolis: Fortress, 2003).

80. Dietrich Bonhoeffer, *Letters and Papers from Prison* (London: Fontana, 1960), p. 163.

81. William R. Moody, *The Life of Dwight L. Moody* (Tappan, NJ: Fleming H. Revell, 1900), unnumbered page, second after title page.

Chapter Nine: The Problem of Morals

1. A. N. Wilson, *Against Religion: Why We Should Try to Live Without It* (London: Chatto and Windus, 1991).

2. A. N. Wilson, "Why I Believe Again," *New Statesman*, April 2, 2009.

3. The first quote is from A. N. Wilson, "Religion of Hatred: Why We Should No Longer Be Cowed by the Chattering Classes Ruling Britain Who Sneer at Christianity," *Daily Mail*, April 10, 2009. The second quote is from A. N. Wilson, "It's the Gospel Truth—So Take It or Leave It," *Telegraph*, December 25, 2013, www.telegraph.co.uk/news/religion/10537285/Its-the -Gospel-truth-so-take-it-or-leave-it.html.

4. Ibid.

5. Wilson, "Why I Believe Again."

6. Fyodor Dostoevsky, *The Brothers Karamazov*, trans. Richard Pevear and Larissa Volokhonsky (New York: Farrar, Straus, and Giroux, 1990), p. 589.

7. See Jonathan Haidt, "Religion Is a Team Sport," in *The Righteous Mind: Why Good People Are Divided by Politics and Religion* (New York: Pantheon, 2012), pp. 246–73. Jonathan Haidt and other social scientists point to studies that show the not surprising finding that strong religious beliefs across a community create much less individual selfishness, and much more social capital and social cohesion, than secularity. He points to the frequently cited research that shows that the more often a person attends religious services, the more generous and charitable they are across the board (p. 267). This research could be used to make a case—and it often is—that religion is crucial for the functioning of a healthy society. It does not, however, prove that secular individuals are less honest and moral than religious individuals.

8. Julian Baggini, "Yes, Life Without God Can Be Bleak. Atheism Is About Facing Up to That," *Guardian*, March 9, 2012, www.theguardian.com/ commen tisfree/2012/mar/09/life-without-god-bleak-atheism.

9. Charles Taylor, *A Secular Age* (Cambridge, MA: Harvard University Press, 2007), p. 695–96.

10. Ibid., p. 588.

11. Ibid., p. 581. "Once human beings took their norms, their goods, their standards of ultimate value from an authority outside of themselves: from God, or the gods, or the nature of Being or the cosmos. But then they came to see that these higher authorities were their own fictions, and they realized that they had to establish their norms and values for themselves, on their own authority. . . . They dictate the ultimate values by which they live" (p. 580).

12. Mari Ruti, *The Call of Character: Living a Life Worth Living* (New York: Columbia University Press, 2014), p. 36.

13. Charles Taylor, *The Malaise of Modernity* (Concord, ON: Anansi, 1991), p. 18.

14. In contemporary academic reflections on ethics and morals, this kind of self-contradictory rhetoric is common. In an introduction to poststructuralism and the work of Jacques Derrida, the question arises: Is there any basis for ethics, any way to talk about "right action in a world without foundational truths to constitute a ground for choice"? Catherine Belsey, *Poststructuralism: A Very Short Introduction* (Oxford: Oxford University Press, 2002), p. 90. After acknowledging that we can no longer ground moral in "universal and ultimate . . . absolute reality" such as "the will of God . . . or the moral law, or . . . the laws of nature," the question remains: Is ethics possible at all? The answer: "Values not only have a history, they differ from themselves. They can therefore be changed in the future, if not in the light of a fixed idea (or Idea) of the good, at least in the hope that the trace of an alternative inscribed in them might one day be realized. Derrida calls this way of thinking 'messianicity': not the promise of a specific messiah, who would fulfill and individual scripture . . . but the hope of a different future 'to some.' . . . Deconstruction, then, is not incompatible with moral . . . choice" (pp. 90–91). This seems to be saying that because we now know all values are changeable, not absolute or ultimate, we are thus free to change them for the better. But how will we know what is better? What lies behind all the changeable socially constructed moral norms that would make it possible to know whether we are moving toward something better than we had before? The only way to know would be if there was Moral behind the morals that, according the poststructuralism, doesn't exist.

15. See Christian Smith, "Morality Adrift," in *Lost in Transition: The Dark Side of Emerging Adulthood* (Oxford, UK: Oxford University Press, 2011), pp. 19–69. Smith's findings are that about 30 percent of younger adults are very strong relativists (p. 27). Most say they believe in morality but define it as behavior that makes people thrive and be happy (p. 51).

16. Ibid., p. 52.

17. Another example of this moral inarticulacy is "Brian Palmer," one of the four persons profiled in Robert Bellah's first chapter of *Habits of the Heart* as representative of our culture's approach to morality and society. After overwork led to the breakup of Brian's first marriage, he chose a new source of meaning and satisfaction in life—not career success and money but instead an affectionate marriage and family marked by mutual affection, complete honesty, and "being involved in the lives of my children" (p. 6). Brian does not justify this shift—from living for his work to living for his family— as being right or as a recognition of "any wider framework of purpose or belief" (p. 6). Rather, he simply found it was not as personally satisfying as devotion to his family. When asked about his value system, he consistently failed to give any explanation for it. For example, when asked why he thought lying was wrong, he says, "I don't know. It just is. . . . It's part of me." Then he says, somewhat inconsistently, "I don't think I would pontificate . . . to establish values for humanity in general . . . [but] if the rest of the world would live by my value system it would be a better place" (p. 7). Bellah concludes that Brian lacks the language to explain his life commitments and so they are

"precarious" (p. 8). They could quite easily shift and change if they don't seem to be "working" for him.

18. My friend's experience and frustration is well explained in James D. Hunter, *The Death of Character: Moral Education in an Age Without Good and Evil* (New York: Basic Books, 2001).

19. Philip Gorski, "Where Do Morals Come From?" *Public Books*, February 15, 2016, www.publicbooks.org//nonfiction/where-do-morals-come-from.

20. Ibid.

21. David Bentley Hart, *The Experience of God: Being, Consciousness, Bliss,* (New Haven, CT: Yale University Press, 2013), p. 252. See also Evans's assessment of the effort to ground moral obligation in evolutionary traits in C. Stephen Evans, *Natural Signs and Knowledge of God: A New Look at Theistic Arguments* (Oxford: Oxford University Press, 2010), pp. 116–21.

22. The "social contract" theory holds that culturally constructed moral intuitions should be seen as authoritative. Thomas Hobbes famously argued in *Leviathan* that if human beings lived according to the laws of the wild, the survival of the fittest, we would be perpetually at war with one another and life would be "solitary, poor, nasty, brutish, and short." Thomas Hobbes, *Leviathan*, ed. Richard Tuck (Cambridge: Cambridge University Press, 1996), p. 89, quoted in Evans, *Natural Signs and Knowledge of God*, p. 121. It is beneficial to everyone that all in a society adhere to moral norms of honesty, peacefulness, self-control, hard work, the honoring of human rights, and so forth. This "social contract" of moral values is so important, and so widely agreed upon, that compliance should be seen as a moral obligation, our duty. However, this view has the same fatal weakness as the effort to find moral obligation in evolutionary traits. If the reason for these moral values is that they serve my self-interest, then what generates my duty to perform them when I feel they do not? Why can I not lay aside society's norms whenever it is of advantage to me? Someone might retort, "If everyone did that, where would you be?" But that, again, is nothing but an appeal to self-interest. It is wrong because it hurts me. All right, if that is what makes an action wrong, then I can do anything that doesn't hurt me, anything that I can get away with. The problem with the social-contract theory is that the moral obligation that is the common experience of the human race does not work like that. When we feel a moral duty, it is that we act in a certain way even though it does not benefit us at all. So the social-contract idea cannot generate moral obligation either. See Evans's assessment of the effort to ground moral obligation in social contract and in "self-legislation" in *Natural Signs and Knowledge of God*, pp. 121–30.

23. Gorski, "Where Do Morals Come From?"

24. Wolterstorff is quoted in Ronald J. Sider and Ben Lowe, *The Future of Our Faith: An Intergenerational Conversation on Critical Issues Facing the Church* (Grand Rapids, MI: Brazos, 2016), p. 44.

25. Gorski, "Where Do Morals Come From?"

26. Robert Nozick, *Anarchy, State, and Utopia*, 2nd ed. (New York: Basic Books, 2013), p. xix. For Leff's discussion, see Arthur Leff, "Unspeakable Ethics, Unnatural Law," *Duke Law Journal*, vol. 1979, no. 6 (December 1979).

27. G. E. M. Anscombe, "Modern Moral Philosophy," *Philosophy* 33, no. 124 (January 1958), Available at www.pitt.edu/~mthompso/readings/mmp.pdf.

28. One typical answer has been what Anscombe calls "consequentialism." Some say something is morally wrong not because it violates some absolute standard but because its consequences practically harm people. But, Anscombe asks, how do you know what hurts people unless you can define what a good and thriving human life is before you evaluate the consequences? And where does that definition come from, given that it is already filled with value judgments before you can check out the consequences? Finally, this approach assumes it is immoral to harm anyone. Many cultures have thought it was permitted to harm some kinds of people, so the no-harm principle is not self-evident. What grounds that assumption? This is all viciously circular reasoning. "Consequentialism" is a broad term for a number of approaches, the most famous of which is utilitarianism, "the greatest good for the greatest number." Anscombe's critique of consequentialism works for utilitarianism as well. For a thorough critique of consequentialism in general and utilitarianism in particular, see Bernard Williams, "A Critique of Utilitarianism," in J.J.C. Smart and Bernard Williams, *Utilitarianism: For and Against* (Cambridge: Cambridge University Press, 1973), pp. 75–150.

29. "This word 'ought,' having become a word of mere mesmeric force, could not, in the character of having that force, be inferred from anything whatever. . . . A real predicate is required; not just a word containing no intelligible thought: a word retaining the suggestion of force, and apt to have a strong psychological effect, but which no longer signifies a real concept at all. For its suggestion is one of a verdict on my action, according as it agrees or disagrees with the description in the 'ought' sentence. And where one does not think there is a judge or a law, the notion of a verdict may retain its psychological effect, but not its meaning." Ibid., pp. 6–7.

30. Ibid. Elizabeth Anscombe had not read or written much in moral philosophy before the mid-1950s, but she was outraged by Oxford's decision to give an honorary doctorate to former U.S. President Harry S. Truman, who had dropped atomic bombs on Japan. Her outrage moved her to begin reading in modern moral philosophy, and the fruit was a series of short, influential exposés of how subjective and thin modern moral reasoning had become. On the connection between the Truman doctorate and her writing, see Duncan Richter, "E. E. M. Anscombe (1919–2001)," *Internet Encyclopedia of Philosophy*, no date, www.iep.utm.edu/anscombe/.

31. MacIntyre acknowledges his debt to Anscombe in *After Virtue: A Study in Moral Theory*, 3rd ed. (Notre Dame, IN: University of Notre Dame Press, 2007), p. 53.

32. Ibid., p. 54.

33. Ibid., p. 55.

34. See chapter 1, "A Disquieting Suggestion," ibid., pp. 1–5.

35. See chapter 5, "Why the Enlightenment Project of Justifying Morality Had to Fail," and chapter 6, "Some Consequences of the Failure of the Enlightenment Project," ibid., pp. 51–78.

36. Ibid., pp. 57–58.

37. Ibid., p. 59.

38. If the secular person responded that human beings do have a *telos,* or purpose—to survive and pass on our genetic code—this would not help in the discovering a basis for morality. If our only purpose is "the survival of the strongest," then any behavior, however cruel, that helped us survive would be "good."

39. Smith, *Lost in Transition,* p. 27.

40. Ibid., p. 28.

41. Friedrich Nietzsche, *Twilight of the Idols,* quoted in Smith, *Lost in Transition,* p. 110.

42. Friedrich Nietzsche, *The Anti-Christ,* cited in Smith, *Lost in Transition,* p. 111.

43. Terry Eagleton, *Culture and the Death of God* (New Haven, CT: Yale University Press, 2014), p. 163. Another early proponent of Nietzsche's position was the Marquis de Sade, in his novel *Juliette.* "Justice has no real existence. . . . So let us abandon our belief in this fiction, it no more exists than does the God of whom fools believe it the image: there is no God in this world, neither is there virtue, neither is there justice. . . . Self-interest . . . is the single rule for defining just and unjust." Marquis de Sade, *Juliette* (New York: Grove, 1968), pp. 605 and 607, quoted in James D. Hunter, *Culture Wars: The Struggle to Define America* (New York: Basic Books, 1991), p. 313.

44. J. L. Mackie, *Ethics: Inventing Right and Wrong* (London: Penguin Books, 1990). See also his chapter "The Argument from Queerness," pp. 38–42. There he argues that moral entities—objective facts and obligations—would be exceedingly "queer," unlike anything else that science can confirm, and because there are no moral facts there can be no moral obligations.

45. Ibid., pp. 30–33.

46. Ronald Dworkin, "What Is a Good Life?" *New York Review of Books,* February 10, 2011, quoted in C. Stephen Evans, *Why Christian Faith Still Makes Sense: A Response to Contemporary Challenges* (Grand Rapids, MI: Baker Academic, 2015), p. 50. The italics are mine.

47. Ibid.

48. Hart, *The Experience of God*, p. 257.

49. See George Mavrodes, "Religion and the Queerness of Morality," in Robert Audi and William Wainwright, *Rationality, Religious Belief, and Moral Commitment* (Ithaca, NY: Cornell University Press, 1986), pp. 213–26; Robert Adams, "Moral Arguments for Theistic Belief," in *The Virtue of Faith and Other Essays in Philosophical Theology* (Oxford: Oxford University Press, 1987), pp. 144–63; Mark D. Linville, "The Moral Argument," in *The Blackwell Companion to Natural Theology*, ed. William Lane Craig and J. P. Moreland (Oxford, UK: Wiley-Blackwell, 2012), pp. 391–448; C. Stephen Evans, *Natural Signs and Knowledge of God: A New Look at Theistic Arguments* (Oxford: Oxford University Press, 2010), pp.107–48. See also C. Stephen Evans, *God and Moral Obligation* (Oxford: Oxford University Press, 2013), which is devoted to making the case for premise number one, that moral obligation depends not necessarily on belief in God but on the existence of God.

50. Evans, *Natural Signs and Knowledge of God*, p. 109. In this section I am following Evans's exposition of the moral argument (pp. 107–48).

51. Mavrodes, "Religion and the Queerness of Morality," pp. 213–26.

52. At the very least, if we believe that "some moral ideals are objectively binding . . . regardless of how we think or feel," then belief in God and the supernatural makes more sense of our world than a secular view. Evans, *Natural Signs and the Knowledge of God*, p. 113.

53. I think testimony to what Mavrodes and C. Stephen Evans are saying can be found in Thomas Nagel's *Mind and Cosmos*, which has the subtitle *Why the Materialist Neo-Darwinian Conception of Nature Is Almost Certainly False*. Nagel agrees that moral value really exists. While continuing to assert his atheism, he concludes that the reductionistic view of the world so dominant now—that life consists of nothing more than physical, chemical, and biological substances—cannot account for human consciousness, the validity of reason, or moral value. He admirably and honestly admits he doesn't have good answers to the many questions this raises. But he concludes that because of moral reality, there must be something more to the universe than we can see now. He denies the current naturalistic (and [Bertrand] Russellian) view of the world. See Thomas Nagel, *Mind and Cosmos: Why the Materialist Neo-Darwinian Conception of Nature Is Almost Certainly False* (Oxford: Oxford University Press, 2012), pp. 97–126.

54. Wilson, "It's the Gospel Truth."

Chapter Ten: A Justice That Does Not Create New Oppressors

1. David O'Reilly, "A Study Asks: What's a Church's Economic Worth?" *Philadelphia Inquirer*, February 1, 2011.

2. On this very important subject see Robert Putnam's *Bowling Alone: The Collapse and Revival of American Community* (New York: Simon & Schuster, 2001), and Robert Bellah, "The House Divided: Preface to the 1996 Edition," in Robert Bellah et al., *Habits of the Heart: Individualism and Commitment in American Life*, pp. xxii–xxviii.

3. See Jeffrey Stout, *Blessed Are the Organized: Grassroots Democracy in America* (Princeton, NJ: Princeton University Press, 2010). See especially chapter 16, "Pastors and Flocks," pp. 196–209. Stout explains that community organizing seeks to mobilize communities of need against the power interests of government and business. To do that requires networking and organizing of not just the poor individuals but also of the institutions and associations within the needy communities. The overwhelming majority of these organizations, which are created by and directed by the poor themselves, are churches. Stout notes that the decline of church in our society spells the decline of community organizing and grassroots democracy. It means growing inequality, with more and more power going to big government and big business.

4. Nicholas Kristof, "A Little Respect for Dr. Foster," *New York Times,* March 28, 2015.

5. Nicholas Wolterstorff, *Justice: Rights and Wrongs* (Princeton, NJ: Princeton University Press, 2008) pp. 4–6.

6. The document is available at www.ohchr.org/EN/UDHR/Documents/UDHR_Translations/eng.pdf.

7. Michael Ignatieff et al., *Human Rights as Politics and Idolatry*, ed. Amy Gutmann (Princeton, NJ: Princeton University Press, 2001).

8. Charles Taylor, *Dilemmas and Connections: Selected Essays* (Cambridge, MA: Belknap, 2011), p. 123.

9. Ibid.

10. Nicholas Wolterstorff, *Journey Toward Justice: Personal Encounters in the Global South* (Grand Rapids, MI: Baker Academic, 2013), p. 131.

11. Ibid., p. 132. For a much more extensive argument that human rights cannot be grounded in "capacities," see Wolterstorff, *Justice:Rights and Wrongs,* chapter 15, "Is a Secular Grounding of Human Rights Possible?" and chapter 16, "A Theistic Grounding of Human Rights," pp. 323–61. See also N. Wolterstorff, "On Secular and Theistic Groundings of Human Rights," in *Understanding Liberal Democracy* (Oxford: Oxford University Press, 2012), pp. 177–200. See also Christian Smith, "Does Naturalism Warrant a Moral Belief in Universal Benevolence and Human Rights?" in *The Believing Primate: Scientific, Philosophical, and Theological Reflections on the Origin of Religion,* ed. J. Schloss and M. Murray (Oxford, UK: Oxford University Press, 2009), pp. 292–317.

12. Wolterstorff, *Justice: Rights and Wrongs,* chapters 2–5, pp. 44–132. See Brian Tierney, *The Idea of Natural Rights: Studies on Natural Rights, Natural Law*

and Church Law 1150–1625 (Atlanta: Scholars Press for Emory University, 1997). Tierney points as an example to the early 1300s, when a dispute arose between the Franciscans and Pope John XXII over the order's vow of poverty and rights to the use of property. A member of the order, William of Ockham, argued that the Franciscans had not simply a "positive right" (one that was created and bestowed by rulers or institutions) but a "natural right" to the use of property in times of extreme need, because such a natural right to basic sustenance could not be renounced and was irrevocable. See Tierney, *Idea of Natural Rights*, p. 122; also cited in Wolterstorff, *Justice: Rights and Wrongs* pp. 46–47. This idea of natural rights, which Tierney argues was not present in Roman jurisprudence, was already evident in the work of some of the church's early fathers. Ockham based his arguments on language in Gratian's *Decretum*, a compendium of canon law writings compiled by canon jurists. Much of the *Decretum* consisted of quotes from the early church fathers. One example is St. Basil the Great, Bishop of Caesarea (AD 329–379) who preached the following to his people: "Tis the bread of the hungry you are holding, the shirt of the naked you put away in your chest, the shoe of the barefooted which rots in your closet, the buried treasure of the poor on which you sit!" Quoted in G. Barrois, "On Mediaeval Charities," in *Service in Christ: Essays Presented to Karl Barth on his 80th Birthday*, ed. J. I. McCord and T. H. L. Parker (Grand Rapids, MI: Wm. B. Eerdmans, 1966), p. 73. Striking a similar note, the great preacher of the Eastern church, John Chrysostom, preaching in AD 388 or 389 in the city of Antioch, challenged his listeners: "This is also theft, not to share one's possessions. . . . To deprive is to take what belongs to another, for it is called deprivation when we take and keep what belongs to others. . . . I beg you to remember this without fail, that not to share our own wealth with the poor is theft from the poor and deprivation of their means of life; we do not possess our own wealth but theirs." Quoted in Wolterstorff, *Justice: Rights and Wrongs* pp. 60–61. Repeatedly the early church fathers told listeners that a failure to give to the poor was not just a lack of charity but theft, because the basic means of sustenance *belongs* to the poor. Drawing on Scripture, they preached that some of their people's wealth they owed to the needy as an obligation. Though Chrysostom and Basil did not use the language of "rights," it was natural for the canon jurists of the *Decretum* and William of Ockham to recognize the concept in the earliest Christian interpretation of the Scriptures. Tierney tells another interesting story in his chapter "Aristotle and the American Indians" (*Idea of Natural Rights*, p. 255). The European discovery of America suddenly moved the relatively abstract discussion about human rights into new territory. A debate arose in Spain over the status of the indigenous peoples they found there, American "Indians." Were these people the natural slaves Aristotle talked about? (Aristotle famously taught that some people were made for servitude.) After all, they were idol worshippers and cannibals. Could the developing concept of human rights be truly universal? Would these rights apply to them? Bartolomé de las Casas argued that "all the races of humankind are one," and from this premise he claimed that the American Indians had the right to liberty, to property, to self-defense, and to their own government. See Brian Tierney, "The Idea of Natural Rights: Origins and Persistence," *Northwestern Journal of International Human Rights* 2 (Spring 2004): 10–11. He was opposed by Juan Ginés de Sepúlveda, who took Aristotle's position and called the indigenous people natural slaves and barbarians. Las Casas wrote an entire shelf of books in defense of the Indians. Though the ultimate foundation of his conviction was his religious beliefs ("They [the Indians] are our brothers, and Christ died for them."), he was carefully grounding his argument in the juridical tradition of natural rights that had been developing, by now, for centuries in Christendom. He drew from Gratian's *Decretum* and said, "Liberty is a right instilled in man from the beginning." Ibid. Tierney points out that though Las Casas and his allies won the debate intellectually, they lost it politically. The Spanish defenders of the "Indians" did not provide much help to the people on the ground, because the ruling powers backed the *conquistadores.* Nevertheless, this debate in Spain gave new life to the idea of natural rights. Elsewhere Tierney traces out how the idea of natural rights, which was a medieval concept based on Christian theology, made its way into the modern world.

13. See John Rawls, *A Theory of Justice,* revised ed. (Cambridge, MA: Belknap Press, 1999), pp. 118–23.

14. Michael Sandel, *Justice: What's the Right Thing to Do?* (New York: Farrar, Straus, and Giroux, 2009), pp. 248 and 261.

15. Sandel lays out three current views of justice, which he calls "maximizing welfare," "respecting freedom," and "promoting virtue." According to the first view, following utilitarianism, the most just action is that which brings the greatest good to the greatest number of people. According to the second view, following Immanuel Kant, the most just action is that which respects the freedom and rights of each individual to live as he or she chooses. According to the last view, following Aristotle, justice is served when people are acting as they *ought* to, in accord with morality and virtue. Ibid., p. 6.

16. There is another problem with Rawls's approach that has often been pointed out. He argued that violating human rights cannot be seen as immoral (because that would be to bring religious/moral values into the argument). Rather, he says, it is irrational. Why? It is so, he says, because if you stood behind the "veil of ignorance," you would want to support human rights, for—who knows?—you might end up being one of the powerless in society and might need to assert those rights for yourself. But when Rawls says that reason would lead us to support human rights, he means we would create them because they serve our interests. We should value the interests of others because it is the best way to secure our own. But this is actually an appeal to selfishness. We should treat others as if they have rights *not* because we are under a moral obligation to respect their worth, not because it is wrong to do otherwise, but because it will benefit us. We should behave this way not because we value others for who they are but because we value ourselves. But if that is the only reason to honor human rights—that it serves our interests— why not trample on somebody's rights if we know we can get away with it? So this effort to create a solid, compelling basis for human rights, without any religious grounding, fails.

17. The sermon was preached by Martin Luther King Jr. at Ebenezer Baptist Church, Atlanta, Georgia, July 4, 1965. It can be accessed at http://kingency clopedia.stanford.edu/encyclopedia/documentsentry/doc_the_american

_dream/. Many Christian thinkers, like Martin Luther King Jr., ground human rights in the *imago Dei*. Wolterstorff makes an interesting and unique argument that two things give human beings their unique worth. See Wolterstorff, *Journey Toward Justice*, pp. 136–39. First is the fact that God wants a relationship with us and has made us all capable of that relationship. The image of God, of course, could be part of what makes humans able to have such a relationship, but Wolterstorff is keen to avoid turning the image of God into just another set of "capacities" (such as rationality, personality, morality, etc.), so that very young or very old or very injured do not have the full image. Second, Jesus Christ, the Son of God and second person of the Trinity, took on our human nature in the Incarnation. "We each have no greater dignity than that. To torture a human being is to torture a creature whose nature he or she shares with the Second Person of the Trinity" (p. 139).

18. Martin Luther King Jr., "I Have a Dream." This speech is available many places on the Internet. See http://www.americanrhetoric.com/speeches/mlkihavea dream.htm.

19. Theodor W. Adorno, *Negative Dialectics* (New York: Seabury, 1973).

20. Stephen E. Bonner, *Critical Theory: A Very Short Introduction* (Oxford, UK: Oxford University Press, 2011), pp. 6–7.

21. Jean-Francois Lyotard, *The Postmodern Condition: A Report on Knowledge* (Minneapolis: University of Minnesota Press, 1984), p. xxiv.

22. Richard Bauckham, "Reading Scripture as a Coherent Story," in *The Art of Reading Scripture*, ed. Richard B. Hays and Ellen F. Davis (Grand Rapids, MI: Wm. B. Eerdmans, 2003), p. 45.

23. Catherine Belsey, *Poststructuralism: A Very Short Introduction* (Oxford: Oxford University Press, 2002), p. 99.

24. See the entirety of *Hedgehog Review* 17, no. 2 (Summer 2015). The issue is titled "The Body in Question."

25. Terry Eagleton, *The Illusions of Postmodernism* (Oxford: Blackwells, 1996), p. 41.

26. Ibid., p. 26.

27. Ibid.

28. Ibid., p. 41.

29. Peter Wood, "The Architecture of Intellectual Freedom," National Association of Scholars, January 26, 2016, www.nas.org/articles/the_architecture_of_in tellectual_freedom.

30. Edward Docx, "Postmodernism Is Dead," *Prospect*, July 20, 2011, www.prospectmagazine.co.uk/features/postmodernism-is-dead-va-exhibition-age-of-authenticism.

31. Ibid. Fuller quote: "For a while, as communism began to collapse, the supremacy of western capitalism seemed best challenged by deploying the ironic tactics of postmodernism. Over time, though, a new difficulty was created: because postmodernism attacks everything, a mood of confusion and uncertainty began to grow and flourish until, in recent years, it became ubiquitous. . . . And so . . . in the absence of any aesthetic criteria, it became more and more useful to assess the value of works according to the profits they yielded. . . . By removing all criteria, we are left with nothing but the market. The opposite of what postmodernism originally intended."

32. Ibid. Richard Bauckham makes a similar criticism: "[Postmodernism] appears liberating in its valorization of consumer lifestyle choices but it is oppressive in the much more realistic sense that affluent postmodern theorists are liable to ignore: it enriches the rich while leaving the poor poor, and it destroys the environment." In this way it continues the kind of oppression that the modern narratives of progress have always legitimated. Bauckham, "Reading Scripture as a Coherent Story," p. 46.

33. Ibid.

34. Simon Critchley, *The Faith of the Faithless: Experiments in Political Theology* (London: Verso Books, 2012).

35. Ibid., p. 24.

36. Ibid., p. 8.

37. Critchley speaks about the "infinite ethical demand" repeatedly in *The Faith of the Faithless.* See pp. 7 and 17 where he introduces it, but then also pp. 146, 220, 227. Terry Eagleton comments that Critchley's book characterizes "a whole current of recent leftist thought" in that it "sees the limits of any entirely secularist worldview" for a politics of social justice. He notes how remarkable it is that a range of prominent left thinkers, "from Badiou, Agamben, and Debray to Derrida, Habermas, and Žižek," have thus turned to "questions of theology," now "speaking in strenuously Protestant terms of the 'claims of infinity,' 'heeding the call,' 'infinite responsibility,' and the like." Terry Eagleton, *Culture and the Death of God* (New Haven, CT: Yale University Press, 2014), pp. 203–4.

38. Bauckham, "Reading Scripture as a Coherent Story," p. 46.

39. Ibid., p. 47.

40. Ibid., pp. 49–50.

41. Ibid., pp. 47–48.

42. Ibid.

43. Ibid., p. 52.

44. Robert Alter, *Genesis: Translation and Commentary* (New York: W. W. Norton, 1996), p. 128.

45. Walter Brueggemann, *Genesis* (Atlanta: John Knox, 1982), p. 215.

46. Psalm 138:6 is quoted from the King James Version. The Old Testament prophets are famous for their denunciations of oppression both inside and outside the believing community. One of the most attractive figures in the Old Testament, Daniel, speaks truth to power, telling a nonbelieving emperor in God's name that he must stop ruling unjustly (Daniel 4:27). In Amos 1, God denounces the nations surrounding Israel for trafficking in human slavery (Amos 1:6,9), for war crimes (slaughtering innocent noncombatants) (Amos 1:11), and for imperialistic foreign policy (Amos 1:13). Then he turns on Israel, the community of faith, but he goes no easier on it. "They trample on the heads of the poor as on the dust of the ground and deny justice to the oppressed" (Amos 2:7).

    Most penetrating is the Old Testament's use of social justice as a gauge of a person's true heart faith in God. When the suffering Job faces friends who are skeptical about his love for and faithfulness to God, he points to his zeal for lifting up the poor. He says, for example, that it would be a terrible sin to think of his goods as belonging to him alone. If he had not shared his bread and assets with the poor and the widow (Job 31:17, 19), it would have been a violation of God's justice (Job 31:23, 28). Had he failed to help the orphan get justice in court, it would have been a great evil (Job 31:21–22). Even more directly, the prophet Isaiah says that God will not regard the prayers of the most religiously observant and otherwise moral people: "When you spread out your hands in prayer, I hide my eyes from you. . . . Your hands are full of blood! . . . Learn to do right; seek justice. Defend the oppressed. Take up the cause of the fatherless; plead the case of the widow" (Isaiah 1:15–17). When some people point out that they have prayed and fasted religiously, God says: "Is not *this* the kind of fasting I have chosen: to loose the chains of injustice and untie the cords of the yoke, to set the oppressed free and break every yoke? Is it not to share your food with the hungry and to provide the poor wanderer with shelter?" (Isaiah 58:6–7).

    Jesus continues and extends the Old Testament emphasis on justice. In Mark 12:40 and Luke 20:47 he denounces the religious leaders who "devour widows' houses" and oppress the poor. This means that, for all their religiosity, they are strangers both to God's grace and to God's heart. If they really saw themselves as spiritually bankrupt and in need of God's free riches of grace, they would be generous and just to those without power or resources (James 2:14–17; 2 Corinthians 8:8–9). According to the Bible, a life poured out in deeds of compassion and justice for the poor is the inevitable sign of a heart changed by the grace of God through faith in Christ.

    One New Testament book that is striking for its emphasis on justice for the vulnerable and poor is the gospel of Luke. It shows Jesus's love and concern for social and racial outcasts such as the immoral woman (Luke 7:37), the collaborators with the Romans (tax collectors) (Luke 19:1-9), and the despised Samaritans (Luke 10:25–37). He infuriates a mob to violence (Luke 4:28) by telling them that God loves other races (Luke 4:25–27), and he says he comes to bring "good news to the poor" (Luke 4:18). Luke records many parables about the importance of giving away one's money and caring for those in need (Luke 14:15–23). Biblical scholar Joel Green summarizes much of the teaching of the gospel of Luke: "The disposition of one's possessions signifies the disposition of one's heart." Joel B. Green, *The Gospel of Luke* (Grand Rapids, MI: Wm. B. Eerdmans, 1997), p. 471. If your heart has been changed by grace, and your identity is in Christ, then money and status are no longer matters of either pride or security.

47. Bauckham, "Reading Scripture as a Coherent Story," p. 52.

48. Ibid.

49. Ibid. Bauckham's illuminating essay provides more inferences regarding how the biblical metanarrative undermines the tendency to domination. Postmodernists claim that a metanarrative or claim of "truth oppresses because it delegitimizes difference" (p. 52). Bauckham points out how the biblical story does not suppress diverse voices and difference. The Hebrew Scriptures, for example, provide multiple perspectives on the same history. So 1–2 Chronicles reports on the same span of history as Genesis through 2 Kings, offering significantly different views and interpretations of events. In addition there are three short stories—Ruth, Esther, and Jonah—that offer significantly different angles and viewpoints on Israel's history from those presented in the other books that cover the same histories. And notice that two of those three books give women's perspectives. The book of Proverbs teaches that, in general, right living produces a good life, but the book of Job speaks of mysterious, innocent suffering and provides a counterpoint. In the New Testament as well the life of Jesus is covered four times by four different authors, providing different emphases and interpretations of the same man's life, not to mention that Paul often gives us his own commentary on the sayings and events of Jesus's history. Bauckham argues effectively that, despite all the diversity, there is a unity, and there is a single story line. The effect of the different voices, genres, and viewpoints of the biblical authors is not ultimately discordant, though it is often striking and challenging and ultimately provides an endless richness of insight and understanding. And so the very character of the Bible as literature makes "the biblical metanarrative . . . a story uniquely unsuited to being an instrument of oppression" (p. 52).

50. Eagleton, *Culture and the Death of God*, pp. 201–8.

Chapter Eleven: Is It Reasonable to Believe in God?

1. See David Bentley Hart, *The Experience of God*, pp. 1–86.

2. C. Stephen Evans, *Why Christian Faith Still Makes Sense: A Response to Contemporary Challenges* (Grand Rapids, MI: Baker Academic, 2015), p. 23.

3. See Richard Swinburne's unpublished academic paper, "The Existence of God," available on the University of Oxford users Web site, http://users.ox.ac .uk/~orie0087/pdf_files/General%20untechnical%20papers/The%20Exis tence%20of%20God.pdf. He writes that theories in physics are considered established by their explanatory power—if they explain what we see. "An inductive argument from phenomena to a cause will be stronger the better the

four criteria are satisfied: (1) the more probable it is that the phenomena will occur if the postulated cause occurred, (2) the less probable it is that the phenomena will occur if the postulated cause did not occur, (3) the simpler is the postulated cause, and (4) the better the explanation fits with background knowledge. The better the criteria are satisfied, the more probable it is that the purported explanation is true." This is how a physical cause can be inductively and rationally inferred from data. In the same way, God as a hypothesis can be compared with other possible accounts of reality.

4. For a thorough exposition of this argument, see Hart, *Experience of God,* pp. 87–151. Also see William Lane Craig, *The Kalam Cosmological Argument* (London: Macmillan, 1979); William Lane Craig and James D. Sinclair, "The *Kalam* Cosmological Argument," in *The Blackwell Companion to Natural Theology,* ed. William Lane Craig and J. P. Moreland, pp. 101–201; C. Stephen Evans, *Natural Signs and Knowledge of God: A New Look at Theistic Arguments* (Oxford: Oxford University Press, 2010), pp. 47–73; Alvin Plantinga, *God and Other Minds: Study of the Rational Justification of Belief in God* (Ithaca, NY: Cornell University Press, 1968), pp. 3–25; William C. Davis, "Theistic Arguments," in *Reason for the Hope Within,* ed. Michael J. Murray (Grand Rapids, MI: Wm. B. Eerdmans, 1997), pp. 20–46; Robert J. Spitzer, *New Proofs for the Existence of God: Contributions of Contemporary Physics and Philosophy* (Grand Rapids, MI: Wm. B. Eerdmans, 2010), pp. 105–43.

5. Evans cites Camus in this way in *Why Christian Faith Still Makes Sense,* pp. 41–42.

6. For a thorough exposition of this argument, see Roger White, "Fine-Tuning and Multiple Universes," *Noûs* 34, no. 2 (2000): 260–76; William Lane Craig, "Design and the Anthropic Fine-Tuning of the Universe," in *God and Design: The Teleological Argument and Modern Science,* ed. Neil Manson (London: Routledge, 2003); Richard Swinburne, "Argument from the Fine-tuning of the Universe," in *Physical Cosmology and Philosophy,* ed. John Leslie (New York: Macmillan, 1990); Richard Swinburne, "The Argument to God from Fine-tuning Reassessed," in Manson, *God and Design;* Robin Collins, "A Scientific Argument for the Existence of God: The Fine-tuning Design Argument," in Murray, *Reason for the Hope Within;* Robin Collins, "The Teleological Argument: An Exploration of the Fine-tuning of the Universe," in Craig and Moreland, *Blackwell Companion to Natural Theology,* pp. 101–201; Evans, *Natural Signs and Knowledge of God,* pp. 74–106; Plantinga, *God and Other Minds,* pp. 95–114; Alvin Plantinga, *Where the Conflict Really Lies: Science, Religion, and Naturalism* (Oxford: Oxford University Press, 2011), pp. 193–306; John C. Lennox, *God's Undertaker: Has Science Buried God?* (Oxford: Lion Hudson, 2009), pp. 57–97; Spitzer, *New Proofs for the Existence of God,* pp. 13–104.

7. Alan Lightman, "The Accidental Universe: Science's Crisis of Faith," *Harper's Magazine,* December 2011, http://harpers.org/archive/2011/12/the -accidental-universe/.

8. Lewis Thomas, "On the Uncertainty of Science," *Key Reporter* 46 (Autumn 1980), quoted in Evans, *Natural Signs and Knowledge of God,* p. 99.

9. Immanuel Kant, *Critique of Pure Reason*, trans. William Kemp Smith (London: Macmillan and Co., 1929), pp. 30–31. The quote is taken from Kant's preface to the second edition, B xxxii–xxxiii, and is also quoted in Evans, *Natural Signs and Knowledge of God*, p. 101.

10. For full expositions of this argument, see Linville, "The Moral Argument," pp. 391–448; Evans, *Natural Signs and Knowledge of God*, pp. 107–48; William C. Davis, "Theistic Arguments," in Murray, *Reason for the Hope Within*, pp. 20–46; Hart, *The Experience of God*, pp. 251–76; George Mavrodes, "Religion and the Queerness of Morality," in *Rationality, Religious Belief, and Moral Commitment*, ed. Robert Audi and William Wainwright (Ithaca, NY: Cornell University Press, 1986), pp. 213–26; Robert Adams, "Moral Arguments for Theistic Belief," in *The Virtue of Faith and Other Essays in Philosophical Theology* (Oxford: Oxford University Press, 1987), pp. 144–63.

11. Evans, *Why Christian Faith Still Makes Sense*, p. 47

12. Thomas Nagel, *Mind and Cosmos: Why the Materialist Neo-Darwinian Conception of Nature Is Almost Certainly False* (Oxford: Oxford University Press, 2012), p. 110.

13. Ibid.

14. Ibid., p. 35.

15. Thomas Nagel, "What Is It Like to Be a Bat?" in *Mortal Questions, Canto Classics* (Cambridge: Cambridge University Press, 2012), p. 166.

16. Hart, *Experience of God*, pp. 172–201.

17. Plantinga, "IV: Mathematics," in *Where the Conflict Really Lies*, pp. 284–91. Plantinga's entire chapter 9, "Deep Concord: Christian Theism and the Deep Roots of Science," gives a number of arguments regarding how the existence of God better explains the human ability to do science and mathematics, learn from experience, do abstraction, and perceive beauty and simplicity. See pp. 265–306.

18. Steven Pinker, *How the Mind Works* (New York: Norton, 1997), pp. 521 and 525, quoted in David Skeel, *True Paradox: How Christianity Makes Sense of Our Complex World* (Downers Grove, IL: IVP Books, 2014), p. 40.

19. Francis Crick, *The Astonishing Hypothesis: The Scientific Search for the Soul* (New York: Simon & Schuster, 1994), p. 3.

20. Skeel, *True Paradox*, p. 44.

21. See also David Bentley Hart, "Consciousness," in *Experience of God*, pp. 238–92; Thomas Nagel, "Consciousness," in *Mind and Cosmos*, pp. 35–70; David Skeel, "Ideas and Idea-making," in *True Paradox*, pp. 37–62; J. P. Moreland, "The Argument from Consciousness," in Craig and Moreland, *Blackwell Companion to Natural Theology*, pp. 282–343; Robert C.

Koons and George Bealer, eds., *The Waning of Materialism* (Oxford: Oxford University Press, 2010).

22. Plantinga's latest published version of this argument is called "The Evolutionary Argument Against Naturalism," in *Where the Conflict Really Lies*, pp. 307–50. See also Victor Reppert, "The Argument from Reason," in Craig and Moreland, *Blackwell Companion to Natural Theology*, pp. 344–90.

23. Quoted in Plantinga, *Where the Conflict Really Lies*, p. 315.

24. Nagel, *Mind and Cosmos*, p. 27.

25. Skeel, *True Paradox*, p. 65.

26. Ibid., p. 67.

27. Hart, *Experience of God*, p. 281. Hart describes the work of Dutton.

28. Ibid., p. 283.

29. Ibid., pp. 279–80.

30. Skeel, *True Paradox*, p. 76.

31. Luc Ferry, *A Brief History of Thought: A Philosophical Guide to Living*, trans. Theo Cuffe (New York: Harper Perennial, 2011), pp. 236–37.

Chapter Twelve: Is It Reasonable to Believe in Christianity?

1. C. Stephen Evans, *Why Christian Faith Still Makes Sense: A Response to Contemporary Challenges* (Grand Rapids, MI: Baker Academic, 2015), p. 27.

2. Ibid., p. 75.

3. See Pew Research Center, "The Future of World Religions: Population Growth Projections, 2010–2015," April 2, 2015, www.pewforum.org/2015/04/02/religious-projections-2010-2050/.

4. Richard Bauckham, *Jesus: A Very Short Introduction* (Oxford: Oxford University Press, 2011), p. 1.

5. Ibid., p. 2.

6. This paragraph is based on material in Bauckham, *Jesus*, p. 3.

7. James Allan Francis, *The Real Jesus and Other Sermons* (Philadelphia: Judson, 1926), p. 124.

8. Even Bart Ehrman, who is highly skeptical of orthodox Christian belief and of traditional Christian interpretations of the Bible, wrote *Does Jesus Exist?*

The Historical Argument for Jesus of Nazareth (New York: HarperOne, 2013). "The view that Jesus existed is held by virtually every [historical] expert on the planet" (p. 4). In the book Ehrman argues very powerfully and vigorously that the evidence for the existence of Jesus is decisive. He also laments that the view that Jesus is a myth is disturbingly resistant to the evidence. Because he himself is agnostic or atheist, he knows that those who hold those views would find it convenient to dismiss Jesus as a mere legendary figure. But, he insists, that is impossible (p. 6).

9. See Craig Blomberg, *The Historical Reliability of the Gospels,* 2nd ed. (Downers Grove, IL: IVP Academic, 2007); Paul R. Eddy and Gregory A. Boyd, *The Jesus Legend: A Case for the Historical Reliability of the Synoptic Jesus Tradition* (Grand Rapids, MI: Baker Academic, 2007); Paul Barnett, *Finding the Historical Christ* (Grand Rapids, MI: Wm. B. Eerdmans, 2009); Richard Bauckham, *Jesus and the Eyewitnesses: The Gospels as Eyewitness Testimony* (Grand Rapids, MI: Wm. B. Eerdmans, 2006). A very short but helpful overview of the critique of form criticism is found in Bauckham, *Jesus,* pp. 6–17.

10. Bauckham, *Jesus,* p. 13.

11. Ibid.

12. Ibid. See also Bauckham, *Jesus and the Eyewitnesses,* pp. 240–89.

13. Bauckham, *Jesus,* p. 14.

14. Ibid., p. 14.

15. Ibid.

16. Bauckham, *Jesus and the Eyewitnesses,* pp. 39–92.

17. Eddy and Boyd, *Jesus Legend,* p. 452.

18. Ibid.

19. Jonathan Edwards, "The Excellency of Jesus Christ," in *The Works of Jonathan Edwards: Sermons and Discourses 1734–1738,* vol. 19, ed. M. X. Lesser (New Haven CT: Yale University Press, 2001), p. 565. The rest of the ideas in this paragraph are from this great sermon by Edwards.

20. It is well known that the episode of Jesus and the woman caught in adultery (John 8:1–11) is not found in the oldest New Testament manuscripts, so most scholars believe it was not originally part of the Gospel of John but rather is a very old account, from another source, that became attached to the Gospel of John. Also, the Greek grammatical constructions and vocabulary do not match well the rest of the book of John. Nevertheless, "there is little reason for doubting that the event here described occurred" and was preserved accurately. D. A. Carson, *The Gospel According to John* (Leicester, UK: Inter-Varsity, 1991), p. 333. It is quite in line with the rest of the Gospels' testimony to Jesus's character.

21. See Craig Blomberg, *Contagious Holiness: Jesus' Meals with Sinners* (Downers Grove, IL: InterVarsity, 2005).

22. Michael Green, *Who Is This Jesus?* (Nashville, TN: Thomas Nelson Publishers, 1990), p. 14. For the ideas in this paragraph I am indebted to Green, pp. 13–14.

23. Spufford, *Unapologetic,* p. 109.

24. Huston Smith, *The World's Religions,* 50th anniversary ed. (New York: HarperOne, 2009), p. 83.

25. Ibid.

26. For the material in these two paragraphs on the claims of Jesus I am indebted to John Stott, "The Claims of Christ," in *Basic Christianity* (London: Inter-Varsity Press, 1958), pp. 21–34.

27. C. S. Lewis, "What Are We to Make of Jesus Christ?" in *God in the Dock* (Grand Rapids, MI: Wm. B. Eerdmans, 1970), p. 168.

28. Cited in Michael F. Bird et al., *How God Became Jesus: The Real Origins of Belief in Jesus' Divine Nature* (Grand Rapids, MI: Zondervan, 2014), p. 14. See also Martin Hengel, "Christology and New Testament Chronology: A Problem in the History of Earliest Christianity" in *Between Jesus and Paul* (London: SCM, 1983), and *The Son of God: The Origin of Christology and the History of Jewish-Hellenistic Religion* (London: SCM, 1975).

29. Bird, et al., *How God Became Jesus,* pp. 13–16. See also Larry Hurtado, *One God, One Lord: Early Christian Devotion and Ancient Jewish Monotheism,* 2nd ed. (London: T&T Clark, 1998); and Richard Bauckham, *God Crucified: Monotheism and Christology in the New Testament* (Carlisle, UK: Paternoster, 1998).

30. See the previously cited works by Hurtado and Bauckham on Christology, as well as N. T. Wright, *The Resurrection of the Son of God* (Minneapolis: Fortress, 2003).

31. Wright, *Resurrection of the Son of God.* Also see the more recent Michael R. Licona, *The Resurrection of Jesus: A New Historiographical Approach* (Downers Grove, IL: InterVarsity, 2010). For an overview of this brief argument in the next few paragraphs, see Bauckham, "Death and a New Beginning," in *Jesus,* pp. 104–09.

32. Celsus (a second-century critic of Christianity), cited in Bauckham, *Jesus,* p. 105.

33. Ibid., p. 109.

34. Quoted in Bauckham, *Jesus,* p. 108.

35. On evil and suffering, see my summary of the Christian responses in "The Challenge to the Secular" and "The Problem of Evil," in *Walking with God*

Through Pain and Suffering (New York: Riverhead Books, 2013), pp. 64–111. On holy war in the Bible, see Paul Copan and Matthew Flannagan, *Did God Really Command Genocide? Coming to Terms with the Justice of God* (Grand Rapids, MI: Baker Books, 2014); and Joshua Ryan Butler, *The Skeletons in God's Closet: The Mercy of Hell, The Surprise of Judgment, The Hope of Holy War* (Nashville, TN: Thomas Nelson, 2014). On the record of the church in history, see David Bentley Hart, *Atheist Delusions: The Christian Revolution and Its Fashionable Enemies* (New Haven, CT: Yale University Press, 2009); and Karen Armstrong, *Fields of Blood: Religion and the History of Violence* (New York: Alfred A. Knopf, 2014). For a variety of objections to Christianity, see Jeffrey Burton Russell, *Exposing Myths About Christianity* (Downers Grove, IL: InterVarsity, 2012).

36. D. A. Carson, *Gospel According to John,* p. 226.

37. Lewis, *God in the Dock*, p. 171.

Epilogue: Only in God

1. Langdon Gilkey, *Shantung Compound: The Story of Men and Women Under Pressure* (New York: Harper and Row, 1966).

2. Ibid., p. 7.

3. Ibid., p. 16.

4. Ibid., p. 14.

5. Ibid., p. 75.

6. Ibid.

7. Ibid., p. 74.

8. Ibid.

9. Ibid., pp. 68–70.

10. Ibid., p. 75.

11. Ibid.

12. Ibid., p. 76.

13. Ibid.

14. Ibid., pp. 77–78.

15. Ibid., p. 115.

16. Ibid., p. 90.

17. Ibid., p. 116.

18. Ibid., p. 92.

19. Ibid., pp. 91–92.

20. Ibid., p. 93.

21. Ibid., p. 242.

22. Ibid., p. 192.

23. Ibid., pp. 197–98.

FURTHER READING

Together the following five books will give readers a good overview of Christian beliefs presented in the context of most contemporary arguments for and against their validity. Each book, however, takes a different approach and addresses somewhat different questions and subjects. I propose that if you pick up one and find its particular topics of less interest, that you take up another that engages you more.

John Dickson, *A Spectator's Guide to Jesus: An Introduction to the Man from Nazareth* (Oxford: Lion Hudson, 2008).

Timothy Keller, *The Reason for God: Belief in an Age of Skepticism* (New York: Dutton, 2008).

John C. Lennox, *Gunning for God: Why the New Atheists Are Missing the Target* (Oxford: Lion Hudson, 2011).

C. S. Lewis, *Mere Christianity* (New York: HarperCollins, 2001).

David Skeel, *True Paradox: How Christianity Makes Sense of Our Complex World* (Downers Grove, IL: IVP Books, 2014).

REDEEMER

REDEEMER

The Redeemer imprint is dedicated to books that address pressing spiritual and social issues of the day in a way that speaks to both the core Christian audience and to seekers and skeptics alike. The mission for the Redeemer imprint is to bring the power of the Christian gospel to every part of life. The name comes from Redeemer Presbyterian Church in New York City, which Tim Keller started in 1989 with his wife, Kathy, and their three sons. Redeemer has begun a movement of contextualized urban ministry, thoughtful preaching, and church planting across America and throughout major world cities.

239   Keller, Timothy,
K   1950-

Making sense of God.

DATE